CULTURE CLUB

Culture Club

The Curious History of the
Boston Athenaeum

Katherine Wolff

University of Massachusetts Press

AMHERST & BOSTON

LC 2009017734
ISBN 978-1-55849-714-6 (paper); 713-9 (library cloth)

Designed by Jack Harrison
Set in Monotype Dante
Printed and bound by Thomson-Shore, Inc.

Library of Congress Cataloging-in-Publication Data

Wolff, Katherine, 1963–
Culture club : the curious history of the Boston Athenaeum / Katherine Wolff.
p. cm.
Includes bibliographical references and index.
ISBN 978-1-55849-713-9 (lib. bdg. : alk. paper) —
ISBN 978-1-55849-714-6 (pbk. : alk. paper)
1. Boston Athenaeum—History.
2. Subscription libraries—Massachusetts—Boston—History.
3. Boston (Mass.)—Intellectual life—19th century.   I. Title.
Z733.B74W65 2009
027'.274461—dc22
2009017734

British Library Cataloguing in Publication data are available.

Portions of Chapter 6 also appear in
Boston Athenaeum: Bicentennial Essays (edited by Richard Wendorf, 2009),
by permission of the Boston Athenaeum.

for my mother
Mary Neave Wolff
&

in memory of my father
Nikolaus Emanuel Wolff
(1921–2007)

CONTENTS

ILLUSTRATIONS

PREFACE

Posh library. Sanctuary for eminent Bostonians. Brahmin enclave. There has always been a mystique surrounding the Boston Athenaeum. For the academic, especially, the place poses a challenge. Founded in 1807, the Athenaeum raises issues about the mood of a young nation and the promise of American cultural institutions.

My initial research questions sounded simple enough. How did the Boston Athenaeum arise? What if one were to use the institution to probe the origins of "high culture" in America? An abstract concept, to be sure. But what needs and desires led to an official site for culture in the antebellum era? Soon the plot thickened. In making an athenaeum the focus of my investigation into capital-C culture, I came to realize that libraries and galleries as research topics in themselves have been neglected. The neglect is due, in part, to the enchantment of such sites and their romanticized role in our life stories. Though it embraced many purposes, the Boston Athenaeum was first and foremost a library. Because a library is the setting in which most other research is pursued, its own richly textured history generally becomes invisible. Just as the field of book history requires, at least temporarily, the disenchantment of the book, so library history demands its own disenchantments. The Athenaeum founders sought the pleasures that come with, as they might have put it, "civilization's ornaments." This book seeks the origins of that impulse; it tracks the elusive idea of American high culture.

The term *culture* is itself problematic.[1] I locate "culture" in the realm of institutionalized learning and the arts, narrowing but also intensifying the term. I try here to resurrect the ideal that early nineteenth-century American men and women held fast. (I say "ideal" because the word "culture" in reference to philosophy, literature, music, and art is somewhat anachronistic for the antebellum United States.)[2] Though they may not have used the word until later, the Athenaeum's founders purposely built a center for culture, a place where they could control chaos and celebrate civility. Yet they also had their own

xi

culture as a community; they had their own ways of living out their shared goal. In describing the habits and rituals of the Athenaeum community, I portray the institution's sometimes quirky internal culture as well.

The most prolific and oft-cited scholar on the subject of culture is the late French sociologist Pierre Bourdieu, who advanced a theory of cultural capital. In brief, his argument is this: one's tacit absorption of gentility and eloquence functions as capital, much like economic capital, which is spent like currency to establish social standing.[3] For him, cultural taste defined social class; he maintained that culture in the sense of education and the arts is always hierarchical. Further, according to Bourdieu, culture can be said to be "coded"; the internalized code is unequally distributed and thus confers distinction upon those who possess it. I find Bourdieu's terms useful but ultimately limiting. In researching and writing about the Boston Athenaeum, I certainly saw cultural capital and cultural coding at work. I borrow the terms freely. Yet the meaning that Athenaeum members sought for themselves transcends sociological categories. Cultural authority—the special power wielded by a city museum or library, for example—originates in an emotional, even psychological, matrix of needs. Founders of elite centers of culture have their own histories that move beyond the single-minded pursuit of status. And consumers of such institutions visit again and again for reasons that might include status-seeking but embrace more idiosyncratic motivations.

Students of American history have puzzled over the idea of cultural authority for decades.[4] Richard Bushman, in *The Refinement of America*, has documented the spread of genteel culture. He concludes convincingly that through emulating the houses, material goods, and manners of the English aristocracy, middle-class Americans in the nineteenth century gained security and solidified their identities. By constructing parlors in their houses (to offer one example), modest homeowners set off a place to welcome guests, as well as to display a few books and perhaps a painting. Parlor culture connected these homeowners—remotely but distinctly—with the leisurely mores of English gentlemen. The emulation reinforced the cultural authority of Great Britain and, at the same time, weakened it: "Once cultural power was invested in chairs and carpets, rather than armies and castles, the aristocracy was vulnerable." Bushman observes elsewhere that in the early republic the project of defining an American high culture led in two directions: boostering American arts and letters that mimicked British culture; heralding a pure, rustic native style. He shows that the former impulse proved to be more influential.[5]

In order to understand the establishment of high-cultural norms, scholars have sometimes focused on institutions. Alan Wallach, in *Exhibiting Contradiction*, explores the history and function of the American art museum. He shows that early American institutions such as athenaeums proclaimed their cultural visions proudly but, because of regionalism and factionalism, often lapsed into clubbiness. In the antebellum era, American collectors differed greatly from the public at large, who tended to view art as entertainment. The evolution of American "high art," according to Wallach, involved relegating plaster cast collections to gallery basements and (by the early 1900s) identifying museums with spectacular displays of connoisseurship. Wallach interests himself in the way museums depict American society and the American past. Through close attention to curatorial details ("the hang," the lighting, the text on exhibit labels), he exposes intellectual problems concealed within the cultural space of the museum—assumptions and ideologies related to nationalism, for example. His work is valuable to any study of institutions that exhibit art.[6]

Other Americanists have indulged in what could be called high-low fetishism. For example, historian Lawrence Levine and sociologist Paul DiMaggio have argued that after the mid-nineteenth century a high culture of carefully prescribed standards and behavior split off from a looser, more democratic middlebrow culture.[7] Levine, especially, writes in an elegiac tone about the erasure of a common culture and the resulting symphonies, parks, and theaters that mirror class distinctions. He argues that a deliberate "sacralization" of cultural forums in the latter part of the nineteenth century reinforced class distinctions beneficial to elites. This train of thought betrays a particularly American preoccupation with the line that separates popular entertainment from high culture. Although there is persuasive evidence that strict norms arose around the consumption of nineteenth-century arts and letters, Levine's conclusions are incomplete and misleading. The elite's role as cultural gatekeeper has been depicted as baldly conspiratorial.

Attributing single intentions to whole institutions (as DiMaggio and Levine risk doing) distorts the rich context out of which life and art spring. Similarly, the univocal missions that emanated from nineteenth-century libraries and museums themselves conceal a complex web of truths. Institutions have multiple intentions, and it is worthwhile to try to unveil them. I wanted to scrutinize the nineteenth-century institutional discourse and reveal more about the people who used such sites: their reading and writing habits, their art and architecture, their domestic situations, their travels, their fears and joys.

My conviction is that ambitious cultural institutions such as the Boston Athenaeum developed in America largely as a result of profound anxiety and confusion—about ethical responsibility, personal and national identity, and aesthetic experimentation. Acknowledging that anxious confusion (and mapping its contours) leads to a better sense of our past. It also leads to a keener awareness of the role of cultural institutions as communities whose stated missions coexist with—and often contradict—personal and political uses. Unlike other historical studies of American high culture, this work illustrates the burdens felt by those who invented an official site for cultural pursuits.[8]

As an institution that was established to collect, preserve, and present books, the Boston Athenaeum offers a unique opportunity to investigate the idea of American high culture. I try to uncover something other than the well-told story of money and power among Boston Brahmins. Until now, scholars of American high culture have approached the subject largely from a sociological perspective. Class as an isolated category has been mined. One need not deny the significance of wealth to recognize other factors that sustained the development of celebrated urban cultural institutions. Approaching the Athenaeum as a phenomenon in the lives of its members reveals American attitudes toward books, art, ethics, and city life. A close study of the Boston Athenaeum allows one to listen to and see, in situ, intellectual influences, political disputes, and aesthetic debates at play in the early republic. This book explores ways in which the institution's coming-of-age embodied tensions of the antebellum era. The Athenaeum serves as a case study of the many uses a self-proclaimed "ornament for the city" had over the first decades of the nineteenth century.[9] It also illuminates the construction of civic as well as personal identities. Indeed, studying the hinge between private and public, between individual readers and a young city (and nation), was, for me, part of the appeal of the project. I am no apologist for elite readers and gallery visitors. Rather, I simply try to recover some of their stories for examination.

Using a blend of textual and formal analyses, this book shows that the Boston Athenaeum stood at the intersection of three themes in American life: the tension between inherited European and emerging American aesthetic models; the relationship between a city and its artificial cultural center; and the persistence of narrative as a means of establishing personal and institutional identity. After an introduction to the elite Bostonians and their agendas, each of the book's six chapters begins with an illustrative anecdote or artifact.

In Chapter 1, "The Collector," a literary club called the Anthology Society prepares us for an interpretation of the life of William Smith Shaw, the man generally acknowledged to be the Boston Athenaeum's founder. Shaw's relationship with a fellow Anthologist led directly to his role as the institution's indefatigable librarian. Born of loneliness and anxiety, the Athenaeum grew more robust under the guidance of Shaw. Of course the pleasures that attended its early life answered the private needs of more than one man. A close reading of the Athenaeum's founding documents yields Chapter 2,

"Sweet Are the Fruits of Letters," which highlights the symbolic apparatus of the institution: its antecedents, its heroes, and its developing reputation. I explore the habitat of the Athenaeum and view its official seal as a means of self-definition. Together, the two chapters in Part One show the origins of a close-knit literary community.

As the Athenaeum matured, men and women who had been skeptical of forging a distinct American cultural identity began to endorse the enterprise. Within the context of the institution, those efforts typically manifested themselves in the artist-patron relationship—a bond I explore through episodes in the paired chapters of Part Two. Chapter 3, "A Woman Framed," shows how Athenaeum readers used the historian Hannah Adams to strengthen the authority of the institution. Adams herself took advantage of the circumstances, artfully advancing her role as an intellectual in spite of the limits placed upon her. "Ornament for the City," Chapter 4, shows that opening the institution to paying gallery visitors was a gamble. Proprietors lost control of the Athenaeum's insulated status, but they gained a reputation in the city. The Athenaeum further institutionalized culture by situating it within the symbolic space of a stately new building on Beacon Street. I read the reception of the Athenaeum Gallery as part of a larger network of responses to urban cultural space. Furthermore, Part Two explains how some of the published aims of the Boston Athenaeum were at odds with the consequences of its initiatives. Specifically, even while it appealed to learned Brahmin gentlemen as a private refuge, the Athenaeum served as something of a laboratory for such new ideas as female scholarship and public art exhibitions.

Eventually, questions about whom the Athenaeum would serve threatened to destroy the institution. In Part Three, I explore ethical dilemmas that the Athenaeum members faced (or avoided): in particular, crises of racial politics and public access. The abolitionist uproar in Boston touched Athenaeum life subtly but significantly; Chapter 5, "The Color of Gentility," discusses the larger social obligations of the institution and—through the lives of Lydia Maria Child and Charles Sumner—illustrates the Athenaeum's passive stance in the fight for abolition. With the fragmentation of cultural authority in the city, members no longer shared a strong sense of the institutional mission; during the late 1840s the very fact of the library and its gallery became a contested idea for many Bostonians. The Athenaeum's rival was the embryonic notion of a public tax–supported library. In "Pamphlet War," Chapter 6, the reasons for and against merging the Athenaeum with the Boston Public Library foreshadow issues that are debated among directors of libraries and museums today: the fear of desecration and theft, the call for aesthetic standards, the imperative to provide access to the tools of self-education. In the case of the Athenaeum, whose shareholders were never directly accountable to the public, the decision to remain independent has resulted in an institution that continues to provoke debate about American cultural authority.

Two ancillary features should be explained. First, the book's prismatic structure—sets of paired chapters that explore the three broad themes of Enterprise, Identity, and Conscience—made a strict timeline of events impossible. The textual divisions trace only a loose history from the Athenaeum's founding in 1807 to its firm establishment in the 1850s at its present site on Beacon Street. So a selective "Chronology" appears at the beginning, to be consulted along the way. In addition, a précis on the book's key historical characters can be found in an appendix called "Biographies."[10]

This study reaches back to a time when reading literature, and conversing about books and art, was not taken for granted. Throughout, I find connections between emotional needs and a larger, authoritative cultural project. Whether the history of the Boston Athenaeum portrays, in miniature, the tortured task of building cultural institutions in the United States is unclear. The Athenaeum, like all subjects, is both representative and unique. Its history cannot provide us with a reliable sense of the nation at large. However, it does expose a collection of forces that have far-reaching effects. For a long time the grand culture of Boston was synonymous with American culture. Pursuing the struggles of the early Boston Athenaeum is one way to trace the origins of the American intellectual elite.

CHRONOLOGY

1798–1803
William Smith Shaw and Arthur Maynard Walter correspond feverishly.

1804
The Monthly Anthology and Boston Review begins publication; Hannah Adams
and Jedidiah Morse discuss their competing histories of New England.

1806
Anthology Reading Room (precursor to Athenaeum) is founded.

1807
Arthur Maynard Walter dies; Anthology Reading Room is incorporated
and renamed Boston Athenaeum.

1811
Anthology Society and its publication cease.

1822
Boston Athenaeum moves to Perkins mansion on Pearl Street.

1826
William Smith Shaw dies; three-story building for lectures and art gallery
is erected behind Pearl Street house.

1827
Book withdrawal is permitted; Athenaeum stages first painting exhibition;
Chester Harding's portrait of Hannah Adams is displayed.

1829
Hannah Adams becomes first woman officially allowed to read
at Athenaeum.

1831
Hannah Adams dies.

1832
Hannah Adams's memoir is published; Lydia Maria Child is granted
Athenaeum privileges.

1833
Lydia Maria Child's *Appeal in Favor of That Class of Americans Called Africans*
is published; Athenaeum allegedly withdraws Child's privileges.

1839
Athenaeum stages first sculpture exhibition.

1845
Architects compete for design of Athenaeum on Beacon Street; Charles
Sumner delivers controversial July Fourth oration.

1848
Massachusetts legislature passes act allowing taxation for a public library.

1850
Athenaeum moves to Beacon Street.

1853
Josiah Quincy and George Ticknor debate future of Athenaeum; proprietors
vote for Athenaeum to remain separate from new city library.

1856
Charles Sumner is physically attacked by opponent on floor
of U.S. Senate.

1876
Boston's Museum of Fine Arts is founded.

1895
Boston Public Library building, designed by McKim Mead & White,
is dedicated.

2000
Athenaeum undergoes $30 million renovation.

CULTURE CLUB

The Athenaeum—exquisite institution. . . . This honoured haunt
of all the most civilized—library, gallery, temple of culture, the
place that was to Boston at large as Boston at large was to the rest of
New England—had it not with peculiar intensity had a
"value," the most charming of its kind, no doubt,
in all the huge country . . . ?

HENRY JAMES
The American Scene
1907

INTRODUCTION
Boston's Conflicted Elite

WHEN THE UNITED STATES was two centuries younger than it is now, all books were considered precious. Book collections grew slowly and required wealth as well as great effort. Those who cared about books were always among the most privileged members of a community, and those who gathered to read together sensed a responsibility, an expectation of leadership with respect to the general citizenry. Books smelled of leather and sometimes even of surf; most were imported from London on cargo boats and retrieved by dealers who met the ships in harbor. Well-traveled symbols of cosmopolitanism, books represented erudition. They reinforced their owners' clout and moral standing.

The Boston Athenaeum dates from this early period in American history. The library was founded in 1807 as a gentlemen's reading room whose proprietors bought shares of membership. At that time Boston was still governed by a town meeting. Merchants and sailors populated the seaside streets, where artisans set up shops for candles, wigs, and sailing supplies. The city had roughly 30,000 inhabitants and was known primarily as a busy port. The ships that crowded the wharves dispensed silk from China, sugar from the Caribbean islands, and that occasional crate of books from London. Most Bostonians lived in modest houses, but a few elegant brick mansions had spread along Beacon Hill's south slope—many designed by architect Charles Bulfinch.[1]

From its inception, the Athenaeum aimed to foster the appreciation of literature, science, and the visual arts. (An athenaeum is a place of learning dedicated to Athena, the Greek goddess of wisdom.) No mark of civilization seemed beyond reach when the founders of the Boston Athenaeum framed an elaborate mission statement to attract subscribers. Its goals, carefully crafted, drew upon the preoccupations of a new nation. The language of the Athenaeum's prospectus echoes the tone of other, more famous American public documents: touting virtue, civic pride, and the proper uses of wealth, the early organizers projected a paradisiacal image of group readership. Bostonians were eager to associate themselves with an enterprise that combined peaceful patriotism with a refined sociability. The institution soon drew enough shareholders to permit the purchase of books and real estate. By 1851 the Athenaeum had moved four times and expanded to include a library of some 50,000 volumes—plus a gallery of paintings and sculpture open to paying visitors.

The Athenaeum still exists; in fact, it thrives. Sitting atop Beacon Hill, near the State House and the Boston Common, the membership library is housed in an elegant neo-Palladian building that was designed expressly for its use in the mid-1840s. Today's Boston Athenaeum is self-defined as "a library and cultural center for members and scholars." Some 7,000 readers enjoy privileges there, many paying annual fees of $230. The library boasts a collection of more than half a million circulating books and a robust endowment.[2] "Welcoming the intellectually curious since 1807," reads a sign by the front entrance. Indeed, the place is welcoming to those who are privileged to know it.

As someone once remarked, the Athenaeum mixes "elements of the Bodleian, Monticello, the frigate Constitution, a greenhouse, and an old New England sitting room."[3] Climbing up the stone steps to a reception desk on your right, you state your affiliation or show your membership card. Past glass doors, high-ceilinged rooms beckon. An exhibition gallery is nestled at one end of the first floor, and an ample lecture hall is set up for one of the week's semipublic events. Displays of recent acquisitions invite readers to browse among book-club standards, cultural commentary, memoirs, new translations, poetry anthologies, and scholarly debuts. Vases of fresh flowers decorate the rooms here and there. Red leather armchairs accommodate a Back Bay matron and a researcher waylaid en route to the rare-book room. You notice art books, along with audio books in categories from cooking to travel, history to mystery. A charmingly antiquated elevator leads to four more levels, including a top story that offers both Wi-Fi and a terrace for brownbagging.

These facilities epitomize Boston's post-Brahmin establishment. Yet at its founding, in the wake of the Revolution, the Athenaeum was just one more desperate—and shaky—American beginning. The Federalists who launched it scrambled to establish a feeling of dignity, of stable cultural ground. The Federalist era spans the years 1790 to 1820. Named for the political party that elected John Adams in 1797, Federalists are often characterized as unwaveringly conservative. According to one historian, in the early 1800s important Boston men routinely met before their midday dinner and "exchanged gossip, made deals, wrote insurance for ships going foreign, and damned the

Democrats."[4] Many Federalists were, in fact, newcomers to Boston, merchants from the seaports in Essex County on the North Shore. They had moved into town eager to bring prosperity to peacetime. They took the places of departed Loyalists and soon became the unofficial social rulers of the city.[5] But life in the decades after the Revolutionary War created strains among Boston's leading men. They were troubled by the demands of brisk commerce, experimental democracy, and their own changing identities.

For Athenaeum men, the task of unifying the nation stirred patriotic sentiments; at the same time Bostonians naturally looked to Europe, specifically England, for patterns of a safe, civilized life. In the aftermath of the French Revolution many Federalists grew to fear American uprisings and Jeffersonian-style francophilia. But the group also embraced a cosmopolitan humanism. Seeing a society unformed but ripe with potential, Federalists were determined to create scientific, artistic, and literary institutions. They were anxious to build an intellectual foundation in order to participate in the established traditions of Europe and advance in the eyes of other nations. John Adams described the new country in terms that underscored the Federalist notion of progress. His generation, Adams maintained, had been devoted to war and politics so that the next generation could have the opportunity to study science and the subsequent generation could then make forays into the arts.[6]

Especially in Boston, so important to the Revolution, men debated among themselves the meaning of independence. *Cultural* independence became a priority, despite the wish in Federalist circles to restore a conciliatory relationship with Great Britain. The act of founding institutions was part of the process of declaring cultural independence. Bostonians had already established the Boston Latin School (1635), Harvard College (1636), and the American Academy of Arts and Sciences (1780). The *Monthly Anthology and Boston Review*, a literary journal started in 1804, eventually spawned the Athenaeum, in many respects the most ambitious of all the Boston educational and cultural enterprises.

What exactly did the Boston Athenaeum mean to its founders? To understand the true appeal of the early Athenaeum, one must consider the core class and its multifaceted agenda. In the immediate post-Revolutionary era, well-to-do Bostonians were a homogeneous group—"mercantile in orientation, Federalist in loyalty," according to one historian.[7] Many were lawyers who then went on to seek public office. The merchants who made their fortunes in foreign trade regularly entered politics, too. In turn, lawyers often specialized in the practice of commercial law, and well-paid ministers preached sermons that soothed anxieties about avarice. This integration of

professions, combined with the Federalist/anti-Jeffersonian rhetoric emphasizing peace and deference to authority, lent the early Bostonian elite an un-
paralleled cohesion.[8]

From 1812 until the end of the 1820s, however, that same sector of Boston
society experienced considerable turbulence. Successful industrialists who
acquired great wealth in textile businesses were absorbed (at first reluctantly)
by the reigning merchant elite. As Ronald Story demonstrates in his history of Harvard University, accommodating self-made textile manufacturers
proved painful to older commercial families. Because of embargoes during
the War of 1812, the competition from British textile imports dissolved; profitable mills opened up north of the city, and the success of the new manufacturers could not be denied. Little by little the established elite made social
and economic investments in these emerging enterprises. Names like Appleton and Lawrence were uttered with increasing admiration, and the old-
guard Bostonians (Lowells, Cabots, Higginsons) slowly acknowledged the
value of a business mentality.[9]

By 1830 the elite had essentially consolidated once again, and the group allowed fewer outsiders to penetrate its ranks. Through entrepreneurship, favorable marriages, and political acumen, prominent Bostonians accumulated wealth and protected their fortunes as never before. These years—from
roughly 1830 until the beginning of the Civil War—marked a period of sustained power for the upper tier of Boston society. Yet the sealed group of key
players (most were leaders within the matrix of medical, financial, and cultural institutions) fretted about their authority.[10] Members of the ruling class
looked for ways to justify and legitimize their own leadership. It was this
spirit of self-definition that inspired many of the Athenaeum's devotees to
trumpet the importance of their reading room.

Although the elite class was strengthened by 1830, individuals within
that larger group had always exhibited distinct interests and orientations.
Some men possessed literary credentials, others academic expertise, still
others legal or business prowess. In addition, the elite-born occasionally
sparred with the parvenu, each group honoring its own trajectory toward
success. Far from monolithic, the antebellum Boston elite reacted to their
circumstances—and to one another—in ways that have been elided by many
histories of this period.

To illustrate the range of archetypes at play, consider this admittedly partial sampling of Athenaeum characters: the administrator, the intellectual,
the businessman, and the amateur. Josiah Quincy, who studied law but never
practiced it, represents the administrator well. A post-Revolutionary man of
rigor and organization, Quincy could boast a colonial pedigree. He was emi-
nently disciplined, and, as mayor and then college president, he forced the

city of Boston and Harvard to establish sound systems of management. Like many elite party leaders, he grew wary of government's volatility as politics became more democratic. This fundamental ambivalence toward public officials colored his later years and eventually placed him at odds with other powerful men such as George Ticknor. A cosmopolitan scholar, Ticknor epitomizes the intellectual. Ticknor was not a Harvard man (he attended Dartmouth), but his passion for Spanish history and literature made him a beloved Harvard professor. Like many other Boston intellectuals, he married into money and enlarged his sphere of influence through his wife, the daughter of wealthy benefactor Samuel Eliot.[11] The archetype of the businessman may be represented by two successful Bostonians: Thomas W. Ward, a financier, and Nathan Appleton, a manufacturer.

Finally, the amateur: vital to an understanding of the Boston Athenaeum, this category serves as a catchall for the frustrated essayist, the eloquent but marginalized divine, the reluctant attorney, and the wide-eyed collector of books and art. One of the hallmarks of the Boston elites was a tendency to experiment with amateur pursuits, such as gardening and architectural drawing, as sidelines to their business enterprises.[12] There were also those who did not excel in politics, academics, or business but nevertheless occupied themselves with the refinements that the age offered. Even if officially employed in the law or the ministry, such men put most of their energy into reading and conversing about books. The label of "amateur" applies to William Smith Shaw, the Athenaeum's first librarian; Arthur Maynard Walter, Shaw's soulmate; and John Kirkland, the author of the Athenaeum's mission statement, among others (including some women).

These archetypes are by no means exhaustive, but they hint at the habits of particular readers and the meaning of the Athenaeum in their lives. An analysis of the "Charging Records" of the library—the now-crumbling ledger books in which librarians noted the titles or authors that proprietors withdrew for home reading—point to a central canon but also striking differences among Athenaeum types. Starting in 1827, the first year circulation was allowed, members took full advantage of the privilege of withdrawing books. During the next twenty years, Josiah Quincy (the administrator) took out much American history, travel literature, and biography; George Ticknor (the intellectual) took out the Koran, Goethe's autobiography, Plato, and much French literature; and Nathan Appleton and Thomas W. Ward (the businessmen) took out novels, biographies, and occasional geology or chemistry texts as well. Granted, these individual cases are selective (and their labels reductive). Yet a Venn diagram would show that the preceding representatives' total book withdrawals overlapped. The overlap helps define the mini-canon of the institution: Cicero, Shakespeare, John Milton, John

Locke, Daniel Defoe, Henry Fielding, Addison and Steele, James Boswell (and all figures in the eighteenth-century Johnsonian circle), Jane Austen, Sir Walter Scott, and a now-obscure British gentleman named William Roscoe. This mini-canon coincides with works that the amateurs—our final archetype—cite most often. In other words, while there was considerable common ground among Athenaeum members, the more professional a member was, the more he ventured into specialized reading matter. Reading priorities exhibited by this brief analysis indicate the range of interests among the Boston elite. And sometimes those interests collided.[13]

Although most conflicts are disguised in the official records, after 1820 an alliance between businessmen and a few serious intellectuals seems to have caused much tension. A subset of Athenaeum shareholders had grown increasingly frustrated with the amateur librarian, William Shaw. According to a committee led by George Ticknor and the mathematician Nathaniel Bowditch (both established experts in their academic fields), the institution sorely needed a long-range plan. The committee men (Ticknor, Bowditch, Ward, Francis C. Gray, and Francis J. Oliver) pushed for a major acquisition program, a library catalogue, book circulation, and other reforms. Presumably the group had the backing of then-president Josiah Quincy, who had been elected to lead the institution as of 1820. In 1828 the dispute came to a head at a heated meeting of the proprietors, resulting in roughly one-third of the group rejecting this aggressive agenda—and even rejecting the men who advocated it.[14]

The year 1828 was a turning point. An effort to acquire books that were "not merely rare and curious" resulted in a $12,000 London shopping spree, urged by Ticknor and company. Almost one-third of the volumes purchased were categorized as "Scientific Works and Transactions from Learned Societies"—quadrupling the number of volumes held in a similar category in 1824.[15] The largest number of volumes purchased fell under the rubric of "Literature and Literary History," with most of the remaining volumes categorized as "History, Biography, Voyages, and Travels." The Athenaeum bought books published in eight languages; as would be expected, the institution spent the most money on English books—but a surprising number were French, German, Spanish, and Italian (not to discount a few Danish, Swedish, and Portuguese volumes). Only a small fraction of the total bill went toward medical books or law texts.[16]

Given that George Ticknor, Nathaniel Bowditch, and other intellectuals at the Athenaeum rarely took out novels or other popular fare, it is interesting that they collaborated so effectively with businessmen, such as Thomas Ward and Francis Gray, who withdrew mostly popular books. Bowditch, the son of a cooper, did not hail from an elite Boston family, nor had Ticknor been born into the urbane set. Perhaps the symbiosis of parvenu thinkers and parvenu patrons (the businessmen were largely from nearby Salem) allowed for the perfect blend of intellect and efficiency.[17] The committee must have realized that by stocking the library with both widely popular literature and the transactions of learned societies, the institution would be able to sustain itself financially. New subscribers were certain to find their tastes gratified. Those who wanted the fruits of scholarship could consult the recently acquired *Transactions of the Royal Societies of London,* and those who wanted Fanny Burney's diary could read that. In the minds of the new hybrid leadership of the Athenaeum, there was little place for the "rare and curious" books sought by William Shaw and his ilk.

Meanwhile, the type I am calling the amateur—Shaw, Arthur Maynard Walter, and John Kirkland, for example—collected avidly and enjoyed the materiality of books. They had anglophilic tastes reflected in their mini-canon but also found pleasure in tracts on such choice topics as toenail shapes and balloon ascents.[18] Mostly, they valued intimacy among true friends, anonymity for their own self-published work, and a leisurely climate for reading together. They appreciated the ideal of the gentleman-author and felt anxious about choosing a profession. Though not by and large famous authors themselves, they admired the wit of Joseph Addison and Richard Steele and wrote passionate essays that attempted to draw attention to Anglo-American literary life. These men took their role as cultural cheerleaders very seriously, but they were not well suited to keeping the Athenaeum's administrative affairs in order. The nuts and bolts of institutional planning was antithetical to their very identity as readers.

However splintered the Boston Athenaeum may have been at various times throughout the first half of the nineteenth century, the outward face of the privileged class remained more or less consistent. Parallel to an evolving Harvard ethos, the Athenaeum ethos was built upon Federalism and Unitarianism.[19] The majority of the institution's leaders emphasized a restrained attitude toward popular democracy. Long after the Federalist Party was dead, Federalist sentiment held sway in Boston. In elite circles, men believed in a gradual uplifting of society through charity and enlightened leadership. As for churchgoing, the Athenaeum members preferred rational religion to the scriptural literalism and finger-wagging of Calvinists. Whereas Calvinism emphasized the powerlessness of man, Arminianism (the proto-Unitarian sect) stressed free will. By 1825, with the founding of the American Unitarian Association, most churches in Boston were Unitarian—that is, they denied the Trinity and accepted the notion of universal salvation. Unitarianism was appealing, in part, because it shunned polemics and refused to revisit theological debates that had proved divisive in the colonial era.[20]

Boston elites helped project an image of decency to the Old World by embracing liberal religion and conservative politics. Indeed, the city's preoccupation with rectitude was celebrated by foreign visitors. About nineteenth-century Boston, Charles Dickens proclaimed, "The institutions . . . of this capital are as nearly perfect as the most considerate wisdom, benevolence, and humanity can make them." Alexis de Tocqueville marveled at the refinements of Boston. "Manners are distinguished, and conversation turns on intellectual matters," he wrote. "One feels oneself delivered from those commercial habits . . . that render society in New York so vulgar." Owing to its position as the center for rational and ethical thought, Boston was often called the Athens of America.[21]

Men such as Athenaeum proprietor Edward Everett, a Greek scholar and later a senator, had been raised on stories of the ancient world. "The noble and elegant arts of Greece," he told a Harvard audience, arose in a "region not unlike our own New England."[22] Everett and his elite friends had learned about the glories of Athens from tutors at the Boston Latin School and Harvard. The idealized Greek city-state embodied for them a stable democratic spirit and an orderly urban life. Athens came to stand for Boston's imagined destiny: a city of statesmen, philosophers, artists, and writers. Early signs of Greek revival architecture on fashionable Beacon Street (and, among some elites, support for Greek independence against the Turks in the 1820s) further excited the leaders of Boston.[23]

Yet the reference to Athens is complicated. On some level, the term "athenaeum" itself underscores the institution's ambivalent attitude toward the new American polity. As the current director of the Boston Athenaeum points out, the athenaeum was actually a Roman invention established by Hadrian, the Greek-loving emperor, around the year 135. The connotations of the a-word point toward the principle of equality within a Greek-style republic (slaves, disenfranchised women, and a hierarchical class structure). In the larger political context of the early American republic, Massachusetts took relatively progressive stances. The state's constitution antedates the federal constitution and was its model. Further, the Massachusetts Supreme Court declared slavery unconstitutional in 1783. As the century turned, however, the Boston elites were not always in line with the state's progressivism. Certainly by the time of the library's 1807 founding, the Athenaeum reading room was considered something of a refuge from messy town affairs. In spite of the enlightened tone of its founders, the Athenaeum danced around notions of universal education and the public good.[24]

So how did readers at the Boston Athenaeum understand moral leadership? It is not enough to imply that the organization tried cagily to have it both

ways, grandstanding about integrity yet harboring discriminatory sentiments. For certain Athenaeum members, moral leadership meant cultural
and aesthetic leadership; establishing standards of taste to combat chaos and
vulgarity was considered tantamount to ethical action. This attitude stood
in contrast to the work of lower-class benevolent societies, which identified
Sabbath-keeping and temperance as the most significant moral issues—the
best way of preserving secular order.[25] No, on the question of moral authority the important players at the Athenaeum were motivated by something
different, something hazier. They feared barbarity and the abuse of raw
wealth. For them, literary patronage would urge the importance of manners
and "catch the softening gleam of humanity."[26] What counted most was the
model of manly excellence known as the gentleman.

The Athenaeum asserted its moral leadership by maximizing the ambigui-
ties inherent in the concept of the gentleman. As Edwin Cady demonstrated
in an enduring study, the *class* of gentry must be considered separately from
the *concept* of the gentleman. The latter is an ideal with a long tradition. In
America, the absence of a hereditary aristocracy created a void. In fact, the
fate of the gentlemanly ideal was a critical question for many leaders after
the Revolution. When in the 1820s an Athenaeum subscriber chose to take
out Hugh Henry Brackenridge's novel *Modern Chivalry*, he read a satirical interpretation of the post-Revolutionary "gentleman crisis." Independence had
been won in the name of simple republican virtue and at the expense of aristocratic privilege and overrefinement; after the war, many men felt shock at
the rough new order that democracy had brought. Even though notions of
bloodlines may have lingered in some regions, for the people of New England acquiring status was subtler. In Boston there was a sense that the elite
could absorb gentlemen of humble background, if only the newcomers could
prove their worthiness. Accordingly, the merchant and eventually the successful manufacturer became analogues of the great noble gentlemen of
Europe.[27]

The true gentleman was always a reader. A love of books was chief among
the qualities of an "esquire" or a "mister," as the early New England gentlemen were known. An Athenaeum reader's identity as a gentleman was vague
and therefore flexible. Elite Bostonians proceeded more cautiously than others when it came to the question of who should lead the city, the state, the
nation. Harvard and the Athenaeum were training grounds.[28] Virtue, learning, and the display of liberality through leisure—all these elements made it
inevitable that a gentleman attend to civic responsibilities. As a close study of
William Roscoe reveals later in this book, the required moral code of a gentleman included a commitment to service, commerce, and bookishness—
and, indeed, the concept brought these ends together.

But not all model gentlemen were created equal. Personal character and cultivation helped distinguish a "natural" Christian gentleman from a superficial, or "fine," gentleman (split ideas that populated novels and journals in the late 1700s and early 1800s). Lord Chesterfield, though criticized for recommending superficiality in his published letters to his son, nevertheless attracted Athenaeum readers with his *Principles of Politeness*. In the meantime novelist Samuel Richardson provided a more appealing model with the eponymous hero of *The History of Sir Charles Grandison*, a virtuous man of feeling and a devoted Christian.[29] Sir Walter Scott offered another variation on the gentlemanly literature to which Athenaeum readers were drawn. George Ticknor admired the Waverly novels for their rich chivalric traditions, and Scott circulated widely among the proprietors.[30]

For the Boston elite, both at the Athenaeum and at Harvard, outward signs of refinement (proper dress, upscale housing) mattered greatly. And so did inward signs.[31] William Atkinson, yet another Athenaeum borrower who admired Sir Walter Scott, offered advice. In his *Letter to a Young Man* (1849), he admits, "It is the hardest thing in life to be a man, but is also the grandest and most satisfactory." Atkinson admonishes his Harvard-bound son to "study the classics thoroughly, but in a large and liberal way. . . . Subordinate the letter to the spirit, but *know the letter well*, or you will lose both letter and spirit." This obsession with equipoise resonates with the reigning Unitarian morality, which, in the words of Daniel Walker Howe, struck a delicate balance: "to arouse the emotions enough to motivate action but not so much as to destroy the primacy of rationality." A recurring theme in advice literature was the need to counteract inner turbulence through habits of hygiene, grooming, and fresh-air ambles.[32]

Athenaeum readers not only urged theirs sons to "walk the walk" of a gentleman; they also urged them to "talk the talk." Elocution was central to the elite education. The frequent circulation of the classical authors required by Harvard's rhetoric curriculum (Cicero, Quintilian) indicates that Athenaeum readers were well acquainted with the teachings of Edward T. Channing, professor of rhetoric after 1819. The Channing rhetorical style combined oratory with moral purpose, emphasizing the idea that only good men can become good speakers. Oratorical authority was derived from Greek and Christian traditions. The speaker acquired eloquence because of who he was, not because of the force of his argument. Edward Channing censured "tawdry expression" and was considered a paragon of the gentlemanly virtues: consistency, sincerity, and restraint. And gentility apparently ran in the Channing family. The Unitarian preacher William Ellery Channing, an Athenaeum proprietor, was also measured and self-controlled, like his brother. His long-awaited abolitionist treatise (1835) suggests that slavery, though an ugly practice, can be abolished without ugliness.[33] (From our vantage point, one cannot help but counter with the Hemingwayesque reply, "Isn't it pretty to think so?") The reputation accorded the Channing brothers stemmed from the elite's multilayered understanding of ethical leadership. At the Athenaeum, sound morals were woven into the very syntax of conversation. But action was sometimes slow to follow.

Members of the cultural elite, and specifically the Athenaeum, did not always respond to moral issues with the rhetorical equivalent of white gloves. Ralph Waldo Emerson, perhaps the most famous of Athenaeum readers, made gentlemanliness a test of every man's "heroic character." Emerson frequented the Athenaeum; his father's library was sold to the Athenaeum; and he spent part of his childhood on the same Beacon Street site where the Athenaeum now stands. In his essay "Manners," he complains that the gentlemen in Walter Scott's fiction "strut and bridle," that even the "dialogue is in costume." Emerson had no patience for poseurs. Striking a characteristically vigorous tone, he insists that "a natural gentleman finds his way in, and will keep the oldest patrician out, who has lost his intrinsic rank." He further explains that "God's gentleman" (as opposed to "Fashion's gentleman") is distinguished by "living blood and a passion of kindness."[34]

From the tenets of sincerity and self-reliance in Emerson to advice from novels and courtesy books, hyperliterate Bostonians reacted to a range of gentlemanly standards while political conflicts festered. The sensibility of the gentleman was like so much elegant background noise. No matter whether an Athenaeum member was an administrator, an intellectual, a businessman, or an amateur, the flexible gentlemanly paradigm allowed him to invest his reading life with moral significance.

As the Athenaeum matured, the early tone of the institution set a precedent for other cultural centers in the city of Boston and beyond. The Athenaeum of the early nineteenth century was frequented by publishers, collectors, authors, reviewers, and other tastemakers—in addition to wealthy funders and high-status educators. The notions of American cultural life emanating from the library and gallery originated within a constellation of friendships, shared literary heroes, and lengthy European tours. The Boston Athenaeum was a dynamic community. Intense relationships among men, reliance upon British models, a cult of bookishness—all these contributed to ideas of what American culture should be. Yet in spite of much talk of national beginnings, Athenaeum readers clung to one another (and to old patterns) for reasons of sentiment, isolation, weakness, or vested interest.[35]

This book explores the relationship between individual, psychological motivations at the Boston Athenaeum and more class-based meanings and functions. Although these two sets of criteria are contradictory at times, they are nonetheless related. Elite Bostonians and their auxiliaries sought to legitimize not only the new nation but also their own place in society. Conflicts existed *within* individual members—conflicts between their private emotions and their public roles as cultural gatekeepers. By examining the concerns Athenaeum readers themselves defined as central, one can start to understand the range of internal division among members. The reading room welcomed intellectuals, merchants, and industrialists—both the parvenu and the old-school elite. On the fringes were readers whose credentials or connections allowed them access. Furthermore, as the first half of the nineteenth century progressed, the Athenaeum's members responded to (and helped bring about) social, economic, and political shifts. Readers' concerns changed over time. A complex microsociety, the Athenaeum accommodated myriad needs and desires.

The task of analyzing the Boston Athenaeum is a formidable one, and no doubt the episodes that follow could have been written many different ways. The sources are varied and plentiful. As one scholar has noted, Bostonians "thought they were important and said so, at great length and in many volumes." In spite of its intimidating self-love, the city of Boston continues to draw new chroniclers.[36] Elizabeth Hardwick tried to capture the "legendary Boston soul" decades ago, observing that "wealth and respectability" result in "a number of diverting individual tics or, at best, instances of high culture." What she concluded serves as a caution: "The old citizens of Boston vehemently hold to the notion that the city and their character are ineffable, unknowable." Still, wrote Hardwick, "wrongheadedness flourishes, the subject fascinates, and the Athenaeum's list of written productions on this topic is nearly endless."[37] So it goes. Here, the famous repository for Boston narratives becomes the subject itself. If the soul of the city is unknowable, we can still spy through the windows of Boston's idiosyncratic library. And there are fresh stories to tell.

Part One
ENTERPRISE

Depend upon it, that the establishment of the Athenaeum, the rooms of which are to be always accessible at all hours of the day, is one of the greatest strides toward intellectual advancement that this country has ever witnessed.

WILLIAM SMITH SHAW,
letter to Joseph Stevens Buckminster,
May 13, 1807

CHAPTER ONE

The Collector

IN THE RAW DAYS OF DECEMBER 1800, twenty-two-year-old William Smith Shaw watched his uncle, President John Adams, relinquish leadership of the United States. Shaw had been serving as his uncle's private secretary for the previous two years—his first position after graduating from Harvard—and his impressions of Philadelphia and the new capital of Washington had, like so much of his early life, been recorded faithfully in letters to his college friend Arthur Maynard Walter. In the recent election, Vice President Thomas Jefferson had campaigned against President Adams. Now the votes were cast, and young Shaw, deeply troubled, used his quill to pray for protection from "ungodly men." He characterized Jefferson as "a man eternally wavering from one extreme to the other." Confiding anxiously to Walter, he wrote: "All this however you better pretty much keep to yourself at present. Let it be decided either way, I suspect we shall have curious times—curious times indeed, when a whole government of a great nation is entrusted to the hands of an unprincipled jacobinic faction."[1]

Like most Federalists, William Smith Shaw was brought up to worry about chaos. The practice of collecting—and its first cousin, preserving—can function as an antidote to chaos; it followed that Shaw, depicted at midlife in a portrait by Gilbert Stuart as a hunched gentleman with a stiff, chalky expression (fig. 1.1), became a passionate collector. He liked coins and medals, but his tastes were eclectic and voluminous: from the turn of the nineteenth century until his death in 1826 he collected as much printed matter as he could—for himself and for others. By all accounts William Shaw suffered from bibliomania. His habit of collecting books and pamphlets bordered on obsession. In fact, he tailored his clothing to accommodate special pockets for books.[2] Public attention to Shaw's peculiar condition ranged from polite references to his "fondness for bibliography" to pure amazement from those who "daily witnessed the zeal and diligence with which he pursued every object he deemed important to be acquired."[3] The chief recipient of Shaw's

FIGURE 1.1 William Smith Shaw in portrait by Gilbert Stuart, 1827. (*Boston Athenaeum*)

books, pamphlets, and manuscripts was the Boston Athenaeum, the library and reading room that would become his raison d'être. The institution fed Shaw's appetite for information and order. It also kept his despair at bay.

Even this first glimpse into the Athenaeum reveals the discrepancy between the official record of the library's origins and a highly personal history of its evolution. The anxieties of early Americans were inextricably linked to the development of their multipurpose cultural institutions. To understand the complexity of the Athenaeum, one needs to recover the filter through which men like Shaw viewed the world, to detect what they believed, rejoiced in, and feared. The cultural legacy of the written correspondence between William Smith Shaw (1778–1826) and Arthur Maynard Walter (1780–1807) becomes apparent after Walter's death, as their words suggest reasons for the mission of the soon-to-be-established Boston Athenaeum, which had a highly emotional foundation. Its exclusivity and conservatism can be traced to Shaw's mournful disposition.

In the late 1790s, when William Smith Shaw began his career as an attorney in Massachusetts, the mood of the young nation was uncertain. An expanding print culture, aftershocks of the revolution, and the accelerated pace of commercial life contributed to widespread disorientation. In the midst of this upheaval, Shaw, who came from an established Braintree, Massachusetts, family, would pursue the twin goals of literature and the law. The legal profession was attractive to men with literary inclinations; in the early republic, learnedness had not yet splintered into the territorial disciplines we know today.[4] Shaw's father, a village minister, died while his son was studying at Harvard. The two reigning women of the family—his aunt, Abigail Adams, and his mother (Abigail's sister), Elizabeth Shaw Peabody—guided Shaw through early adulthood. In 1798 he had become a personal secretary to his uncle, President Adams. Returning to Massachusetts in 1801 after Jefferson's election, Shaw set up a Boston law practice in proximity to friends and family.[5]

During the first years of the 1800s, Federalists made no secret of their attachment to all things British.[6] Even in Boston, the cradle of the Revolution, the conflict had been only political, never cultural. Separation from England was difficult, if not impossible. In the writing of Shaw's dearest friend, for example, one can detect tension between the traditions of Great Britain and an emerging American identity. Shaw's Harvard classmate Arthur Maynard Walter certainly felt the pull toward British traditions. Walter had always nurtured a desire to participate in a life of letters. The son of a Loyalist rector of Boston's Trinity Church who had taken refuge in Nova Scotia during the Revolution, Walter dreamed of moving to England.[7] In 1798, he confessed ("this, Shaw, between you and I") that he wished he could sit in an English study and "write to my dear friends, to hear from them and live over the scenes of youth, where our affections have ripened and our habits of virtue been confirmed." Recalling one of the aims of the *Life of Johnson*, in which James Boswell invokes Cato (in lines popularized by Joseph Addison: "To make mankind in conscious virtue bold / Live o'er each scene, and be what they behold"), Walter had absorbed the mood of the Johnsonian circle so thoroughly that the reference was merely implied.[8] Noteworthy is Walter's addition—the "ripening of affection"—a notion whose free expression over a decade of correspondence would further distinguish this small group of Boston gentlemen and make evident the intensity of the friendships among Shaw, Walter, and others.

Soon his dream was refined, and Walter yearned less for relocation to the motherland than for importation from it. In fashioning his personal goals in the United States, he looked to prototypes that were decidedly British. "My dear Shaw," wrote Walter,

> One of the most pleasing thoughts of my future life is the happiness I might enjoy from an establishment of a Literary Club. You know how the wits of G. Britain enjoyed themselves from an institution of this kind, founded by Reynolds and Johnson and which is still in existence. Sinclair, the Pursuits of Literature says, has something of this kind at his house every week. This, Shaw, must be capital recreation after the tumult of business is over. Nothing I think would have been more delightful than to have talked with such a Leviathan as Johnson, or such a genius as Beauclerk. Even when I am talking with persons who are only a little acquainted with the secrets of Muses I glow with a sort of inward feeling, which is too good.[9]

Shaw, like Walter, sought refuge in a collaborative literary enterprise, and good fortune afforded both men an opportunity to experiment with this idea. During 1804 a loose collection of gentlemen that included Shaw and Walter took over a failing magazine and inaugurated the *Monthly Anthology and Boston Review* (fig. 1.2), making it both a miscellany and an ill-defined forum for literary criticism. Edited in piecemeal fashion for six years (from 1805 until 1811) and resulting in ten octavo volumes, the *Anthology* was always financially unstable. None of its five printers was able to make it profitable, and subscription figures never reached 500. (A parallel effort in Philadelphia, Joseph Dennie's *Port Folio*, boasted 1,500 subscribers.) The dozen or so members of the Anthology Society—as the group came to call itself—displayed a penchant for eighteenth-century comprehensiveness. On subjects ranging from "the necessity of revelation" to "the purring of cats," the faithful Anthologists (many ministers, a few lawyers, some statesmen and businessmen) entertained mysteries large and small. Perhaps more important, they also devoted a section to reviews of works by and about Americans.[10]

The Anthology Society's method of reading manuscripts aloud was part of the tradition of belles-lettres circles, which had thrived in the colonies as well as in England.[11] Many of the published pieces were written by friends of the Anthologists or by the members themselves. (The Reverend William Emerson, father of Ralph Waldo, was an early participant; he became a founder of the Athenaeum and its first vice president.) The group's reaction to submissions is captured in the journal of the society, which gives the flavor of each meeting. For example, according to an entry from 1810, one gentleman "presented an

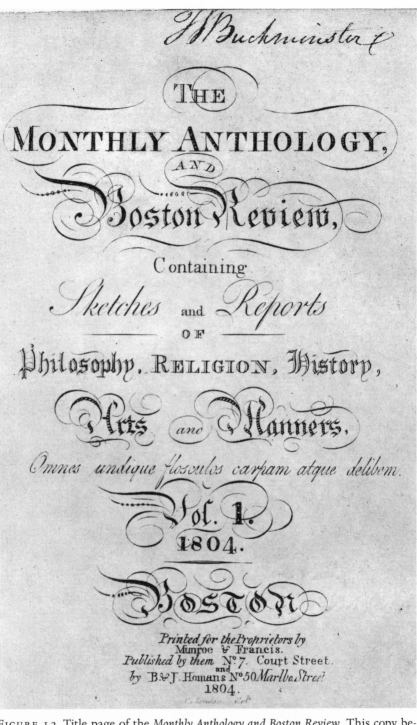

FIGURE 1.2 Title page of the *Monthly Anthology and Boston Review*. This copy belonged to the Reverend Joseph Buckminster. (*Boston Athenaeum*)

Essay on the Superiority of justice to generosity; but he read it so ill, or it was so stupid that the frequent interruptions compelled him to stop, and nobody moved for its acceptance."[12] Attendance was sporadic, and editorial direction negligible.

But there were benefits to these gatherings. As Lewis Simpson notes in his edition of selections from the *Anthology*, the gentlemen sought to "join intellectual and social pleasures," to be "clubbable" in the Johnsonian sense. With Walter as secretary and Shaw as treasurer, the group established semiregular dinner meetings at members' homes. The journal of the society points to conflicting aims; typically, one member tried to "save the *Anthology*" while another simply tried to "save the evening." Often the meetings would be successful only in the social sense, with members eating "a mongrel goose of surpassing beauty," for example, and staying until "a vulgar hour." On one evening when the venue was new to the group, a meeting was cut short. In this characteristic excerpt from the society's journal, priorities become apparent: "No other business was transacted, the members feeling rather wild in a strange room. The beef was good and the wine bad. Every man did not carry his own segars, as had been previously voted."[13]

The Boston Athenaeum owes its existence to the convivial, confused Anthology Society. In the spring of 1806, William Shaw accepted an appointment as clerk of the federal district court. Freed from the stresses of his regular law practice, he worked with his fellow Anthologists to draft a prospectus for a "reading-room in Boston, to be called the Anthology Reading-Room." Convenience was paramount. The group sought "an agreeable place of resort," "opportunities of literary intercourse," and "the pleasure of perusing the principal European and American periodical publications, at an expense not exceeding that of a single daily paper."[14] Robert Hallowell Gardiner, a fellow Anthologist, recalled the evolution of the reading room this way:

> As the circulation of the Anthology increased, so the Periodicals we received in exchange accumulated, and books, both original and republications of English works, were constantly sent to us to be reviewed. All these required a place of deposit, and we hired a convenient room in Congress Street. . . . And as there was then no public reading room in Boston, we opened ours to the Public by the payment of a moderate fee, the receipts, after paying the expenses of the room, being appropriated to obtaining valuable Periodicals that we did not receive in exchange for the Anthology, and thus adding to its attraction.

Each member was to donate books, Gardiner continued. "Walter, Shaw, and myself removed the books ourselves to our new rooms and arranged them on the shelves."[15]

Soon the Anthologists set up generous hours of operation (nine to nine) for an annual fee (ten dollars). By the following January the Anthology Reading Room had transformed itself into a small institution "similar to the Athenaeum and Lyceum of Liverpool in Great Britain." The proprietors issued formal regulations and announced more than 160 subscribers. Formally incorporated in 1807, the renamed "Athenaeum" elected trustees and solicited subscribers through a "memoir" eloquently advancing its mission. "Shaw entered most heartily into the plan," Gardiner recalled, "was made Librarian, and not being troubled with diffidence, became a sturdy beggar for the Athenaeum, applying for donations of books and pamphlets wherever there was the least prospect of obtaining them, and was very successful. His exertions procured for him the soubriquet of Athenaeum Shaw."[16]

Official institutional accounts acknowledge Shaw's unusually prominent role in securing the Athenaeum's future and even allude to his overzealous book collecting. But his behavior remains mysterious. For the few years during which the Anthology Society overlapped with the Athenaeum, there was "much animated controversy" at club meetings about "rights and privileges in the Athenaeum," according to the young George Ticknor, a budding scholar. "W. Shaw would not speak on the subject, because it seemed criminal to doubt the honourable observance of the engagements of the [Athenaeum] Trustees." In his *History of the Boston Athenaeum*, Josiah Quincy (1772–1864) would later write that "the Athenaeum became the almost exclusive object of [Shaw's] thoughts, and not so much a desire as a passion." Quincy's frustration lurks between the lines, as we learn that Shaw mixed his own books and pamphlets among the archives of the library "with little regard to preserve the evidence of his right to property in these collections; so completely did he identify his own interests with its success." The trustees eventually tried to obtain an account of what was due him, but "a love of ease, which nothing could awaken to activity, but the desire to collect books, pamphlets, and articles," prevented him from separating his property from that of the Athenaeum. Even his brother-in-law, Joseph Felt, remarked on Shaw's stubbornness: "While he considered their request as proper, he did not so feel the necessity of it as to comply."[17] Shaw's failing health caused Athenaeum officials to abandon any effort to sort through the collections, fearing that further inquiries would upset and weaken him. It seems that Shaw's employment at the Athenaeum called for special pleading. Handling his temperament necessitated sensitivity, an understanding of the gains and losses of coddling a devoted institutional fixture.

Privately, people were somewhat less circumspect. With a sampling of more casually written assessments of William Shaw comes a small chorus of voices that speak to the man's peculiar nature. As early as 1804, none other than his dear friend Walter hinted at Shaw's inertia, hiding his own worries behind those of their mutual friend Benjamin Welles. "He thinks that Shaw will do nothing; that his habits are against him," Walter wrote in his journal. "I fear there is too much truth in these [predictions]." In 1817, the biographer Samuel Knapp wrote of Shaw, "He fastens on every thing new, rare, and antique, with an earnestness which baffles all denial."[18] And the author and diplomat William Tudor indulged in this spirited sketch of Shaw:

> That fellow Shaw is not unlike the wolf in the desert he goes about seeking what he can devour—not in the night time to be sure (although some folks say he ought to) but in the day time, in the burning heat of the meridian sun. Why gentlemen . . . that dog Shaw goes everywhere. He knows everybody. Everybody knows him. If he sees a book pamphlet or manuscript—Oh! Sir! The Athenaeum must have this. Well, have it he will & have it he must & have it he does—for he seldom goes out of a house without having something under his arm & his large pockets, made on purpose, all crammed. Now he never refuses any thing whatever. With him a book is a book pamphlet a pamphlet manuscript a manuscript &c &c. If I had given it to any of you gentlemen, you would have put it into your pockets and some days after you accidentally would have found something there all in atoms, about which you knew nothing. Now that Shaw will preserve them like the apple of his eye—[19]

A brief but fascinating account of Shaw's career appears in the "Reminiscences" of Robert Hallowell Gardiner. To balance a vice, Gardiner offers a corresponding virtue; to counter a virtue, he notes a vice. The chiasmus ends in a rhetorical shrug, with an admission that the librarian was summarily fired. "Shaw was uncouth in mind and body," writes Gardiner, "but was indefatigable in his labours for promoting the success of the work in which we were engaged. His very great and disinterested exertions for the Institution palliated his eccentricities and gaucheries, and he continued Librarian till the unfortunate habit of intemperance made him incapable of attending to the decencies of life, and the Trustees were obliged to dismiss him."

Uncouth. Unhinged. Intemperate. Insatiable. What was it about William Smith Shaw that moved people to expressions of pity, judgment, even alarm? To answer this question is to introduce the special origins of the Boston Athenaeum. Its earliest documents mask important aspects of the institution's founder and his cohort. Shaw was indeed something of a misfit in the company of ambitious merchants and methodical scholars. He felt most comfortable among his college friends. The intensity of his relationship with Arthur Maynard Walter, especially, would color Shaw's work long after Walter's death. Two years Shaw's junior, Walter—eighteen as their correspondence begins in earnest—was finishing his undergraduate studies and would, like his friend, eventually study the law. He had come to know Shaw, along with the precocious Joseph Stevens Buckminster (1784–1812), at Harvard.[20] All in their late teens or early twenties, these men were just beginning to make their way in the world: Buckminster became an influential intellectual, whereas Shaw and Walter were amateur men of letters.

From the correspondence of their youth, one can understand the conditions that drove Shaw and his friends to exalt the balm of literature and to demand so much affection from one another. The letters offer conversations on paper as these men speak in the private, unmediated realm of the page.[21] Here, in one written in 1798, the autumn after Shaw graduated from Harvard, Walter tries to secure a promise from his friend. He adopts a persuasive manner, reinforcing common desires while pushing an agenda. By the very act of writing, Walter argues for a quid pro quo:

> I have now written a long *dispatch*. If you knew, Shaw, the pleasure I took in reading letters, especially such as your last, you would exert yourself in giving comfort to a classmate, alone and unknown. I certainly am punctual in returning answers, as are you. But I write as often as you will allow me. I will confess you are much taken up with business; but I should think you could steal a little time and converse with me by letter. If you cannot, when you do write, you must write long. I have no enjoyment equal to opening a letter from any one, and you have told me you receive an unknown sensation when you break a seal and find in the form of a letter the features of a friend.[22]

The distinguishing trait of the correspondence between Shaw and Walter is a plea for intimacy. The "unknown sensation" to which Walter refers is what the Federalists called "sympathetick feeling"—a cluster of emotions that combine understanding and empathy with relief from isolation and worry. One scholar has noted that in the antebellum era the personal letter functioned as an "emotional conveyance."[23] More than mere vessels, however, the letters these Federalists exchanged helped create their writers through an experimental display of wit, intellect, and passion. Guides for letter-writing were plentiful at the time, and both Walter and Shaw wanted to perform well by the standards of this genteel art. Still, the conventions of the genre also allowed for improvisation. Neither man was a master of the form, but their respective epistolary styles can be tentatively characterized. For Shaw, letter-writing began as an exercise but increasingly betrayed his loneliness; for Walter, writing to Shaw meant that he could play the role of a true littérateur.[24]

Their epistolary conversations display a close, passionate bond—one that approximates, but does not equal, romantic love. Gentlemen in this era and social class experienced especially intense friendships, typically forged in college, where the all-male environment and a period of insecurity created a charged atmosphere conducive to closeness. Certainly Shaw and Walter fit that scenario, but their bond differs from that same-sex cultural norm in a few respects. Both men became distanced from their fathers (Shaw's father died early, and Walter's father suffered his son's rejection of the ministry); they therefore sought male support elsewhere. Neither man married, which, in the eyes of Federalist society, suspended indefinitely a phase of their life cycles. And, last, the emphasis, shared in letters, on the interior experience of reading magnified the private realm in which the men dwelled; they deepened their attachment through their written correspondence. It would, however, be a mistake to assume that Walter and Shaw were lovers in the twenty-first-century sense; theirs was most likely not a sexual relationship, and it loses its most subtle features when the reductive question of physical contact is put to it.[25]

Yet the correspondence employs the topoi of the love letter. Jealousy, poetic imagery, and fantasies of erasing time and space in order to be together are all on exhibit. Staying up "as long as half a candle lasts," Walter would dream of college days, when "we drank punch on your window seat." And his friend would join him. "My God! What would I give if I could spend one single evening with you in your chamber—it would be too good—how much spleen we would vent—how much happiness enjoy!!" Shaw conveys with dashes and exclamation points the breathlessness of animated speech. Walter answers with his wish that Shaw "could spend a few hours" in *his* chamber: "When I sit over my dying coals during the evening, I only want your company to be completely happy." Dismissing the compensatory pleasures of "girls," Walter continues to conjure his Harvard friends on the page, recreating his collegiate self in the third person: "The wild, random, laughter loving Walter was never made for such scenes of pleasure. He wants Shaw, Channing, Buckminster to be with him, to smoke the segar, drink brandy and water, and laugh like heroes." When Walter pouts about Shaw having answered another classmate's letter before answering his, Shaw soothes him with poetic language ("I have wanted to fly to you on the wings of the wind & shew you my whole heart") and then regresses to childish scorekeeping: "You begin your letter by saying you 'never mean to write a long letter to a short one' but you have written a short one to me in answer to a very long one, mine was 4 leaves of large letter paper & yours only 2 pages of very small paper." The frank measurement of the written output corresponds to the veiled measurement of friendship.[26]

The manipulation, the testing of each other's emotions, was part of a pattern. Years later, in an issue of the *Monthly Anthology*, these same men would endorse the publication of an essay on friendship: "Probably the height at which [friendship] arrives in one who cultivates it is proportional to the strength of the mind. You are not to upbraid your friend with want of sincerity."[27] The essay goes on to imply that men incapable of proper friendship are to be pitied. Friendship was a serious project, one which exposed intellect as well as moral fiber. And Shaw and Walter encouraged each other's progress. "Friendship ought to be a plant of slow growth," Walter writes. "Whether this has not been the case with us, comparatively speaking, I leave you to determine. True in the beginning there was cautious and prudent conduct used, which afterwards led on to a knowledge of dispositions almost similar and a development of character, new and interesting. But what secured our embrio friendship was sympathy of nature. This, my dear fellow, . . . gave the finishing stroke to our sentiments and has made a friendship perfect as human nature will admit." Conceived together, their "embrio" friendship would have its own history and its own achievements. The letters produced the proper environment, the "sympathy of nature," to nourish that creation. "Letters breathe," Shaw writes. "They express the warm effusions of a benevolent heart, . . . and are the happy medium by which you may enjoy the 'feast of reason and the flow of the soul' with your friend, although hills and vallies should separate you." With a strange fervor, Shaw and Walter promoted the notion of sympathy and inscribed their own social niche.[28]

The letters exploit and synthesize various traditions, including the idea of "moral taste" developed by the so-called Common Sense philosophers.[29] The Scottish rhetorician Hugh Blair gave the work of moral philosophers Francis Hutchison and Thomas Reid a prescriptive turn in his widely read manual, *Lectures on Rhetoric and Belles Lettres*, first published in 1783. "Taste is certainly not an arbitrary principle, which is subject to the fancy of every individual," Blair wrote, "and which admits no criterion for determining whether it be true or false. Its foundation is the same in every human mind. It is built upon sentiments and perceptions, which are inseparable from our nature." Required reading at Harvard at the beginning of the nineteenth century, the text was so popular that in 1953 a researcher found twenty-six printings on Harvard's shelves, all issued between 1789 and 1832. Certainly both Shaw and Walter were familiar with the teachings of this handbook on rhetoric. In his guide, Blair recommended that men of fine taste consult their own imagination and attend to the feelings of others. The cultivation of social virtues is inherently moral, Blair maintained. "Compassion, mildness, and generosity," he implied, aid the appreciation of fine writing; ethos is emphasized over logos. (Writing in his London journal in 1803, Walter would later assert, "The heart influences us more than the head."[30]) Blair's book touched upon Homer's epics, Cicero's rhetoric, and Joseph Addison's style; it linked the refinement of one's taste with the awakening of pleasure. Taste is a faculty that can be trained, it has a moral component, and it finds its proper climate in the company of true friends—these assumptions speak to the Federalist culture in which reading and writing were learned.[31]

For Shaw and Walter, the relentless pursuit of sympathy and taste was narrated in the context of their responsibilities as sons and citizens. The correspondence served at least three purposes. First, it functioned as a tether, grounding their emotions as they ventured into adulthood. Further, it allowed the men to exercise a life of belles-lettres, an epistolary esprit de corps that would later be formalized in the Anthology Society; this purpose blurs and overlaps with the first, as the Federalists' idea of intimacy defined and was defined by the ideals of literature. But perhaps most striking is the extent to which their correspondence served to reinforce the identities of Shaw and Walter. Their letter-writing selves evolved as they adopted and adapted to distinct roles. Each correspondent experimented with articulating concerns about political chaos, marriage, and professional choice.

William Shaw wanted to believe that he and Walter were alike in all ways, but in fact their differences were pronounced. In a diary written as Walter embarked on his long-anticipated journey abroad, Shaw stresses their commonalities: "Our habits of living—our talents—our studies and our professions are nearly similar." Yet in the early moments of their scattered eight-year correspondence, one sees the two men serving as each other's foil, so divergent were their outlooks and styles. Walter emerged as the darling and Shaw the dyspeptic, as their identities were linked through a subtle staging of subject matter and tone. Walter directed their exchanges with enthusiasm, baiting Shaw to write at length. As in his "long *dispatch*" to Shaw on the obligations and pleasures of the genre (quoted above), Walter was purposeful in his epistolary efforts. About the possibility of corresponding with Shaw from England, he suggests, "I would write you Literature and you would give me Politics in return. This would be a complete reciprocity and I should like to experience its advantages."[32]

Shaw, threatened by the political instability he observed at close range, offered his share of outbursts. In letters such as this one, written right before he started work for his uncle, President John Adams, he seems to hiss with venomous rage: "I got into the stage the morning after I left you about seven o'clock. I had not rode far before I perceived that the company were all bloody-minded Jacobins. After scandalizing Washington, they immediately began their encomiums on [Franklin]. They called him the political savior &c. I told them I ever had considered him as an enemy of the country, one whose hobby-horse had been France, whose object the destruction of the government & constitution of America. This they could hardly swallow. . . . My blood finally boiled in my veins." "Jacobinism" referred not only to French

Jacobins but also to their American apologists, advocates of popular politics who hid under what Shaw called "the insidious cloak of patriotism."[33]

Partisanship structured the public discussion of how to stabilize the new nation, but beneath the rhetoric of Federalism and Republicanism ran more elemental forces. Later, riding in carriages with President Adams gave Shaw an opportunity "to feel all the climates of the human mind and to see all the variety of the human species." What he perceived was "much virtue but more vice—much politeness but more impertinence and much wisdom but more folly." In measured phrases, Shaw cancels out each claim of progress, finally tipping the balance toward dystopia. As Lewis Simpson has shown, for Federalists such as Shaw and Walter there was a pull in two directions: the promise of progress was matched by its opposite, the dread of decay. The letters mediate between two visions of the American cultural landscape: civilization and barbarism. Walter also watched the political upheaval in Europe with trepidation, "hating Frenchmen," but his interests led him elsewhere. "We will leave these lurid subjects," he announces to Shaw in a clear shift, "and talk of the elegant pursuits of literature and life."[34]

As the exchange of letters continued, Walter became, quite deliberately, Shaw's better half. Walter's performance vis-à-vis a young woman in Philadelphia would forecast other ways in which he completed, or balanced, his friend. "Shaw, I am interested in your welfare and you must tell me the progress you make in the heart of Miss Wilson," he insists. "Repose all your anxious cares in my bosom. I will assuage your grief and perhaps I may be able to assist you." Embracing the role of confidant, he writes, "I hope I shall one day have the pleasure of telling Mrs. Shaw the anxieties you have suffered on her account." He redefines the privileges of friendship: "Now do Shaw tell me what you feel on the subject. As your friend I have a right to it and will claim it. If you do not I shall be induced to write to your young correspondent and tell them unreservedly of your heart. . . . Tell me then Miss Wilson's direction and whether you will carry the letter, which I will write. Sincerely, I will plead on your behalf. That you may not be deceived I will send the letter unsealed and you may read it, provided you will be engaged to send it to her afterwards."[35]

The romance was either nonexistent or doomed. That Walter insinuated himself into this potential affair indicates how entitled he felt to Shaw's heart. He teases Shaw about women: "It is bad to indulge your fancy too much with the white bosoms and fair ancles of your inamoratas." And when he finally comes close to meeting Miss Wilson, Walter reports on her in a letter that expresses devotion to his friend: "Into your bosom I love to have all my thoughts & I think you will not refuse them." On the subject of the woman, a shred of gossip now suffices: "[They say] she was not handsome."

The demonstrative Walter vies for the position of Mrs. Shaw through sheer provocation. Elsewhere, he tweaks Boston society with remarks on a baby born soon after the mother was wed: "Population is the bulwark of any nation, and we are great patriots, you know, in New England. Indeed, if we can alter nature's course and make four, instead of nine months, the usual period of gestation, there must be a great saving in time." With Shaw as his audience, Walter winks at all that is left unsaid.[36]

In the letters Walter served as a ventriloquist, giving voice to hopes and fears that Shaw apparently silenced. About his own future with women, Walter confesses, "I can never enjoy the bliss of a wife and the prattle of children." He fears that a wife of his would "find poverty staring her in the face." Walter also articulates his concerns about choosing a profession: "I dread the thought of studying law, or writing sermons. Ambition actuates me little." When his father received a letter from Walter about his final decision to pursue law over the ministry, a poignant scene unfolded. Walter's sister told him that their father, the Reverend William Walter, read the letter on a Sunday. "Preaching in the afternoon he could hardly articulate his words," writes Walter. "This, Shaw, was indeed distressing." The gentleman-author as a type prevailed well into midcentury. Even though Shaw and Walter would not produce long (or many) pieces, they sought out a subculture that privileged anonymity and leisure with respect to literature. Their connection to merchants and other Boston men of business was sometimes strained. As Lewis Simpson argues, they liked to imagine a "countereconomy" of literary pursuits that would balance the growing trend of commercialism. Like Walter, Shaw was the son of a minister; he wanted a life of letters; and he certainly knew the demands a family would have placed on him. Legal careers offered both men more latitude. And later a kind of self-patronage within the Anthology Society would allow them the independence they craved. One can only assume that Walter expressed many of Shaw's worries about the traditional expectations of marriage and work.[37]

On the subject of the deficiencies of American literature, however, Shaw was more vocal than Walter. His wish for America to "rescue herself" and attain "literary fame" was alternately dizzying and depressing. In 1800 he took a grim inventory of his reading material in the new capital city of Washington: "A *few books* which I sent round by water & which never arrived till this evening & a *few*, which I borrowed and purchased at Philadelphia & a *few* which I borrow of the heads of Department constitute all my library." The reason for these conditions seemed clear to him: "Certain it is that at present the inordinate pursuit of wealth, excluding all cultivation of mind, most criminally arrests the attention of our Countrymen." Shaw was aware of his curmudgeonly tendencies and the manner in which such statements were received. "I have frequently been told," he admits to his friend, "that I am too open in avowing my partialities for some and my prejudices against others—that my exclusive preferences are unauthorized by the rules of politeness."[38]

Shaw bemoaned the state of American letters and politics, indulging in dark, abstract assessments. Walter, meanwhile, revealed more private anxieties, needling his reserved correspondent about romance and worrying about his own uncertain place in society. By inviting Shaw to participate in his struggles, I argue, Walter became a spokesman for Shaw. But that was not to last. The relief Shaw enjoyed from his customary gloom—the sympathy he had with a friend who compensated for his sullen nature—ended suddenly. After an illness so short that there is scarcely a mention of it in any of the correspondence among their circle, Walter died of consumption in January 1807. He was twenty-six years old.[39]

"Walter dead!" Joseph Buckminster wrote Shaw from London upon learning the news. "O, my dear friend. My heart is full of anguish. . . . I suspect the last letter he ever wrote was addressed to me. Alas! I cannot read it without tears. I have been writing to him by every opportunity. Ah, they are letters he will never read!" An intimate of both Shaw and Walter from their Harvard days, Joseph Buckminster became a famous Boston minister who popularized sermon-writing in the first decades of the nineteenth century. Buckminster seems to have mourned the correspondence as much as the man, an indication of how completely letters represented their authors. Shaw no doubt felt the loss even more acutely. "My dear friend is dead!" he finally wrote to Buckminster in a melancholy echo. "There was no good I ever enjoyed, there was no pleasure I ever anticipated, with which Walter was not intimately associated." Friends knew what Walter's death would mean for William Shaw, and the letters that appeared in the ensuing months stand as further evidence of the intimacy the two had enjoyed. "I condole with you, my friend, in your loss," wrote Josiah Quincy, adopting the tone of one comforting the recently widowed. "Such men as your Walter was, are rare."[40] Tributes by fellow Anthologists also appeared, as the tight circle pulled even closer. It was in the aftermath of Walter's death that Shaw dedicated himself to the work of the Athenaeum, whose early distinguishing features— exclusivity, anglophilia, a certain hauteur—had also been dominant elements in the correspondence. Shaw's contribution to the Athenaeum both reflected and distorted ideals he and Walter had championed together.

Walter had left his friend a bequest that referred to their shared commitments. Some two weeks after his death, this note arrived for Shaw: "The brothers of your deceased friend, A. M. Walter, ask your acceptance of his

gold watch as a mark of his esteem and as a continual proof of the friend-
ship which subsisted between you. They also carry into effect his wish of
October 4, 1802, as expressed in his letter on going to Europe, thus: 'If the
Supreme Being should take me from among the children of men, I request
that my Tully should be presented to William S. Shaw, for I love him.'"[41]
"Tully" was a familiar term for Marcus Tullius Cicero, Roman statesman and
orator, whose book on friendship would have been well known to both men.
In addition, the section on epistolary writing in Hugh Blair's primer upheld
Cicero as the master of the epistolary art and emphasized "ease" and "familiarity" in the writing of letters: "Cicero's epistles are the most valuable collection of letters, extant, in any language. They are composed with purity and
elegance, but without the least affectation." Cicero's dominant teaching was
that to be a good orator one must first become a good man.[42]

For Shaw and his contemporaries, the ancients offered healthy models for
public life. "The goal," historian Gordon Wood writes about the years following the American Revolution, "was not to create a leveled society, but an
organic hierarchy led by natural aristocrats who would resemble not the
luxury-loving, money-mongering lackeys of British officialdom but the stoi-
cal and disinterested heroes of antiquity—men like Washington, who seemed
to Americans to embody perfectly the classical ideal of the Republican
leader."[43] When people gained the power of eloquence without learning duty,
according to Cicero, corruption—in individuals and in government—
resulted. Thus, for Federalists, the Ciceronian brand of rhetoric united epistolary excellence with morality; it also stood for protection against the dangers of Republicanism. Clearly, Walter had left his most cherished book to
Shaw. Homosocial relations in this era were predicated on the exchange of
beloved authors.[44] Shaw and Walter had tried to fashion an alternate literary
world in which friendship, not marriage, mattered above all.

The public legacy of Shaw's interrupted relationship with Walter unfolded
over the first decade of the Boston Athenaeum's life, during which Shaw led
the institution almost single-handedly. Extreme grief helps explain Shaw's
absorption in its daily operations. Gradually, he became indispensable to—
and coterminous with—the Athenaeum. Although the reading room started
from a communal base, it grew into a lone production. During the first year
it was not unusual for Shaw, both secretary and librarian, to be the sole
trustee in attendance at quarterly meetings. Repeatedly, the Athenaeum's
public record adumbrates the loneliness of the whole enterprise: "Present no
one but the Secretary" is a refrain in the trustees' book. The words, written
in Shaw's spidery script, almost sigh with disappointment. Indeed, in 1812,
the first year of the war with Great Britain, interest in the Athenaeum dwin-
dled. Of six trustees' meetings, only one had a quorum for transacting busi-

ness. As his brother-in-law wrote, "At this critical juncture, Mr. Shaw redoubled his diligence, and necessarily took on himself the entire superintendence of the institution."[45]

One of the ideals that had excited Shaw, Walter, and the other amateurs was that of an American man of letters. "Man of letters" was a porous term that admitted legal, scientific, and philosophical writing in addition to poetry, sermons, and personal correspondence.[46] In a disquisition titled "The Dangers and Duties of Men of Letters," Joseph Buckminster supplied his contemporaries with the image of a scholar who was also accountable to the world at large. Again, the ubiquitous Cicero was the model: Buckminster points to Cicero and his "regular course of public service" in contrast to the Greek rhetorician Atticus, who wandered "among the ruins of Athens, purchasing up statues and antiques." Buckminster concludes with these cautionary words: "You, then, . . . who seek in learned seclusion that moral security, which is the reward of virtuous resolution, remember, you do not escape from temptations, much less from responsibility, by retiring to the repose and silence of your libraries."[47]

Yet in practice the Anthologists did largely retreat to the safety of their intellectual pursuits.[48] Though undeniably learned, William Shaw was lauded neither as a lawyer nor as a writer. Buckminster's model of the American man of letters must have haunted him, as the librarian's storied bibliomania replaced a more virtuous application of bookishness. Instead of following the Ciceronian imperative, Shaw collected ardently. The collector, it is said, "*invests in objects all that he finds impossible to invest in human relationships.*"[49] Applying few discernible criteria, Shaw routinely acquired published works with desperate letters like this one: "I cannot urge upon you too strongly to spare no pains to send me the interesting books published in NYork as soon as possible."[50] Like Charles Willson Peale, whose taxonomic efforts were legendary, Shaw collected natural specimens as well.[51] One can imagine that collecting—in all its forms—distracted him from melancholy. Eventually, the duties of the paradigmatic man of letters mutated into a scribbled list of "Duties To Be Performed at the Boston Athenaeum & Not To Be Omitted." Far from glamorous, the responsibilities included collecting "all the Periodical works to bind" and "sending a letter of introduction to all the Booksellers of Boston." "Every morning," wrote Shaw, "Sweep News-rooms/dust the tables, chairs &c and the Library-room—After breakfast, clean the Lamps & Lamp-room, see that the books are in their places and even with the shelves."[52]

The gap between the Anthologists' original ambitions and Shaw's gradual alienation was wide. In 1807 the Athenaeum's prospectus, which Shaw had helped craft, emphasized a public spirit behind the institution's mission: "Besides the dignity and satisfaction associated with the cultivation of letters and the arts, and which constitute their worth to the individual, they have unlimited uses in respect to the community. . . . Where the love of pleasure and the means of it are continually augmenting, and where expense is not grudged to amusements of a different nature, it is presumed this institution will be thought to deserve the countenance of the wise and patriotic." Benefits to the citizenry are extolled. Ambiguous language swells with noble purpose. And if we turn to Quincy's *History of the Boston Athenaeum*, we read much about the founders' "generosity" and "enlightenment." Not surprisingly, an institutional voice pervades Quincy's history, where, for the most part, the librarian's problematic "zeal" conveniently collapses into the nickname Athenaeum Shaw.[53] But the angst and the solace Shaw experienced— to which readers of his letters are an audience—tell a more complicated story. Fearing the worst for America (anarchy, barbarism), Shaw cleaved first to Walter, then to the life of the Athenaeum. The basis for his singular dedication was personal anxiety, as he struggled to gain composure in the cultural turbulence of his time.

When Joseph Buckminster died in 1812, Shaw's mother—whose epistolary "maternal counsels" had been a constant for Shaw since his Harvard years— acknowledged his pain: "Friend after friend, my dear son, is severed from your heart. May you meditate thereon, and learn to consider your own frailty."[54] Emotionally amputated yet again, Shaw, now thirty-four, cast about for comfort. That book collecting would become a substitute for the lost friends of his youth makes sense. Years before, as secretary to President Adams, he had felt exiled in the swampy new capital and had devised a similar solution:

> Unless I can find society whose habits and feelings correspond nearly with my own, . . . [I] infinitely prefer none, but to cultivate with increased industry friendship for my books, in whose society I can always recognize friends that are delightful to me. [They] come at my call and return when I desire them— they are never out of humor and they answer all my questions with readiness. Some present in review before me the memory of past ages, while others reveal to me the secrets of nature—these teach me how to live and those how to die.[55]

Here, contrary to what the Athenaeum's prospectus would later insist upon, books do not promote a good society; they *are* good society. Unless one is with perfect friends, Shaw decides, books are preferable to people—a sentiment that hints at the origins of the institution's exclusivity.[56]

The story behind the story of the Athenaeum's founding is an example of how private lives become publicly expressed. The Boston Athenaeum had a personal foundation, based in large part on fear, love, and loss. The early papers of the Athenaeum shield from view the idiosyncratic, often erratic behavior of William Shaw. Contrasting two readings of the institution's history—one official, the other intimate—exposes how underreported the emotional life is in historical discourse.[57] Fundamental to every institution is a myth of its own origins. Such stories depend on ethical appeals and compensatory gestures; they play with authorship and audience. By arguing that Shaw used the Athenaeum to relieve anxiety about his place in the new nation, I offer a corrective to the founding myth. The counternarrative gives rise to fresh inquiries—about assumptions and motivations, about convenient reasons versus real reasons.[58] What unintended roles did the Athenaeum play in the city? How did its exclusivity sit with members who supported marginalized groups? Why was the Athenaeum's own identity shaped and molded so meticulously?

One is struck by the difference between the minutes of the Anthology Society and those of the Boston Athenaeum. The sociability of the former, with its well-documented drinking and laughing, was all but erased in the dry businesslike records of the emergent Athenaeum. Once the latter was incorporated, the wit and warmth of the Anthologists' minutes evaporated into the Athenaeum's formal documents. Whereas the Anthology served its members as a club of friends, the early Athenaeum seemed, stiffly, to feel itself watched by the city. Perhaps this difference relates to the self-conscious use of money from shares purchased after the prospectus was circulated. The Athenaeum's scope was ambitious, and the former Anthologists—whose relaxed meetings had celebrated the intellectual play of the amateur—no doubt felt a new burden of public accountability. As David Shields writes about the earliest American reading groups, "Anything that institutionalized social relationships in the new Republic . . . had to answer to the needs of society at large, had to avoid private interest or frivolity, and had to withstand moral scrutiny."[59]

The strategies that Shaw and others employed to develop the library, and the traditions that aided them in that enterprise, wait to be explored. In the meantime, the Athenaeum had clearly emerged as Shaw's true home. Other American athenaeums—in Philadelphia, Salem, Nahant—were being founded or revived at the time. In fact, one gentleman from Albany wrote to Shaw, "We may consider you the father of the whole progeny, which is to spring up." Asking for donations to aid his "infant institution," Shaw encouraged the parental metaphor. The most suitable image for his attachment to the place, however, is a marital one. As with the devotion between Walter and Shaw, the library demanded and repaid Shaw's kindnesses. Only one year after the Athenaeum's incorporation, his fidelity to the institution was well known. "Dear Shaw," wrote a friend from Philadelphia, "I rec'd Mr. Buckminster's Sermon under your direction, for which I am much obliged to you.

Should have been glad if your Grecian wife would have permitted a moment's interval in your attention to her, that I might have received other tokens of your remembrance than what is to be discerned in your handwriting." At the very least, the Boston Athenaeum's early reliance on William Shaw points to a coincidence of needs: Shaw required a new passion, and the new reading room required a steward. Soon the number of volumes deposited in the library approached twenty thousand. By the early 1820s, even Shaw would be unable to deny that the Athenaeum was firmly established. His "Grecian wife" had arrived.[60]

CHAPTER TWO

Sweet Are the Fruits of Letters

THE BOSTON ATHENAEUM was invented by men who understood the power of symbols. In nineteenth-century America it was customary for a new institution to choose an emblem, a seal or "device," for official purposes. By the spring of 1812, five years after incorporating, Athenaeum members had begun to entertain various designs. A few ideas were passed back and forth before trustees approved the final prototype: an image of three putti harvesting fruit in an idyllic orchard, with the motto *literarum fructus dulces* ("sweet are the fruits of letters") festooning the scene (fig. 2.1).[1] To state that an institution's emblem is emblematic seems flagrantly tautological. Yet the humanistic iconography of the Athenaeum seal says much about the enterprise. The emblem serves as a kind of visual manifesto, a starting point from which to explore three aspects of the institution's history: namely, transatlantic bonds, a fervor for collecting (which extended well beyond William Shaw's obsession), and the quest for the ideal setting for study and repose. The symbolic underpinnings of the Boston Athenaeum lead directly to analyses of its public image—an image that sometimes conflicted with the attitudes and practices of its members.

The Athenaeum seal belongs to a larger emblem tradition that employs a highly abbreviated visual language. Typically, the lemma, or motto, and the picture together address an ideal reader—often a patron, to whom the creation is dedicated and for whom a longer explanatory text is written. Whoever chose the Athenaeum's device was familiar with an Italian folio of "Antique Gems" illustrated by Michelangelo de La Chausse. Dedicated to his prince in the year 1700, the album includes an image the artist calls "albero con amorini" (fig. 2.2). The Latin gloss provided for the original—*litterarum radices amarae, fructus autem dulces* ("the roots of learning are bitter, but the fruit is sweet")—implies toil, risk, even distaste on the path to enlightenment. Sanitized in the Athenaeum's adaptation, learnedness only pleases. The benign Athenaeum image includes a grassy foreground in a friendlier

FIGURE 2.1 The current
Athenaeum seal, originally
approved in 1814. (*Boston
Athenaeum*)

FIGURE 2.2 Inspiration
for the Athenaeum seal,
from an Italian book of
emblems published in
1700. (*Boston Athenaeum*)

orchard, a tree generously weighted down with more fruit, and, where the winged beings in the original have muscular male bodies, the Athenaeum's putti are innocent, asexual, idealized—clearly not of this world. Emblems dating back to the early sixteenth century have always spoken to a specific community in the interest of a common cause. Unlike other early American seals—which depict the act of civilizing Indians or include pieces of the wilderness (a cornhusk, a fish, an eagle)—the Athenaeum's seal emphasizes a safely contained activity of self-culture: the putti use the urn as a repository for their harvest, and their aspiration is rewarded.[2]

Taking a cue, then, from the Athenaeum's emblem, its most ubiquitous symbol, one can read the device as a clear, if whispered, expression of Athenaeum values. The values evoked—improvement on Old World models, deliberate collection, paradisiacal space—protected the idea of the Athenaeum and together represent a scaffold on which one notion of a sanctioned American culture was built.

Unlike many of his friends, William Smith Shaw never yearned to travel abroad—because, perhaps, of a lame ankle and an overprotective mother.[3] It is an undisputed fact, however, that Shaw's Athenaeum borrowed its symbolic apparatus directly from British and Continental models. The social circle around Shaw was colored by a sensibility gained from lengthy tours of Europe. In their writings, members of the Anthology Society had expressed skepticism about the idea of an American cultural identity. (For example, J. S. J. Gardiner, a minister and schoolteacher, insisted that Americans rely on the authors of Great Britain "till we can produce equal excellence.")[4] The Anthologists adopted an outlook that had its origins in Europe—principally Great Britain, but, as demonstrated by the institution's seal, Italy as well.[5] Shaw and his friends seized upon the goal of aligning the upper reaches of Boston society with certain handpicked icons of European civilization. The reigning aesthetic imperative—"the progress of the arts"—asserted that the growth of literature progressed from ancient times to the present, and from the East to the West. It was a convention that emphasized both improvement and movement. In his poem "On the Prospect of Planting Arts and Learning in America," British bishop and sometime Rhode Island resident George Berkeley wrote, "Westward the course of empire takes its way."[6] The "progress of the arts" trope insisted that universals such as beauty and justice be carried to the next site; these ideals were accessible to all and ready for a fresh flowering in the hands of Americans, whose conditions seemed to cry out for cultural definition. As Gordon Wood writes of the Anthologists' immediate forebears, "The Revolutionaries aimed not at becoming more American but at becoming more enlightened."[7] For the organizers of the Athenaeum, as for their fathers, enlightenment was something to be grasped from afar and shared through travel-worn accounts and shreds of conversational anecdote. These gentlemen were most intrigued by British men of letters who succeeded in combining civic duty with cultural authority. Contemporaries praised as models included literary scholars William Jones and William Shepherd. Most conspicuous are references to yet another William: a Liverpudlian banker-cum-historian named Roscoe.

William Roscoe, an Englishman whose support of the Liverpool Athenaeum (founded in 1798) inspired imitation among Bostonians, is a colorful character in recent histories of the Federalist era. Roscoe (1753–1831) was a liberal Whig Member of Parliament, a critic of the slave trade, and an early proponent of prison reform; in addition, he was the author of two Renaissance biographies: the lives of Lorenzo de' Medici and, later, of Pope Leo X. Scholars laboring in the field of American cultural history mention Roscoe chiefly to illustrate Bostonians' admiration for upwardly mobile Brits. In his essay on the Athenaeum's role in forming the Boston upper class, Ronald Story adopts a traditional three-part explanation of the Athenaeum's founding: a man (Roscoe), a plan (the Liverpool Athenaeum), an institution (the Boston Athenaeum).[8] In Anthony Mann's more recent article which convincingly portrays wealthy Americans' subtle criticism of the motherland, Roscoe stands as a legitimate model for searching Bostonians, the premier example of the "liberal, non-conformist elite of provincial Britain."[9] Although Roscoe's influential role in the Athenaeum has been acknowledged, it has never been satisfactorily understood. Here I consider the significance of what might be called the Roscoe cult.

For decades starting around the turn of the nineteenth century, Roscoe received enthusiastic praise from the Boston gentlemen who founded the Athenaeum. During the years of the institution's infancy, the name Roscoe peppered letters, diaries, and the borrowers' records at the reading room.[10] As early as 1800, Arthur Maynard Walter excitedly mentions in a letter to his friend Shaw that a new work by Roscoe is expected and, two years later, writes Shaw from Liverpool that he "shall see Roscoe."[11] In his diary, the minister Francis Parkman, father of historian Francis Parkman, recalls a visit to Allerton Hall, Roscoe's country house: "Mr. Roscoe most kindly showed me his favourite pieces of taste, his best paintings and rarest books. I enjoyed the greatest pleasure from this visit. I saw how well Mr. Roscoe deserved all his fame."[12] So widespread was Roscoe's reputation that at least two Bostonians— the banker George Livermore and the shipper G. E. Thayer—named their sons after him.[13]

George Ticknor (1791–1871), an Anthologist, a key supporter of the Athenaeum, and, later, a Harvard professor, visited Roscoe twice. About his first visit, in 1815, he writes to a friend:

Of the acquaintances whom I found or formed in Liverpool, I know not that you will be much interested to hear of any but Mr. Roscoe, whom you already know as an author. . . . He is a lover of, and a proficient in, the fine arts, and has done more to encourage and patronize learning than all his fellow-citizens put together. But he is now beginning to bend with age, and has retired from active pursuits, both as a man of letters and as a banker. . . . He lives in a style of splendor suited to his ample fortune; and, what is singular, he lives on the very estate where his father was gardener and his mother housekeeper. There I passed one day with him afterwards and spent a couple of hours, and found him exceedingly simple in his manners, and uncommonly pleasant in his conversation.[14]

On his second visit to Roscoe, in 1819, Ticknor met the gentleman for dinner. During the intervening years, Roscoe had, in the words of his son, experienced "pecuniary embarrassments": his bank had invested overzealously in mining properties, and Roscoe was forced to sell his personal collections, as well as his house, to pay creditors. "His circumstances have changed entirely since I passed a day with him in Allerton," Ticknor writes in his journal. "He now lives in a small house, simply and even sparely, but I was delighted to find that poverty had not chilled the warmth of his affections, or diminished his interest in the world and the studies that formerly occupied him. He spoke of his misfortunes incidentally, of the loss of his library, with a blush which was only of regret."[15]

Roscoe's life was most famously codified in a chapter of Washington Irving's popular collection, *The Sketchbook of Geoffrey Crayon, Gentleman*, first published in seven paperback installments (between June 1819 and September 1820) and read by men at the Athenaeum.[16] The chapter on Roscoe follows the baggy form of secular hagiography. Analysis of the piece, titled simply "Roscoe," shows how a cult of personality took shape. Conventional hagiography adheres to a structure recognized for centuries: the author begins with a confession of his unsuitability for the task of writing the saint's life (a mock humility), then proceeds to the subject's portents of greatness, an account of the subject's "holy living," reports of a miracle, some sermonizing, and an account of the subject's "holy dying."[17] In Irving's "Account of Himself," the first piece in the *Sketchbook*, the author claims not to possess "the eye of a philosopher" but admits instead to having "the sauntering gaze with which humble lovers of the picturesque stroll from the window of one print shop to another." In "Roscoe," Irving begins by offering this glimpse of his subject, caught in the Liverpool Athenaeum reading room:

He was advanced in life, tall, and of a form that might once have been commanding, but it was a little bowed by time—perhaps by care. He had a noble Roman style of countenance; a head that would have pleased a painter; and though some slight furrows on his brow showed that wasting thought had

been busy there, yet his eyes still beamed with a poetic soul. There was something in his whole appearance that indicated a being of a different order from
the bustling race around him.[18]

Inverting the convention of predicting greatness from tales of the subject's
childhood, the author hints of this aging gentleman's spent glory. An emphasis on Roscoe's noble traits and his appropriateness as a portraitist's subject is
tempered by a note of "care" in his posture and "furrows on his brow." Later
there would even be visual evidence of the Roscoe cult: distinguishing features of the most famous portrait of Roscoe (fig. 2.3), painted by Martin Archer Shee in 1815, would reappear in a Gilbert Stuart portrait of Athenaeum
benefactor James Perkins (fig. 2.4) seven years later.[19]

Irving's biographical portrait proceeds to condense Roscoe's life, merging
the hagiographic elements of holy living, miraculous event, and sermonizing
into a sympathetic explanation of the inhospitable circumstances under
which the young Roscoe read and wrote. The saintliness accorded him in
this popular tribute centers on the near-miracle of Roscoe's mind as a "chance
production" despite "a thousand obstacles." More remarkable still is the fact
of his philanthropy: "Born in a place apparently ungenial to the growth of
literary talent; in the very marketplace of trade; without fortune, family connections, or patronage; self-prompted, self-sustained, and almost self-taught,
he has conquered every obstacle, achieved his way to eminence, and, having
become one of the ornaments of the nation, has turned the whole force of his
talents and influence to advantage and embellish his native town." The les-
son is one of fine choices: Roscoe "presents a picture of active, yet simple
and imitable virtues, which are within every man's reach, but which, unfortunately, are not exercised by many, or this world would be a paradise." A
true hagiography includes an account of holy dying. Irving ends instead
(Roscoe did not, in fact, die until 1831) with the reversal of fortune, his *financial* death. As with George Ticknor's second visit with Roscoe, the tone
in Irving's sketch shifts to honor a man who suffered losses admirably.
Roscoe's house "was now silent and deserted," and "his library had passed
under the hammer of the auctioneer, and was dispersed about the country."
The sketch ends with a posthumous salute—not from Irving to Roscoe, as
would befit a standard hagiographic treatment, but from Roscoe to his lost
books. Irving recovers a sonnet the banker-author had written in honor of
the tools of learnedness: "Teachers of wisdom, who could once beguile / My
tedious hours, and lighten every toil, / I now resign you. . . ." Parting from
his books, writes Irving, "seems to have touched upon his tenderest feelings,
and to have been the only circumstance that could provoke the notice of his
muse"—though in fact, Roscoe had published much other poetry.[20] (There is

FIGURE 2.3 William Roscoe in portrait by Sir Martin Shee, 1815. (*Walker Art Gallery, National Museums, Liverpool*)

reason to believe that Irving's own financial straits influenced his overstatement here; he had been traumatized by the ordeal of bankruptcy since the collapse of his family's import firm in 1818.) Throughout the short piece, features of Roscoe's life expand and contract to emphasize the gentleman's special goodness.[21]

So how are we to understand the Roscoe cult? One reason for Roscoe's celebrity was that his merits met the needs of his audience. Michael Wentworth

FIGURE 2.4 James Perkins in portrait by Gilbert Stuart, 1822. (*Boston Athenaeum*)

describes the earliest Athenaeum establishment as "masculine, mercantile, and middle-class." Yet among the officers and trustees from 1816 to 1830, roughly 70 percent were businessmen who, in terms of net worth, were in the top 1 percent of the population.[22] Regular Athenaeum readers enjoyed great social advantages, but they also struggled to find their place in the new nation. One who eavesdrops on the concerns voiced in the correspondence between William Smith Shaw and his friend Arthur Maynard Walter knows something of the anglophilia so widespread in post-Revolutionary Boston.

Enamored of the Johnsonian circle, Shaw and the men around him were hungry for models to emulate; Athenaeum regulars searched for contemporary British figures who provided a learned yet civic-minded style. William Roscoe answered the conflicting desires of these men: as a banker, he came from the mercantile class, yet he had cultivated a gentility with his book collecting and his mastery of botany and landscape gardening. He had come to embody the ideal of the gentleman so important to the Athenaeum's understanding of moral leadership. Roscoe's best-known biographical subject (Lorenzo de' Medici) reflected an interest in historical precedents for the correct management of wealth. The embodiment of a new man of letters, Roscoe appealed to Bostonians who were launching an exclusive reading room.[23]

A more subtle and satisfying explanation for the interest in Roscoe comes from an understanding of so-called culture heroes. "Anthropologists and historians of art have observed that societies often create . . . 'culture heroes,' in terms of whom normative histories may be constructed," writes Adrian Johns.[24] As another scholar has observed, societies in great flux require "a new common language and common points of reference."[25] In volatile Federalist Boston, Roscoe became a conveniently remote figurehead whose deeds seemed to stabilize the competing demands of public service, bookishness, and commerce. He was the protagonist in a shared public story, his legend fueled by repeated references to him and his aesthetic taste. Allerton Hall, Roscoe's elegant Georgian country house, was featured in *Views of the Seats of Noblemen and Gentlemen in England, Wales, Scotland, and Ireland* (1818–1823), an illustrated work by J. P. Neale; the book was prized by the Boston Athenaeum. (It is unclear whether Allerton Hall had an impact on country houses built by Bostonians. Certainly, the house and its owner together stood as an example of gracious country living.)[26] And the 1816 catalogue of the auctioned collection of Roscoe's drawings and pictures also settled into the Athenaeum's holdings. It is almost as if the relics from his happiest times were enshrined by his most reverential admirers. The uses of Roscoe's life reveal an emphasis on his exemplary character and his love for arts and letters. These two qualities—character and taste—were seized upon and, more important, *molded* by well-heeled Bostonians.

William Roscoe's renown illustrates the role that civility plays in the development of cultural institutions. Pilgrimages and epistolary niceties made him, in effect, a patron of the Boston Athenaeum in absentia. Bostonians knew well that Roscoe had been a leader in founding the Liverpool Athenaeum, "a handsome room for the reading of Newspapers and Magazines, with a good library," wrote Arthur Maynard Walter from Liverpool in 1802. "The genteel part of the Inhabitants frequent the Library and read from Books [that] are not allowed to be taken away." In the 1807 plan for the Boston

Athenaeum, the library in Liverpool rises as the primary antecedent: "The Athenaeum of Liverpool has been visited with delight and admiration by numbers of our countrymen." And in the years before and after, Shaw and others urged their friends to procure sample regulations from Roscoe's Athenaeum.[27] The communal adulation of Roscoe drew the Boston founders even closer to one another; by identifying with the values circulated in his mythologized life, Athenaeum readers enjoyed well-trod common ground. The structures of civility in early nineteenth-century Boston favored a redis-covered naturalness in manners. Accordingly, Roscoe's quiet dignity is pre-served in the accounts of his gracious demeanor after his bankruptcy. By stressing "the warmth of his affections" and his "poetic soul," for example, Ticknor and Irving uphold the inner life over externals such as one's house and private library. Irving, especially, addresses a readership of elite Ameri-cans whose attitude toward business and books was complex. The preoccu-pation with personal character in the Roscoe story functions as an ethical appeal to readers.[28] It was the manufacture of his potent reputation, more than his actual achievements, that made Roscoe exciting to the men of the Athenaeum. The popular image that they helped create supplied these Bos-tonians with a compelling story to absorb and live out.

This explanation—the idea of a self-fashioned imprimatur, a flesh-and-blood seal of approval to complement and reinforce the seal found in an Italian album—goes a long way toward answering the question of the Roscoe cult, but it does not go far enough. In the *Sketchbook* and in other accounts of Ros-coe, his home library occupies a hallowed place; it inspires more commentary than does his family. Even though Roscoe suffered the shame of bankruptcy, his life—as told by and for the merchant princes of Boston—never serves as a cautionary tale about a fallen prince. And even though financial speculation was considered by his American peers to be the greatest sin, there is no scold-ing of Roscoe's acquisitiveness, only silence or sorrow.[29] (In fact, no popular retelling of Roscoe's story provides full details of his spectacular business fail-ure.) Rather, if the story can be said to have a dominant message it must be the importance of books, especially when all else is lost. Here was a man who had failed in business, who had overreached, and whose library was repossessed. Yet the story's moral is clear: the true badge of learnedness, one's character, remains invulnerable to the vicissitudes of commerce. William Roscoe stood for cultivation without dandyism, gentility without airs. He was a kind of shibboleth, a watchword for certain Bostonians. And the bookishness he rep-resented served the Athenaeum as valuable cultural currency.

In the early nineteenth century, though books were still scarce in America, bibliomania was no rare disease. The same transatlantic pipeline that brought news of William Roscoe's excellent character fed a growing appetite for books, pamphlets, and magazines. Like Roscoe, for whom the "arrangement and cataloging of books . . . afforded the greatest pleasure," William Smith Shaw fell victim to a "bibliomaniacal affection." Both men became familiar with the work of the Reverend Thomas Frognall Dibdin, for example, whose playful 1809 volume *The Bibliomania: Or, Book-Madness; Containing Some Account of the History, Symptoms, and Cure of This Fatal Disease*, ushered in what one commentator has called the heroic age of book collecting. Most of Shaw's intimate friends shared his habit. Epitomized by the harvesting activity of the Athenaeum's emblematic putti, collecting was popular among amateur men of letters such as Shaw and Walter.[30] And it was to London that these collectors looked. In 1810, as the gentlewoman Anne Cabot Lowell writes to a friend, "even those who cherish other prejudices have none against the literature of G. Britain—they look there for all their models. They despise an American book."[31]

Accordingly, Arthur Maynard Walter's book lust, never hidden in his correspondence with Shaw, took on a more confident tone when he crossed the Atlantic in 1802:

> Literature is my object. I shall buy a good library in London. I shall expend $1,500 in law books and a private, choice collection. I mean to buy the cornerstones of my learning. These must support the building; and others, gradually attained, must contribute to its strength and beauty. The gigantic names of Cudworth, Locke, Milton, Selden, and others will be obtained, and, if money be sufficient, my library will not be small. There is a pathway open in this country to a goodly land. I mean to offer my passport at the turnpike-gate.[32]

Employing metaphors from both architecture and exploration, Walter's announcement is typical of the jumbled excitement that characterized book purchasing at this time. The last two sentences imply special access, an entrée into heretofore forbidden territory. Walter's eagerness to be let into London's storied bookstores is matched only by his bravado in declaring that his large budget should meet his needs. He is an informed collector, but he clearly wants to return with as many books as possible. For men set on accumulating private libraries, size did matter.

Many scholars have commented on the hidden psychology of collecting, claiming, for example, that "the ubiquity of collecting is one of the most telling facts of nineteenth-century upper-class history." While undoubtedly a source of pleasure and prestige, collecting is also said to be the individual's way of compensating for real or imagined failures, an effort to reduce anxiety, an experiment in self-healing.[33] Certainly, a review of William Smith Shaw's life shows that such impulses were at play there: the loss of a beloved friend pinched Shaw's heart and concentrated his focus on collecting, for himself as well as for the young reading room. The despair associated with the low status of American letters, a despair voiced by Shaw and others, motivated the men in his circle to help him in his cause. Although its origins were ultimately personal, the Boston Athenaeum gradually adopted a public face. In the collecting efforts made on its behalf, one detects a shared institutional drive to amass the tokens of learning—and to assert Americans' worthiness as cultural consumers.[34]

The mechanics of William Shaw's long-distance collecting reveals anxieties inherent in the task. Instead of dealing directly with London booksellers, Shaw worked through agents who bought the books and had them sent back on merchant ships. (One such vessel, the *Amelia*, was, conveniently, owned by a friend of the Athenaeum who charged no fee for the literary cargo.)[35] Shaw's correspondence with his longtime friend Joseph Buckminster, the Athenaeum's first official "book scout," helps us understand the obstacles encountered. Buckminster had traveled to Europe seeking a cure for his worsening epilepsy. A popular Boston minister who enjoyed a reputation for energizing biblical scholarship until his death in 1812, at age twenty-eight, Buckminster was the more remote member of the friendly triad that had included Walter and Shaw.[36] According to book historian James Raven, whose study of the Charleston Library Society chronicles another early American institution's participation in the transatlantic book trade, "Social imperatives loomed large in maintaining the attraction of imported books. American book imports were lifelines of identity, and they were direct material links to a present and past European culture." The phrase "lifelines to identity" tantalizes with connotations of a high-stakes rescue mission. Shaw's desperation becomes evident in the text of his correspondence. If, as David Hall asserts, "the history of learned culture is a history of the strategies that scholars, reformers, and intellectual entrepreneurs devised to overcome the scarcity of resources and the absence of centers of authority," then it pays to trace the strategies represented in Shaw's letters abroad.[37]

His methods were Machiavellian. Supplied with information from periodicals and catalogues, Shaw composed a long wish list of British books, including the reference works desired by merchants, "as most of our subscribers are of this class." In 1806 he wrote from Boston, dictating to Buckminster a plan for acquiring books:

> I would beg leave to suggest to you the expediency of selecting a confidential bookseller in London—promise that we will purchase all our books from him—let him supply us with all our newspapers magazines &c, in short every thing we shall want from England—tell him that our institution promises to be a permanent one—that we shall probably send to England from one thou-

sand to fifteen hundred dollars per year to be expended in books—With such inducements, I should think someone might be persuaded to make considerable exertions to comply with our requests.[38]

The uncomfortable posture Shaw adopts seems both necessary and painful. Inducement, persuasion, confidentiality, and promises abound. With a contortionist's skill, he distorts the facts of the Athenaeum to impress a distant audience. It was disingenuous to guarantee the institution's permanence and to promise a single bookseller that he alone will "supply us with . . . everything we shall want from England." Shaw knew both assertions were highly speculative. Efforts were already being made to commission other agents, who would no doubt contact other booksellers. And the Massachusetts legislature had not yet officially recognized the Athenaeum as a city institution. Nevertheless, Shaw urges his friend to push the Athenaeum's agenda with "every generous American" there. "I think it is your duty," he writes, unabashedly. "The gentlemen of the Anthology society desire to be particularly remembered to you," he continues. "We now meet in Congress Street under the same roof with the reading room—Our subscribers gradually increase and the publication seems to be rising in reputation. The booksellers and printers begin to think us of some consequence and send us most of their publications."[39] The impression of the Anthology Society that Shaw conveys to Buckminster here, in December of 1806, is also misleading. The fiscal health of the group and its *Monthly Anthology* was in decline. Just a few months earlier, the *Anthology*'s publishers, Munroe and Francis, had written to Shaw that in their opinion the publication must cease unless it could win more subscribers.[40]

Anticipating the expectations of a London audience, Shaw's correspondence with Buckminster was strained by bald exaggeration and unspoken worry. Shaw wrote what he believed Londoners needed to hear in order to grant Americans respect—and, of course, books. The boasts continued into the spring of 1807, as Shaw intones to his friend, "Depend upon it, that the establishment of the Athenaeum, the rooms of which are to be always accessible at all hours of the day, is one of the greatest strides toward intellectual advancement that this country has ever witnessed." The exceptionalism of the Athenaeum was to be its selling point: the place is represented as groundbreaking and newsworthy. One senses hope in this claim but also hyperbole beyond what would be expected of its librarian. From the beginning of this correspondence, Shaw's efforts on behalf of the Athenaeum were linked with his own emotional stake in the enterprise. He mixed business with pleasure by requesting from Buckminster books for his personal library as well: "I send you one hundred dollars on my own account with which I wish you to procure for me the best edition of Shakespears plays with all the prefaces notes commentaries &c which I suppose to be Reids—Dr. Aikens edition of Dr. Johnsons Dictionary in 4 vols & both to be well bound in calf—Dibdins bibliographical work and if these would not amount to one hundred dollars any other books you may please to procure for me." Access to London bookdealers was evidently too fine a thing to pass up. These few letters from Shaw to Buckminster underscore the fragility of the American self-image, and the feverish need to fill shelves.[41]

In the decade that followed there would be much public handwringing about "the literary delinquency of America." A short detour into the discourse of the Boston-based *North American Review* shows that intellectuals of the time searched self-consciously for the causes of their reliance on European literature. In an unsigned article published in 1815, the author writes, "The truth is, we have wanted literary enterprise, and been sadly deficient in general intellectual courage. . . . The literary dependence to which we have been long reconciled, has become so much a part of our character that the individual who ventures to talk about surmounting it is thought the wildest schemer." The article seems to be as much about American authorship and publishing as it is about libraries and other centers of learning. With a nod to William Roscoe, the piece despairs further: "Even a banker of Liverpool has amassed for us the literary wealth of Italy." The author entertains reasons for this situation, dismissing explanations such as the lack of financial resources and a saturated literary market. Three additional causes are considered, and it is here that one senses the author's determination to identify his nation's true handicaps: "*We want a remote antiquity.* Our heroes are not yet dead. We are all acquainted with them, or feel so. . . . Is it because *we are a communal people*, and thus the mind of the nation is thus necessarily diverted from the pursuits of literature? . . . Our best writers have been unfortunate in the vehicles they have chosen as depositories of their intellectual productions. *Pamphlets and newspapers are ephemeral and temporary*" (emphasis added). Finally, as part of a remedy, the piece offers a "suggestion of topicks"—including "the complete history of the United States of America" and "a collection of all that has been done for poetry among us (including a bibliography of our poets)." One can see that, in the mind of the anonymous author at least, an American literary life required deliberate, pioneering effort.[42]

In spite of these concerns, there were, in fact, many small libraries in America by the beginning of the nineteenth century, and Americans were reading voraciously. In Philadelphia, Benjamin Franklin's successful lending library, founded in 1731, appealed to young tradesmen, who were willing to pay forty shillings to join and ten shillings in annual dues.[43] Other libraries would cater to different classes. A simple taxonomy of those of the early national era includes social, or subscription, libraries; institutional libraries (such as that of Harvard College); and circulating, or commercial, libraries—the latter principally owned by booksellers who turned overstock into an asset by renting books for a nominal fee.[44] Especially in port towns like Boston, news had become central to commercial life; it was among merchants that social libraries with reading rooms first had real utility. Subscription libraries in Newport, Charleston, and New York City had developed by the mid-1700s. And the Boston Library Society, founded in 1794, became an interesting alternative to the Athenaeum: six of its dozen or so founders were women, and the circulation of books was its chief object. (The Athenaeum would not allow books to circulate until 1827, and female readers were rare until the mid–nineteenth century.) The proliferation of small libraries meant that it was becoming fashionable to read in the United States. Yet literacy did not necessarily lead to a shared public culture, as books were used very differently from setting to setting.[45] Debate would continue to rage among the intelligentsia about the problem of fostering exemplary libraries nationwide.[46]

Given the preoccupation with library development, why did the Athenaeum, in particular, flourish? According to the *North American Review*, in 1826 the institution, "one of the earliest of the kind in the United States, . . . now bids fair to become the most important." Simpson writes that the library owed its success in large part to Buckminster's early decision to buy popular and useful books instead of the more specialized publications to which Shaw was chiefly attracted. "We must, at least for some time, think of popularity," Buckminster told Shaw, "and I know of no method so likely to procure it, as to keep our rooms furnished with an abundance of magazines, pamphlets, and new books."[47] Even elite subscription libraries such as the Athenaeum were forced to consider the reading market and to ascertain the most effective means of exploiting it.

As Ronald Story documents, the business and family connections among the wealthiest subscribers all but guaranteed money to fund acquisitions. By the late 1820s a powerful alliance of businessmen and a few intellectuals (led by George Ticknor and Nathaniel Bowditch) pushed forward administrative reforms and shrewd book purchases. In fact, this same group advocated the circulation of books among proprietors and the hiring of a professional librarian, Seth Bass, to whom a respectable salary was paid.[48] But there were some atypical influences on the Athenaeum's development. In the language of the official documentation, a veil of harmony seems to decorate the institution. The Athenaeum promulgated a seductive mission and created a pleasing cultural environment. Moreover, the reading context—the tacit knowledge about where books originated and how they were to be read—has always been part of the proper understanding of texts.[49] A library, and later a gallery, the Athenaeum held special status as a center for the storage, organization, and use of the arts.

The notion of the Athenaeum as utopian space, as a protected resort apart from the world, would be central to its success. Near pastureland and private gardens, "innocent of traffic and its turmoil," the Athenaeum of the 1820s, '30s, and '40s was situated on Pearl Street (fig. 2.5) in a mansion donated by James Perkins (1761–1822), a merchant who had made his fortune in the China trade. The previous home of the Athenaeum—the Rufus Amory House, on Tremont Street—had proved to be too cramped and too loud by 1821. After accepting the Federal-style Pearl Street house, which comprised more than a dozen rooms on three floors, the institution expanded to include a lecture hall as well. (Although the house was in the style of Charles Bulfinch, there is no evidence that Bulfinch designed it.)[50] According to the deed Perkins gave to the Athenaeum, the gift came from a genuinely charitable impulse inspired by a love of libraries. A bookish man himself (and one who sought out reading material even in the remote locales to which his mercantile business led him), Perkins wanted to promote the growth of "public libraries" and "reading rooms." He planned to move to a new house he had built for himself on the corner of Pearl and High Streets, but, unfortunately, he died of pneumonia soon after the transfer of his mansion. The donated Pearl Street house stood in a residential neighborhood called Fort Hill, the site of the present Post Office Square.[51] One former assistant librarian, Charles Fairbanks, would recall the property in terms that evoke an Edenic calm: "The Athenaeum, surrounded by horse-chestnut trees, stood there in aristocratic dignity and repose, which it seemed almost sacrilegious to disturb with the noise of our childish sports."[52]

Such a site was in keeping with the original impetus for a reading room. In the new nation, the Anthologists had craved permanence and privacy in their intellectual pursuits. Joseph Buckminster, for example, had contrasted Liverpool's idyllic Athenaeum with that same city's Lyceum. He praised the former for encouraging the consultation of "folios" that stayed put, as opposed to the latter's emphasis on circulating "miscellanies." Whereas a "Cornhill apprentice," he said, might be comfortable at the Lyceum, where the fee of half a guinea allowed access to only *"wooden* books," William Roscoe and other "choice spirits" cherished the more exclusive Liverpool Athenaeum and its collection.[53] In the necessary transition from private passion to public mission, the Boston Athenaeum would emphasize democratic ideals

FIGURE 2.5 The Boston Athenaeum on Pearl Street, as depicted on a plate, 1829. This mansion, donated by James Perkins, was the institution's penultimate home. (*Boston Athenaeum*)

but insist that they be sought within the safety of a highly controlled environment. As already noted, Roscoe's carefully fashioned imprimatur helped anchor the Boston enterprise, and the activity of book importation inspired William Shaw to assert the Athenaeum's importance.

The prospectus, or memoir, which was circulated to prospective subscribers, describes yet another aspect of the institution's efforts at self-definition. Printed in 1807, it is an example of the "arcane genre of public document" and, as such, rewards a close reading. Crafted to attract the most respectable citizens while frustrating nay-sayers, the document advances a catalogue of goals—among them, civic pride, Christian virtue, and a peaceful brand of patriotism—and also a catalogue of beneficiaries: "the man of business," "the man of leisure," "the inquisitive merchant," politicians, historians, learned gentlemen, men of letters, young people, and "ladies" (indirectly via their husbands and directly via lectures). Consider this sample from the discourse, which depends on the bold presumption of purpose:

> When we admit the dignity and use of the science of the learned, the taste of the refined, and the improved and cultivated character of the citizens at large, we must also admit that these objects require a fostering care, and will not be obtained without adequate means and incentives. That the institution here proposed, if well begun and liberally supported, must prove in a high degree auxiliary to these purposes, will not, it is presumed, be called into question.

What can be said about the founding documents of the nation can also be said, to some extent, about the founding document of the Athenaeum: in Robert Ferguson's words, "Leaders respond to the uncertainty and flimsiness of their new social forms by inscribing fundamental law more generally, more frequently, more compulsively."[54]

The repetition of themes (virtue, dignity, uses of prosperity, social intercourse) and the employment of syllogism (as in the passage quoted above) lend an air of inevitability to the claims. A need to "address beginnings, instead of allowing them to be implicit," further characterizes such official documents. Years after the Boston Athenaeum was founded, in a lecture called "The History and Uses of Athenaeums," a German-born political philosopher named Francis Lieber outlined the whole history of learning before he reached his immediate subject; in Lieber's speech (to an audience in South Carolina), the glory of Western civilization becomes the glory of the athenaeum.[55] In its prospectus, too, the Boston Athenaeum seems to carry the weight of all culture. Another hallmark, then, of these elaborate mission statements is their comprehensiveness. The notional Athenaeum of 1807 embraced a panoply of uses: Reading Room, Library, Museum or Cabinet, Repository of Arts, Laboratory, and Apparatus for Experiments. The prospectus presents the Athenaeum as a kind of one-stop, full-service cultural spa. It is simultaneously ostentatious and benevolent. And its tone of unanimity ("the value of learning is admitted by all") promotes a sense of cohesion and shared belief.[56]

The prospectus exhibits a grand ethos, inviting the reader to become a member of an ideal "imagined community."[57] Such documents were typically composed by men of letters who wrote for a circumscribed audience of peers and left their work unsigned. Yet if the author's identity goes unrecognized in the official "memoir," it need not go unrecognized here. John Thornton Kirkland, a minister and, later, a president of Harvard College, had been reared among Indians in New York and western Massachusetts. That the author of the Athenaeum's mission statement was the son of a missionary is oddly appropriate; bred "roughly and hardily in the wilderness," Kirkland would have been familiar with advertised paths to salvation. Like a minister's promise of heaven, Kirkland's prospectus and its generic relatives preserve "the tenuous bond between aspiration and realization."[58] The prospectus helped transform the ill-defined Athenaeum into a thinking man's paradise—a notion that would be reinforced in practice among its community of readers.

Decisions about noise, surveillance, permitted guests—all these contributed to the early Athenaeum members' understanding of how best to read.[59] Even before the move to Pearl Street, the trustees fretted about the proper climate in which to digest books. In the official records one detects an effort to strike a balance between liberty and constraint. "Voted that the restrictions as to silence in the Library room be taken off in the evenings and conversation be permitted and that the rooms be made convenient for that purpose," reports the trustees' log of 1810. Four years later, the trustees voiced concern about afternoon visits by teenage boys who were creating a disturbance and injuring books. By October 1822, with the Athenaeum transferred to the Perkins mansion on Pearl Street (a move due, in part, to noisy carriages in the alley near the Tremont Street site), a more refined idea of the perfect reading climate emerged. The trustees voted against supervising members' reading. It was deemed "unpleasant" to read only in one room, and with all other readers, all the time. "Quiet retirement and freedom" must not be compromised, the trustees asserted. Through experimentation, members determined that reading required at least the opportunity for solitude.[60]

It was among the chief aims of the Athenaeum in its early years, then, to encourage reading in the right physical surroundings. Just as the prospectus announced a mission with puffed-up purpose and the trustees complained about noise pollution, so Athenaeum leaders arranged the Pearl Street space—with its specific "hang" of art and its careful choreography of chairs around fireplaces—to underscore the institution's cultural authority. One might say that any given setting promotes a certain kind of reading and inhibits other kinds. But beyond privileging silence, how can a library shape reading practices? We do know that the large reading room taking up the southern half of the first floor was said to be "admirably well adapted to its object, being warm in the winter, airy in the summer, and pleasant at all times."[61] And Fairbanks, the former library assistant, left a few clues to the scene in the reading room, where, he writes, "learning was a quiet, comfortable, select sort of thing." Members ("some of them even wore knee breeches and queues and powder") sat on either side of the fireplace, "undisturbed for hours." Quiet was "never broken, save by the long breathing of some venerable frequenter of the place, enjoying his afternoon nap."[62] The setting mirrored that of a domestic library; evidently, even sleeping was permitted. Yet there were interruptions over the years. In 1825 the librarian Seth Bass reported to the trustees, "Intruders . . . still frequent the Reading Room. Strangers are numerous and are found in all parts of the house." Bass called this a "serious evil" and a subject "of the greatest importance!" As a remedy, more rooms were kept locked to secure the safety of the collections (evidently, during this period there was no guard at the door).[63] The peace of the Athenaeum was occasionally broken by members, too. In a journal he kept while employed by the library, Fairbanks notes: "3 o'clock P.M. Mr. Warren drunk in the Reading Room."[64] From these exceptions one can infer that the library was silent, staid, and relatively secure as a rule.

The Athenaeum's practices of display and classification made visible an idea of elevated culture. The considered placement of books and works of art contributed to a loose narrative of objects.[65] No complete floor plans or interior views of the mansion survive, but the reports of the Examining Committee, whose members took an inventory of all holdings for the trustees in 1825, reveal something about the installations. The sheer size of the Pearl Street mansion meant that, for the first time, collections could be thoughtfully organized with little regard for efficient use of space.

The lower story—consisting of the reading room, a "conversation room," and a periodicals room between them—exhibited Gilbert Stuart's portrait of benefactor James Perkins (fig. 2.4), whose home the building had been. The place of prominence given to the Perkins portrait pays tribute to one of the Athenaeum's most generous patrons. Recall that Perkins's pose reaches back to that of William Roscoe in the 1815 portrait of that famous Liverpudlian (fig. 2.3). In 1822 the Athenaeum had commissioned Gilbert Stuart to copy a portrait of James Perkins that the artist was working on for the Perkins family.[66] Stuart and Perkins were already well acquainted. In fact, "the hours given to sittings had been passed in conversation," according to Perkins's grandson, and the sittings had resulted in nothing but a sketch when Perkins died that year. Stuart surprised the family by finishing the portrait from memory, and he copied the painting for the Athenaeum soon thereafter.[67] One might speculate about what passed between Perkins and Stuart during those hours. Perhaps William Roscoe was a topic of conversation, as both Stuart and Perkins would have been familiar with Roscoe's legendary reputation. And the Athenaeum wanted to honor Perkins with a portrait largely because of the merchant's Roscoe-like generosity and commitment to libraries. Indeed, it was one of Stuart's former students, Martin Archer Shee, who had painted Roscoe's portrait seven years earlier.[68]

Both the Roscoe and Perkins portraits show men at ease with the trappings of a domestic library; both men appear to have been interrupted in the midst of their studies, and they represent unfettered access to self-education. In the portrait of Roscoe, Shee depicts his subject ensconced in his famous home library and treats in a fetishistic way the gentleman-scholar's signature objects: globe, lit partially so as to suggest worldly enlightenment; and bust, of Roscoe's political hero, Charles James Fox.[69] Both bust and globe appear larger than Roscoe's head, almost insisting that the viewer first acknowledge these luxury objects that signify cosmopolitanism. The books and papers casually arrayed around Roscoe's desk convey the sitter's intimacy with scarce printed works, a feature of Gilbert Stuart's portrait of James Perkins as well. In many ways, Stuart's portrait is a distillation and intensification of Shee's. The pretentious column-curtain combination appears in both, as does the background motif of the tiered shelves of a home library. Yet Stuart shows Perkins only to the waist, aggrandizing the sitter and rendering his setting more abstract and suggestive.[70] Perkins was a book collector and undoubtedly had a book room in his house; he was a quiet man whose reading of the English poets functioned as an escape from the demands of business. Following well-established stereotypes, Stuart depicts the patrician Perkins as a calm, rational gentlemen in full possession of his role in society.[71] The Perkins portrait would certainly have affected the Athenaeum visitor's experience, as it models proper gentlemanly behavior: like Roscoe, Perkins, also a successful merchant, sits at his cluttered desk, grasping reading matter in one hand and gazing out with an expression of thoughtful consideration.

Other art objects in the reading room communicated similar ideas about the ideal conditions for learnedness. In 1822, Ralph Waldo Emerson remarked to a friend that the Pearl Street house was "royally fitted up for elegance & comfort," and that the reading room's recently donated casts of ancient statues "attract the eye in every corner from the tedious joys of writing & reading." The casts, described as "lordly strangers," spur on the reader, who "instantly feels the spirit of the connoisseur stealing over him."[72]

It is tempting to attribute too much meaning to the choice and placement of artifacts. Yet focusing on the rare occasion when a library reordered its books can tell us something about how readers related to them. When setting up the Pearl Street space, the Athenaeum's organizers numbered the empty chambers, devoting each to a field of learning. The circuit began in the eastern half of the second story, with North & South America; Politics, Government & Military Science; and History, Travels & Biography taking up three neighboring rooms. The western half housed Theology & Metaphysics, and

Belles-Lettres (by far the two most voluminous categories). Tucked away on the third floor were rooms devoted to Botany and Arts & Sciences (books on inventions and experimental work).[73] Perhaps the second floor's arrangement reflects the priorities of the Athenaeum's (mostly merchant) subscribers: a morning perusal of worldly topics in the east-facing rooms might have freed the member of obligation; the reader might have later retired to the western rooms to address more intimate subjects in the angled afternoon light. The most practical topics seem to have had least importance, as books relating to chemistry, biology, and the use of scientific apparatus were placed on the remote top floor. Though conjectural of course, these musings hint at the intellectual hierarchies assigned by early Athenaeum readers and suggest some ways in which the particular arrangement of books and art objects might have been experienced. Because of its broad mission and comfortable environment, the Athenaeum admitted competing uses in practice. Some scholars argue that elites embraced cultural pursuits during the post-Revolutionary era as a psychological ameliorative for the excesses of an increasingly luxurious society.[74] The Athenaeum, especially, offered men a compensatory value to combat growing materialism.

Many diaries kept by Athenaeum readers echo that of the wealthy merchant William Appleton, who expresses concern about avarice: "I want no man's money, but it gives me an unpleasant sensation to have others more successful than myself. These are feelings I am ashamed of. . . . It is mean and unaccountable that our desire for property or power is so great, when we reflect on the entire uselessness of it for the little time which we can remain with it."[75] If Appleton worried about the ultimate uselessness of money and the swift passage of life on earth, he would certainly have agreed with the prevailing social judgment about amusements such as assemblies and stage dramas. The Athenaeum prospectus, explicitly claims that the institution will counter the "passion for amusement," an evil that accompanies "prosperity and affluence."[76] The fear of such entertainments was consistent with the condemnation of fiction so widespread in Federalist literary circles. Athenaeum readers often privately contradicted the values that they asserted, however. Following an autodidactic habit, members selected books for themselves (and sometimes their families), and borrowers' records reveal that their reading was often not in keeping with the mission of the institution—or even with their anxious diaries. Once books were allowed to circulate, William Appleton, for one, borrowed frivolous fare. In the spring of 1827, he signed out (among volumes on Goethe's life and statistical analysis) *The Flowers of Wit; or, A Choice Collection of Bon Mots*, several issues of a fashion periodical called *La belle assemblée*, and Susan Ferrier's novel *Marriage*. One can imagine that these titles were devoured by Mrs. Appleton, not her husband. Still, other proprietors regularly withdrew fiction, and to assume that only their wives read novels would be naive.[77]

The circulation of books allowed for intense individual experiences. Among amateur men of letters, for example, certain British authors were evidently very much admired. Those of the Johnsonian circle (James Boswell, Edmund Burke, even Fanny Burney) appear frequently in the borrowing records. Jane Austen's novels also reign supreme. As noted earlier, the recurring titles for all types of Athenaeum readers (businessmen, administrators, intellectuals, and so-called amateurs) constitute a kind of mini-canon that includes Cicero, Daniel Defoe, John Locke, Robert Southey, and Sir Walter Scott. The Athenaeum devotees seem to have read intensively as well as extensively, borrowing many of the same titles repeatedly. Real reading habits, however, are difficult to ascertain, in part because many proprietors had large home libraries to which they undoubtedly turned for their most beloved volumes.[78] But the institution was always there to answer emerging needs. Athenaeum librarians indulged readers' personal interests, too, fielding queries about the sources of a poetic phrase or a Latin aphorism.[79] Although the smallest rituals that made up the early life of the reading room lent a sense of order and authority to the place, within those constraints the readers enjoyed the freedom to pursue their own aesthetic tastes.

The pleasures of the Athenaeum were a muted version of the pleasures of the Anthology Society. Like other elite subscription libraries, the Athenaeum manufactured a sense of "literary and social belonging." What James Raven writes about the Charleston Library Society is true of the Boston Athenaeum as well: "The abstraction of a community that reached back and forth across the Atlantic, fueled and supplied by texts and ships, was designed to counter the fear of loss by the extension and consolidation of an intellectual heritage."[80] The institution established a symbolic apparatus that elevated it above the quotidian existence of the new nation. In the landscape of emotional and symbolic "club membership," the signs of belonging—the sanitized emblem, the salute to Roscoe, the imperative to collect books, and the fuss over conditions under which to read—mattered more to Athenaeum members than the formal statutes of the organization. The significance of these small gestures inheres precisely in their vague reinforcement of what it meant to be native to the Athenaeum.[81]

Any public mission brings added responsibility and heightened scrutiny to an organization. Expectations are raised, and accountability demanded. No sooner had the Athenaeum's fame been claimed than it was freely interpreted by others in the larger community. One voice from its earliest years gives an idea of the rejection felt by those who pushed at its borders. A week before Christmas in 1817, John Kirkland, the author of the Athenaeum's prospectus, asked that a young man named John Everett be permitted to use the Athenaeum, then on Tremont Street. (Everett's identity is unclear, but he was most likely the Harvard student who went on to win the Bowdoin Prize in 1818.)[82] When his request for permission to read at the Athenaeum was denied, Everett himself delivered this outburst to William Smith Shaw:

> I think the idea you go upon of the propriety to support the Institution is erroneous. It is or is not what we call a Publick Library, an establishment for the general benefit of the persons of literary taste in its vicinity. If it is not I shall show, I think, hereafter that the object for which it was instituted . . . will never be attained. If it *is* a publick library, it is ridiculous to extort from every one who is placed in a situation where it will be necessary or convenient to employ it, pecuniary assistance, even if it were possible for all to render it. . . . If the object [of the proprietors] was to obtain exclusive literary advantages for themselves or their relations, they should be told that learning disdains to aid those who would willingly keep those around them in blind ignorance. This indeed is I fear an operation of a Spirit in the vicinity which is seen in a thousand instances of prejudice and meanness, which has brought our literature, which has never been in a very exalted situation, almost beneath contempt, which has reduced the state of the country for learning instead of elevated it, and continues to drive abroad all the young men who wish to acquire an education and who would have been, at this period of our country's prosperity, possessed of sufficient advantage at home. . . . As to the depredations you mention, believe me things of this sort will continue, until we learn to consider literature less as money and to set some value on it besides that which belongs to the binder and engraver. In fine I express the sentiment once more that till a more liberal spirit is diffused among us, the objects of the A. or of any other similar institution will never be answered.[83]

The letter discloses attitudes toward privilege and toward books: how Everett, as a self-professed marginalized reader, expresses his own ethos of learning; that the word "public" eludes clear meaning; that national pride and social justice can serve complementary ends; how closely education (especially self-education) is bound up with an imperative to help the less fortunate; and that respect for the *materiality* of books begins with respect for the *content* of books (presumably "depredation" refers to the Athenaeum's fear of injury to the collection).

There is none so native to an institution as one who guards its customs, and William Shaw, the gatekeeper to whom this plea was addressed, inhabited that role. John Everett's eloquent protest, though it likely caused not a ripple, points to the vexing relationship between democracy and culture. One is left to wonder whether access was ever granted to Everett—and how the outcome sat with Kirkland, the missionary's son. Broad-minded statements of intent wear thin, and in spite of engagement in the more mainstream aesthetic and intellectual debates of the coming decades, the Boston Athenaeum would remain fundamentally exclusive, a refuge from the noisier realities of antebellum life. From the winged figures on its seal to the "intruders" in its reading room, the institution contained ambivalent and powerful ideas about culture. Eventually there would be trouble in paradise.

Part Two
IDENTITY

Public taste [has become] more discriminating and critical
and of course more difficult to satisfy.

Report of the Committee of Fine Arts
Boston Athenaeum
1833

CHAPTER THREE

A Woman Framed

From a half-length portrait on a wall of the Trustees' Room in the Boston Athenaeum, the author Hannah Adams halts her reading momentarily and stares into the middle distance. Her painted image provides clues about the workings of cultural capital, the way status can be acquired through the display of distinct taste. Unlike most portrait subjects on exhibit at the present-day Athenaeum, Miss Adams (1755–1831) looks as though she could have been a servant or a housekeeper (fig. 3.1). Never married, she is elderly and plain—paradoxically, both delicate and durable. In this painting, she is all goodness. She wears a large white bonnet and an expression of kind, steady intelligence.[1] Hannah Adams's cerebral nature is conveyed through her familiarity with the books around her. An elbow rests near a voluminous Bible, as her finger on the page of a slimmer volume (perhaps the controversial abridgment of her *History of New-England*) marks the text that prompts her thought. There is no swagger here, no sense of entitlement. The portraitist has treated the muslin shawl and the dark background in a vague, painterly way, focusing the viewer's attention instead on the book in Miss Adams's hands and the seriousness of her face as she absorbs what she reads. "The face deeply impressed me. It was that of an old woman as old women were old in 1827, when it was painted," wrote a journalist decades after both painter and subject had died. "The broad rustic face was entirely surrounded by an antique cap. . . . The general effect was one of some good-natured and countrified old granny whose descendants had had her painted for affection's and not for pride's sake."[2]

That affection, and not pride, was behind this painting is an idea that resonates with the small archive of material on Hannah Adams. The portrait by Chester Harding was exhibited in the Athenaeum's first gallery show, in 1827, and then donated to the institution anonymously by "several ladies" who raised funds to purchase it. But what made the mild septuagenarian a suitable face for the Athenaeum's walls? The answer leads to a deeper understanding

FIGURE 3.1 Hannah Adams in portrait by Chester Harding, 1827. (*Boston Athenaeum*)

of one case of literary patronage in the early republic. Specifically, the alliance of the Athenaeum with a respected female author—and one associated with secularized religion (Adams sympathized with Unitarians)—helped redefine cultural authority in the city. The men of the Athenaeum acted charitably toward Adams, and she lent them her quiet, studious, even religious dignity. Her portrait emphasizes traits that distinguish her from learned male subjects of portraits commissioned in this era. Adams often described herself as "a mere woman."[3] It was, evidently, important that she not distance herself from modesty and the other essential characteristics of her sex. Yet Adams was a pioneer: in 1829 she became the first female to be granted formal access to the reading room of the Boston Athenaeum. For decades afterward, only a handful of other women would officially be given permission to use the library (women were not routinely welcomed into the reading room until after 1856).[4] Even before Adams was admitted to the Athenaeum on Pearl Street, when she had felt herself wronged by a fellow historian, wealthy Bostonians came to her defense, opened their personal libraries to her, and, encouraged by their wives and sisters, supplied her with an annuity for life. A subset of Athenaeum members recognized Hannah Adams's cultural value and seized upon it. These elite gentlemen enhanced their own sense of self through her reputation.

An autodidact, Hannah Adams had overcome poverty to write a dictionary of American religion, *An Alphabetical Compendium of the Various Sects* (1784). Like this early work, her subsequent publications—*A Summary History of New-England* (1799), *A View of Religions* (1801), *The History of the Jews* (1812), and *Letters on the Gospels* (1824)—usually appeared only after supporters among the Boston elite had collected subscriptions on her behalf. Though not an infrequent practice, such subscriptions were rarely collected for women authors. Hannah Adams was apparently a distant relative of John Adams (and, hence, of his nephew, Athenaeum librarian William Smith Shaw). This connection was mentioned by the former president himself, after Hannah dedicated one of her works to him; John Adams told Hannah that they were "undoubtedly related by birth."[5] But her special treatment by Boston society is attributable to more than remote nepotistic ties. By serving as her patrons, members of the Athenaeum benefited from Adams's virtuous reputation and lifted the image of their male community.

To the extent that the patronage of Hannah Adams has been analyzed, opinion holds that men at the Athenaeum were moved to support the lady historian for charitable reasons, for chivalrous reasons (to protect an innocent woman from ill use), and, some claim, for reasons of opposing religious orthodoxy more effectively. These readings of the author-patron relationship assume both clear intention on the patron's side and a remarkable passivity on the author's side. To correct this incomplete understanding, one must attend to at least three sources of evidence: Hannah Adams's own written expressions, the terms in which the elites voiced support for Adams, and the larger contexts within which the author and her patrons were engaged. Adams's autobiography reveals a strong authorial agency and a highly sophisticated appreciation for the nuances of her situation. Further, close attention to the Athenaeum patrons shows that they exhibited distress about their own identity in a growing urban democracy. By embracing a female such as

Hannah Adams, the Athenaeum experimented with new mechanisms of culture. But the institution's self-definition through patronage could not be scripted, and the precedent exposes a network of connections among intellectuals, benefactors, and their multiple audiences.

Hannah Adams was both pawn and player. Her lifework sheds light on the negotiations behind cultural entrepreneurship in the young nation. Throughout the historical record, a sense of her unusual reputation prevails. To be a female author was a novelty in the early nineteenth century, and Adams aroused much interest. In documents written by her patrons and in her own memoir, one encounters adjectives that, taken together, create a verbal portrait: at various times she was considered "uncommon," "perceptive," "distracted," "timid," and "peculiar." Like Harding's painting, these words reinforce the image of Hannah Adams as an almost pitiable oxymoron: the intellectual woman.[6] She experienced loss and hardship during her early life, and in the end she was as rocked by controversy as she was buoyed by support. The professional life of Hannah Adams—and its intersection with the Athenaeum—illuminates the concealed motives of both patron and author.

Hannah Adams represented a kind of ideal beneficiary. Her gender, her preferred genre (history), and her personal situation combined to offer gentlemen supporters at the Athenaeum a most advantageous vehicle for their benevolence and their worldview. But Hannah Adams was also a potent agent of her own image. The early part of the nineteenth century was a confusing era for American patrons, and the arrangements for support proved to be far from straightforward. Before assessing the patron-author bond from the perspective of the Athenaeum, one must consider Adams on her own terms—as a suffering daughter and sister who from an early age was drawn irresistibly to the written word.

Born in a farmhouse in Medfield, Massachusetts, Hannah Adams was reared in a household where books were valued. Her father was a failed farmer and sometime bookseller (his shop, known as English Goods and Books, was too remotely situated to tempt much business traffic). During the Revolutionary War, Adams wove lace to help support her family. As her memoir attests, her life was punctuated by loss: her mother died when she was a girl; her sister died soon after she published her first book. She also suffered a loss of eyesight—though a home remedy (bathing her failing eye in a solution of opium, alcohol, and sea water) seemed to effect a full recovery. In short, the deliberate, patient historian tells of a life in which she achieved much in spite of grief and illness.[7]

Her memoir, written at the end of a full life and published posthumously in 1832, explains her anomalous achievement. Hannah Adams writes that her father encouraged her literary pursuits. She tells how it happened that a modest and unassuming woman became a published writer. Her style is plain; she accepts neither credit nor blame for the freakish event of her literary talent. "As I always read with great rapidity," Adams writes, "perhaps few of my sex have perused more books at the age of twenty than I had." Notwithstanding factual statements about her reading habit, the memoir appears as a standard record of female self-effacement. Her "feebleness" and "ignorance of the established rules of propriety" lend a rueful tone to the text, as she gently pleads with the reader for compassion. In a lengthy postscript written by a friend, Adams is quoted as saying, "I never was taught how to hold my pen."[8] The remark suggests that the pen is a synecdoche standing for all original expression; perhaps we are meant to think that had she only learned to hold her pen (or her tongue) she would have known not to become an author. Throughout her memoir, we can see a range of contradictory emotions. We can also see how Adams navigates herself expertly through a maze of social assumption and prejudice. An awareness of audience permeates her story, as the text is mediated by conventions that shaped the popular literature of the time.

A Memoir of Miss Hannah Adams draws from a number of autobiographical traditions—starting with what historian Ann Fabian would call the beggar's tale.[9] "It was poverty, not ambition or vanity, that first induced me to become an author, or rather a compiler," Adams writes toward the beginning of her autobiography, attempting with this sentence to bury all personal aspiration. The appositional phrase "or rather a compiler" enhances the humble tone, rounding out the statement that began so abjectly. Defining herself as poor explains away her ambition. She insists that her bookishness exhibited itself out of necessity, almost against her will. Dropped into the text are references to "deriving little profit" and, finally, "paying debts." Poverty, however, made room for philanthropy. Adams's subsequent praise for her financial supporters underscores her keen sense of the mechanics of patronage. Pages of "lively gratitude" for the "powerful minds" of "generous benefactors" follow one upon the other. Adams may have anticipated a type of woman professional that, according to Jill Ker Conway, "tells her story as a philanthropic romance." Conway, writing of a certain social type, continues, "She seems to have chanced upon causes which elicit a lifetime commitment from her. She never acknowledges strategizing about how to advance the cause; she is surprised as anyone else when success is at hand."[10] Certainly Hannah Adams, working in the early 1800s, had good reason to redirect the attention of her audience from her ill-held pen to the decency of almsgiving.

Given the popularity of crime stories and conduct manuals, Adams would have also been aware of these commercial genres.[11] Her memoir emphasizes the dangerous influences of her youthful novel reading to such a degree that at times the text takes on the voice of a criminal confessing. If, like many biographical texts of the era, her memoir was designed to edify, it is not meant to instruct through imitation; rather, Adams offers a counterexample for young women to avoid. Because her mind was not "mature" enough to "make a proper selection," she "gratified her inclinations" indiscriminately:

> I was passionately fond of novels; and, as I lived in a state of seclusion, I acquired false ideas of life. . . . My passions were naturally strong, and this kind of reading heightened my sensibility, by calling forth to realize scenes of imaginary distress. . . . My reading was very desultory, and novels engaged too much of my attention. Though my seclusion from the world preserved me from many temptations which are incident to young people, I was perhaps more exposed to errors of the understanding. . . . Time and experience have led me to see the falsity of many of my early opinions and ideas, and made me sensible that they were the source of a large share of the misfortunes of my following life.[12]

Warnings to young women that they should avoid novel reading appear throughout the antebellum period.[13] Here, however, the sins of the fictive imagination are writ large. Adams plays the antiheroine, a woman whose poor choices—caught early, thankfully, and corrected—contributed to the crime of bad reading.

The conversion narrative is yet another source for Adams's memoir. The role of the author as a kind of convert, though understated, no doubt made the contemporary reader more appreciative of Adams's intellectual drive. It seems that after his wife's death, her father took in as boarders divinity students affiliated with the local parish. Young Hannah, then in her early twenties, was instructed in Greek and Latin by a few of these men, one of whom had with him a "small manuscript from Broughton's Dictionary, giving an account of Arminians, Calvinists, and several other denominations which were most common." Having been shielded from religious controversy in her isolated surroundings, she was shocked by infighting and became disgusted with the bigotry of authors who threw out the terms "heretics, fanatics, enthusiasts &c."[14] She was awakened, from that moment on, to the destructiveness of religious propaganda, and thus began her project of assembling her first book, *An Alphabetical Compendium of the Various Sects*, an anthology of denominations published in 1784. She wished only to inject a sense of equipoise into the discussion of religious difference. All the writing Adams did after that book, she claims, flowed from her original intent: to compile what is known on a given subject so as to further understanding and minimize dispute. Like the beggar's tale, the crime story, and the advice manual, the conversion narrative had currency in the early decades of the nineteenth century; all such formulas were polite conventions that encouraged readers to recognize and learn from threatening experiences.

If one considers the tone of her memoir, it seems incongruous that the defining event of Adams's life involved a highly publicized dispute with a theologian, geographer, and historian named Jedidiah Morse (1761–1826).[15] The facts are these. In September of 1804, Morse (fig. 3.2), a Yale-educated minister with a parish in Charlestown, Massachusetts, had just published his *Compendious History of New England* when, at a lecture in Boston, he was approached by Hannah Adams. The Congregationalist was already known as a contentious disputant for criticizing those who dissented from orthodox Trinitarian theology. Soon after having earned a tidy sum from his best-selling *Geography Made Easy* (1784), Morse developed what many of his contemporaries viewed as paranoid behavior; he took a xenophobic stance against atheist members of a group called the Bavarian Illuminati, and he claimed that renegade Unitarians had upset the so-called Standing Order.[16]

It was an ordinary Thursday when Adams approached Morse. She later explained that, in speaking to him, she merely wanted to show the minister a courtesy by informing him that she would be abridging her *Summary History of New-England*, which had been published in 1799. Morse's *Compendious History* had not yet appeared in abridged form. (It was common for authors to provide abridgments for school use.) That the marketplace could not support two abbreviated American histories was obvious to Adams, and she meant to stake her claim. But later that month Morse sent her a letter arguing that her abridgment "would look too much like rivalship," and he discouraged her plan.[17] Hannah Adams charged interference and looked around for allies. The Unitarian-led membership of the Boston Athenaeum, learning more about certain inequitable publishing agreements that Adams had entered into with her other books, took her side.[18] Indeed, after a team of legal "referees" nominated by Morse himself recommended that he defer to the authoress, most public sympathy rested squarely with Hannah Adams. (As a legal case, the affair was muddy: no statute protected Adams against "interference" in her publishing plan, so her lawyers were limited in their recourse.)

The stubborn Morse admitted no wrongdoing; he insisted that Adams never made her intentions about the abridgment clear. Adams and Morse proceeded to publish abridged versions of their histories (in 1805 and 1809, respectively), and the controversy grew; each party wrote an elaborate self-defense. Eventually, starting in late 1809, Athenaeum leaders and their female relatives took action to sponsor Adams financially. It is no wonder that, even late in the century, one observer reduced Hannah Adams's life to a thin catalogue of injustices: "She was of humble birth, poor all her life, cheated by publishers, robbed by printers, outwitted and defrauded by a brother author,

FIGURE 3.2 Jedidiah Morse in portrait by his son Samuel F. B. Morse, 1809. (*Yale University Art Gallery; gift of Miss Helen E. Carpenter*)

and saved from abject penury at last only by the kindness of friends, mostly females, who contributed to give her a comfortable annuity."[19]

What can one make of Hannah Adams's story? And how did she win the support of the most powerful circle in Boston? Putting aside for the moment the quality of her work and even the coincidence of Morse's virulent orthodoxy, a number of factors contributed to her acceptance as a worthy beneficiary. Intentionally or not, Hannah Adams played along with a latent suspicion of female readers (and writers) by emphasizing her vulnerability. The authorial strategies in her memoir show that she was capable of great cir-

cumspection. At the midpoint of her life plot, where one would expect a climactic event, Adams alludes to her dispute with Morse in only the vaguest
terms:

> The profit I hoped to derive from [the abridgment of A Summary History of
> New-England] seemed to me to constitute all I had to depend upon in fu-
> ture. . . . While I entertained these hopes, in which I was made sanguine by
> my knowledge of the success with which books for schools had been printed,
> can it be a subject of blame, or reproach, to a person in my situation, that I felt
> extremely grieved, and hurt, when I found my design was anticipated by a
> reverend gentleman whose calling and indefatigable industry are highly
> respectable?[20]

The masked reference to Morse conceals her own agency and rhetorically in-
vites readers to render a judgment about a case that is never fully delineated.
Adams seems simply to lay the situation out for examination. Yet it is not that
she feigns passivity; rather, she embraces passivity so heartily that she is, arguably, no longer passive. In this passage, her ill treatment by even a "highly respectable" gentleman allows her to pose as the ultimate victim who asks for
the least of favors: that she be permitted to *feel* "grieved" and "hurt."

The success of Adams's self-fashioning—in her life and in her memoir—is
evident not only from her modest financial awards but also from the notices
she received in reviews and, later, in posthumous tributes. "Brilliancy of
imagination and sparkling manner are by no means the characteristics of
Miss Adams," admits a correspondent for the *Ladies' Magazine* of 1828. "Originality is not her aim," the piece continues; she is said to write from the *"store
house"* of understanding, rather than the *work shop* of the imagination." Of her
memoir, a contemporary reviewer in the *Christian Examiner* writes, "The
autobiography bears marks of that trembling diffidence and delicate sensibility which were Miss Adams's peculiarities." Perhaps she anticipated critics
who might have otherwise viewed her as overreaching, because Adams's
plainness flowed back to her in a stream of faint praise. "She wove honest
homespun, when she might have spun fine silk shot with gold," according to
the *New York Times* decades after her death: "Written with quaint simplicity, . . . somewhat in the profile style of the silhouette of her day," the memoir was meant not to satisfy some vain wish but merely to "secure a profit for
an aged sister." And what Ann Fabian says about unschooled writers of personal narratives can be said of Hannah Adams: her success depended on her
ability to "balance contradictory demands of the self-effacement that is humility and the self-assertion that is publication."[21]

Critical responses to her work imply that Adams's choice of genre—
history, both sacred and secular—was central to this success. "She presented
truth and fact to her readers, in their every day dress; without the gloss of

ornament," writes the *Ladies' Magazine* commentator, indirectly contrasting Adams's work to that of a novelist. "In short, she is considered as a useful, not a showy, writer, as a valuable, not a versatile author. . . . [She] has done much for the literary character of her sex." According to William Charvat, before Walter Scott and James Fenimore Cooper rescued fiction by marrying it to history, reading historical books was recommended as an "antidote to the novel."[22] Writing history, as opposed to writing fiction, allowed Adams to participate in the preferred American form. Not only was history the first genre to be published on profitable terms, but it also enjoyed considerable prestige because it was both informative and instructive. Interpreting the deeds of forefathers became essential to an emerging American identity.

Hannah Adams's work, though praised for its artlessness, was occasionally recognized for its originality, too.[23] In a belated review of her first book, for example, an anonymous writer for the *North American Review* commented on its singular arrangement of material and the author's "sagacious" reflections. In all her books, Adams chose information from reliable volumes and compiled anthologies and summaries that, through thoughtful selection and ordering, aimed for accessibility. She approached the task of compilation with a thinly veiled confidence. (In a third-person preface to *A Summary History of New-England*, she writes, "She hopes . . . that the public will view with candor the assiduous though, perhaps, unsuccessful efforts of a female pen.") Even though she was working within the subgenre of religious history, Adams contributed a note of objectivity to the young tradition of American historiography; according to Michael Vella, "by parroting the polyphony of male theologians," she could "argue a sum . . . larger than its sectarian parts."[24] Adams's belief in conscience and free will made her especially attuned to remedying discrimination against her. She apparently appreciated this statement made by another writer: "The penalties and discouragements attending the profession of an author fall upon women with a double weight; to the curiosity of the idle and the envy of the malicious their sex affords a peculiar excitement. Arraigned not merely as writers, but as women, their characters, their conduct, even their personal endowments become the objects of severe inquisition."[25]

After having entered into unfair contracts with printers, in 1790 she had joined others in petitioning Congress for "a general law to be passed which would secure to authors the exclusive right of their publications." Thus, in addition to a shrewd understanding of authorial image, Hannah Adams possessed intellectual vision, an unwillingness to accept male abuse, and a hard-earned business sense. Yet because of her sex (and her station), without substantial patronage such qualities would have remained hidden. In the defining struggle of her writing life, Adams called upon William Smith Shaw, "a most generous and noble friend to support me against oppression," and this friend did much to aid her. Through Shaw, she gained an ally in her dispute with Jedidiah Morse, to be sure, but she also benefited from an annuity, access to libraries, legal counsel on contracts, and a wider audience for her work.[26]

What attracted William Shaw and his cohort to Adams has never been fully explored, but a host of reasons suggest themselves. Starting as early as 1805, the plight of Hannah Adams polarized Boston's learned community for close to a decade. Adams may initially have sought Shaw's help in order to buttress her defense against Jedidiah Morse, but *his* attraction to *her* appears considerably subtler. Shaw himself offered these good reasons for adopting Hannah Adams's cause: "I first became interested in favour of Miss Adams from regard towards a respectable but destitute female. After some time, my interest was so much increased by the peculiar *misfortunes*, as well as uncommon worth, of this self-educated lady, whose writings have done so much honour to her native state, and whose simplicity of character had exposed her to loss in the publication of most of her works."[27]

William Shaw knew another highly educated (though considerably more fortunate) woman in the figure of Abigail Adams, his aunt, and he and his friend Arthur Maynard Walter had corresponded on the issue of women's roles. In 1799, some six years before the Adams-Morse controversy erupted, Walter had written Shaw: "Female education is miserable in this country. . . . Something surely must be done on this very interesting subject. Woman was never made solely to toil in the kitchen and sooth in the night but was instead for the partner of our joys and sorrows and the partaker of intellectual pleasures, as well as of those merely physical pleasures which thrill and enliven."[28]

Perhaps Hannah Adams, aware of Shaw's respect for his aunt and claiming kinship (however remote) with both Shaw and that former first lady, saw in the Athenaeum librarian a ready sympathizer. In a letter to Shaw, she unburdens herself on the topic of her misuse by Morse: "To reconcile myself to my fate? I consider that what is *morally right* and necessary to be done in the situation . . . cannot be *itself improper.*"[29] With Adams's eyes failing, her father too old to assist in business transactions, and her histories in various states of reprinted editions, Shaw became the center of her patronage network.[30] Even if he and his fellow Athenaeum members did truly wish to assist a deserving woman, it is likely that there were other motives at work.

The most widely disseminated charge concerning the Athenaeum's patronage of Adams originated, predictably, with Jedidiah Morse himself, who complained that William Shaw and his friends—Unitarian sympathizers all—were punishing him for his orthodox beliefs. In short, his notion swells to this claim: that secularized clergymen were uniting with wealthy merchants in order to enhance their power in the city, and that this alliance was solidified publicly through the Athenaeum's patronage of Hannah Adams.[31] Instability in local Congregationalist churches such as Morse's First Church of Charlestown was the result of a gradual secularization across New England; the fault lines were not only theological but political and cultural. (By 1819, even Morse's own parish had dismissed him in favor of a more liberal pastor.)[32] It must have been agonizing for Morse to accept the decline of sacred society, the end of a united community led by ministers like himself. His *Appeal* went on for more than two hundred pages, and his son Sidney followed his father's self-defense with a pamphlet of his own. Morse the younger, incensed by the attacks against his father (that he was a "penny-catching, worldly-minded man" and that his reputation was "obtained not by his *merits* but by his *arts*"), posed a question that recalls his father's paranoid tendencies: "Can the accusers of Dr. Morse convince the public, can they convince themselves, that these false charges, this misrepresentation of motives, this distortion of virtues, grows easily and naturally out of the controversy with Miss Adams?" Sidney Morse does not shrink from reasserting his father's unpopular views, such as that "Unitarianism is the genuine Jacobinism of Christianity." But, he maintains, such opinions do not justify slander from "noisy men [devoid] of sense or wisdom."[33]

So how much of the Athenaeum's patronage was *for* Hannah Adams and how much of it was *against* Jedidiah Morse? After explaining that in 1809 "a subscription was made for an annuity for this lady," Shaw, in the preface to Adams's *Narrative of the Controversy*, alludes to the problem of religious difference: "It would be sufficient to confound Dr. Morse, who has attributed unworthy motives to these subscribers, if delicacy permitted me to publish the names. . . . There were many (of both sexes), without any distinction of religious sentiment."[34] Whatever the motives, Shaw and his friends seemed determined to undermine Morse. Subscribers constituted an automatic audience for Adams's books. Indeed, the patrons had an arsenal of publishing weapons at their disposal. Early on, the spirited *Monthly Anthology*, which would soon spawn the Athenaeum proper, launched critical explosives when the abridged histories appeared in print. Adams's New England history was praised as "correct, comprehensive, popular." Morse's version earned this review: "Because there is something peculiar in the history of Newengland, it is not necessary that every Newenglandman who is capable of putting sentences and paragraphs together should become the historian of his country. In the act therefore of opening the book before us, we adventure to predict that it will not generally be read. . . . [The author] condescended to avail [himself] of important information contained in [Adams's history]."[35] As wounding as this was to Morse, the most disturbing comment was undoubtedly the hint of plagiarism, which led to an outpouring of ink and venom for the next decade.

Yet one would be wrong to accept that the sponsorship of Adams was merely an elaborate act of animosity toward a villainous Jedidiah Morse. At this stage in the investigation, it is useful to consider author-patron relationships in the more general terms of Alan Wallach, who has studied patrons and their passions. (Although he addresses the patronage of visual artists, his rubric would presumably apply to authors, too.) According to Wallach, two motives typically govern patronage: the ideology of the work or of its creator (that is, whether the beneficiary "reflects or promotes" a patron's Weltanschauung); and the enhanced status of the patron (that is, whether support of the work in question elevates the patron's reputation).[36] In practice, the two motives usually overlap. In his explanation for supporting Hannah Adams, William Shaw claims foremost to have had a charitable, gentlemanly motive ("regard toward a respectable but destitute female"), and he mentions a patriotic motive as well (her writings "have done much honor to her native state"). Nowhere is the *content* of her books mentioned. Nor is ideology specifically cited—or, for that matter, aesthetic or intellectual compatibility. Behind Shaw's stated reasons lies a recognition of Hannah Adams's cultural value. That is, the sought-after status to which Wallach points in his second governing motive of patronage will prove to be all-important. But the peculiar nature of the Adams case will stretch the conventional meaning of "status."

By briefly contrasting the portraits of Adams and Morse (figs. 3.1. and 3.2), one can better understand how personal reputations were cultivated in this era. With a pose and a costume similar to those in portraits of Boston's liberal gentlemen-scholars, Jedidiah Morse is positioned as a secular leader in society. The portrait was not a commission but was painted by his son, Samuel F. B. Morse (who would live to become a highly regarded artist as well as the inventor of the telegraph). Completed in 1809, by which point the controversy with Hannah Adams was well under way, it is the first of two portraits of his father. It seems likely that the artist wished to rehabilitate his father's reputation and align him with more universally admired gentlemen. Morse the younger crowds the picture space with drapery and volumes—seven of Jedidiah's published works appear, rendering the portrait, among other things, an elaborate book promotion. Jedidiah Morse is meant to appear as a scholar rather than a pastor, since he is dressed in a fancy study robe as opposed to plainer ministerial garb. Bold in color and characterized by a stiff, linear manner (the subject's head is perfectly vertical, aligned with his books on the shelves), the Morse portrait offers a stark contrast to the portrait of Hannah Adams. As noted above, artist Chester Harding portrayed Adams as a modest soul engaged in deep thought. Whereas Adams reads and absorbs, Morse, with pen in hand, writes and produces. Yet these images reinforce more than gender stereotypes. They cement for the viewer a sense of character. Morse appears to overreach in his portrait, advertising his achievements and laying claim to greater authority. The bonneted Adams humbly marks her place in her book and gazes out dreamily.[37]

The reputation of Hannah Adams as an odd but wholly sincere woman enabled her patrons to benefit from reflected virtue. Gossipy anecdotes in the popular press and even in the memoir's postscript contributed to her promotion as a "personality." Depicted as "glowing with gratitude," she was said to possess a "childlike simplicity." Well-worn stories accumulated over the decades—such as the one about how "she staid a week at a house but could never find her way back from the garden," and the one about her father "riding about the country on a bony old white horse with saddlebags filled with his daughter's books, which he peddled from town to town." She was promoted as honest, "out of this world," an absentminded sage who stood apart. A caricature of Adams emerged—admittedly, one that the author herself helped sketch with her self-deprecatory phrases.[38]

William Shaw and his amateur friends at the Athenaeum probably felt a kinship with Adams because she, too, longed to be part of a protected group of book lovers. For other elites of Boston (merchants and lawyers who were also leaders at the Athenaeum), Adams's neutral piety and gentleness were the status symbols they might have felt they needed. Perhaps, as evidence suggests, compensatory energy spent on such pursuits as small-scale farming alleviated somewhat the widespread anxiety about the correct uses of wealth. Greed and avarice required constant opposition among an elite whose fortunes were staggeringly large.[39] Hannah's kinsman John Adams once argued, "The more elegance, the less virtue."[40] If one accepts that maxim, then what means could the Athenaeum (housed during these years in the stylish Pearl Street mansion) employ to add virtue to its elegance? Hannah Adams's reputed lack of dissimulation and absence of status-seeking lent substance to all who supported her. Her widely advertised innocence enhanced the Athenaeum's emerging identity as a public-spirited but apolitical institution.

As if to reinforce the point, Adams's patrons congratulated themselves publicly on their good taste and their goodwill. The framing documents of her memoir—the preface and the postscript—give the reader proof of her benefactors' goodness:

[This memoir] will explain to those who did not know her what was the charm that drew genius and wealth and youth and beauty to minister with so much interest to the infirmities of a poor old woman. . . . It is honorable to the community in which she lived that an individual, destitute as she was of all adventitious claims to distinction, should have been properly estimated and respected.

It would be injustice . . . not to refer to the disinterested and liberal assistance [Hannah Adams] received from those friends who enabled her to reserve a part of her laborious earnings for the benefit of a suffering relative.

The patrons' self-love reaches a climax with lengthy descriptions of the young Reverend Joseph Buckminster's habit of opening his private library to her around 1810, almost two decades before she was admitted to the Athenaeum's reading room. Buckminster was widely recognized as a brilliant scholar; in his role as Unitarian pastor of the Brattle Street Church, he regularly welcomed guests to the parsonage library after services to discuss art, literature, and science.[41] "It is impossible not to look back with admiration upon the benevolence that prompted these kind attentions," begins the breathy incantation of Buckminster's charitable attitude toward Hannah Adams. "It is not a difficult effort of the imagination to enter [Buckminster's] library, and to view these laborious and dissimilar students together." The passage continues: "Who would not be touched by the spectacle of a young man of distinguished talents, equally sought by the world of *science*, and of *fashion*, extending a helping hand, and devoting a portion of his valuable time, to a timid and helpless female shrinking from the ills of life?" Even if such fulsomeness was a commonplace of the time, the rhetoric rewards a closer reading. Cultured status seems to depend upon the patron's ability to discern which men and women ought to be encouraged. The exaggerated awkwardness of Hannah Adams functions as the perfect foil for distinguished Boston gentlemen. Framing devices, coupled with the styling of the author as an eccentric, resulted in a highly artificial construct: an invented audience appreciating an invented author. Thus the response of Adams's patrons—their ostentatious performance of benevolence—becomes, in turn, a barometer of their own cultivation.[42]

The significance of gender has featured prominently in our examination of Hannah Adams so far, but a few important patterns have yet to be highlighted.[43] Federalists such as William Smith Shaw (and his dear friend Arthur Maynard Walter) believed that friendships among men—especially, male friendships that centered on shared appreciation of literature—were the highest form of virtuous activity and refinement. The intensity of their emotions was, to them, dependent upon the exclusion of wives and sisters. As a woman who read seriously, then, Hannah Adams potentially disturbed the established order. Even though in one sense, Adams became for her Athenaeum

patrons a female paragon of typically male virtues, she was haunted by conde-
scension: her intellectual focus was "absent-minded," her bibliophilia "awkward." The hybridity of her nature confused onlookers, so Shaw and his
friends rhetorically neutralized her. Hannah Adams "seemed more a phenomenon than a woman," according to a more recent observer. Indeed, she was
rendered impotent. "Male patrons were not greatly upset by her presence in
the library," explains another commentator. "A woman with scholarly interests may have struck [Athenaeum members] as a curiosity, unlikely to be followed by others of her kind."[44] Adams attracted patrons as would a rare object
to be collected and displayed (hence Chester Harding's portrait and, ultimately, a monument in Mount Auburn Cemetery).[45] Given the tacit prohibi-
tion against learned women, the example of the older, virtuous (and virginal)
Miss Adams offered a celebrated oddity to the public.

But to say that Hannah Adams was the exception that proved the rule
about women in this era does not adequately capture the cultural dynamics
of her time and place. In early nineteenth-century Boston, men severely limited female participation in learned pursuits and at the same time paid hom-
age to women's virtue. The moral suasion that women brought to bear as
republican wives and mothers has been well documented.[46] Hannah Adams
(though never a mother and effectively motherless herself) adopted a thoughtful and often authoritative voice through writing and publishing. Yet although William Shaw showed her respect in some venues, and certainly
championed her cause, he also joined the amused audience when she was
made into a spectacle. At one meeting of the Anthology Society in 1809, for
example, "Mr. Buckminster read an acrostick on Miss Hannah Adams, which
I believe was rejected, for we were in such a roar of laughter that no vote
could easily be taken, or remembered."[47] Clearly the Athenaeum men had
need of both positive and negative images of femininity.

In fact, Hannah Adams was patronized in two senses of the word. "Much
of the work gender does in forming communities and identities," Catherine
Kaplan argues, "is done on the margins—through jokes, casual phrases, and
associations and images which are relied on despite also being disavowed
and even mocked."[48] One of the most frequently repeated anecdotes about
Hannah Adams serves to illustrate this contention. The postscript to her
memoir includes a much-quoted story: "It is said . . . that the Athenaeum librarian, after some ineffectual attempts to disengage her from her book,
would lock the door, go home to his dinner, and return again to find her in
the same spot, unconscious either of his absence or that the dinner hour was
past."[49] This one anecdote tells of the control that patrons and editors sought.
Yes, she must have needed to maximize her time in the library, and perhaps

she became absorbed in her reading; presumably, the Athenaeum staff felt uneasy about her being left unsupervised. However, the sheer repetition of the anecdote mocks her ambitions. By locking her in, figuratively as much as literally, her male supporters contained her and froze her into *their* narrative of female intelligence.

Athenaeum patrons may have appropriated Hannah Adams, but she in turn appropriated the reigning patriarchal schema to advance her intellectual interests. There is a permeable membrane between dominant and subordinate cultures.[50] As a single woman, Adams needed male cosigners for all legal documents. Yet how she attracted the attention of the Boston elite is a tale full of dramatic irony. A woman whose sensibilities were offended by religious controversy entered into a controversy so heated that it played out for more than a decade and inspired arguments on both sides. But she resisted her male handlers, too, through disguising and softening the agency behind her work. For example, she styles her self-defensive statement in the Morse controversy as a "narrative," whereas Morse calls his an "appeal." And in her memoir she addresses her position on the issue of liberal religion, the so-called Unitarian debate, with characteristic balance:

> After removing to Boston, and residing in that city while the disputes upon Unitarian sentiments were warmly agitated, I read all that came my way upon both sides of the question and carefully examined the New Testament, with, I think, a sincere and ardent desire to know the truth. I deeply felt the difficulties upon both sides of the question, yet prevailingly give the preference to that class of Unitarians who adopt the highest idea of the Greatness and dignity of the Son of God.[51]

She appears to be choosing sides, returning the favor her elite Unitarian patrons had paid her, yet she equivocates even here, adding that she "never arrived to that degree of decision that some have attained on the subject." Only through a strategy of ambiguity could she remain independent from her male patrons.

Even in her own time Hannah Adams belonged to more than one community. Aged but never infirm, she would survive Shaw, her most significant male patron, by five years. During the last decade of her life, especially, she stood as a model of intellectual courage to a circle of Boston women. Unfortunately, little is known about either the sitting or the artist's contract for the 1827 portrait by Chester Harding. To honor the marginalized figure can be subtly subversive in portraiture, and as a portrait subject Adams challenged social expectation.[52] Surely she meant something different to the "several ladies" who purchased her portrait than she did to either William Smith Shaw or Jedidiah Morse.

As the Athenaeum would discover, there are unintended consequences for institutions when they invite outsiders in. Neither wife nor mother, Hannah Adams disturbed the social order as a female historian. She used the cultural coin of her time expertly, improvising within her inherited constraints, and was the earliest direct beneficiary of Athenaeum patronage. Yet she was not given formal access to the Athenaeum library until 1829, two years after her portrait was painted and two years before her death. Still, the tentative experiment of supporting a female historian in the early 1800s prepared the institution for other forays into public beneficence and outreach. Any example of patronage both reinforces a frame and manufactures an audience. The discussion of frames and audiences leads to an investigation into the Athenaeum Gallery and its role in Boston society. As the institution embraced not only books but the fine arts, styles of patronage proliferated, and audiences grew even more important.

CHAPTER FOUR

Ornament for the City

DURING THE SUMMER OF 1823 the painter Chester Harding was riding, as he put it, "the top wave of fortune." His studio on Beacon Street, near the site of the present Athenaeum, was cluttered with the faces of Boston's most powerful citizens. Pictures leaned here and there throughout the largest room. "I can see the portraits ranged on the floor, for they succeeded each other so rapidly there was no time to frame and hang them," wrote a family friend to one of the artist's ten children.[1] Indeed, "Harding fever," as fellow artist Gilbert Stuart would call it, raged in Boston throughout the 1820s and '30s. Some fifty people per day would flock to Harding's studio to admire his completed pictures and apply for sittings of their own. Others who had already been painted by the artist "stood by to challenge a resemblance."[2]

Chester Harding (1792–1866) arrived in Boston via Kentucky and Pittsburgh roughly two decades after the Athenaeum's library and reading room were launched. He was only thirty years old. One newspaper would later call him "our first artist in portraits."[3] Even with the interruption of a two-year pilgrimage to Europe, Harding enjoyed huge popularity in Boston. It was upon his return, in 1826, that plans for painting the historian Hannah Adams were probably made. No records of the sitting appear to have survived. The old woman's portrait, displayed in the Athenaeum Gallery's inaugural 1827 exhibition at the Pearl Street site, drew at least one early response: "somewhat *historical* . . . the likeness vividly accurate."[4] As a purveyor of culture, the Athenaeum would foster a new kind of social experience in Boston with its formal art exhibitions.

Though he was never an Athenaeum member, Chester Harding provides a view of the institution from yet another perspective—that of the American painter, for whom the cultural forum of the Athenaeum Gallery offered promise but delivered not a little frustration. The Athenaeum would provide significant income for Harding; still, there was friction between the portraitist and some of the members. The figure of Chester Harding, as an advocate for working artists, unlike many of the art collectors who ran the gallery, introduces issues central to understanding the institution's position in the antebellum cultural scene. Harding's early career touches upon the influence of London exhibitions, the European aesthetic theories known to Americans, and the practice of attracting audiences with the Old Masters instead of promoting American artists exclusively—all factors that contributed to the character of the Athenaeum Gallery.

Harding's time abroad parallels the experiences of other Bostonians who hungered for contact with accomplished artists and patrons. On his first voyage to England in August 1823, high winds and violent rainstorms shook the confidence of everyone on board, including the ship's captain. Once safely in Liverpool, Harding "felt so ridiculously happy" to put his foot on shore again that he "laughed heartily without knowing why." In his memoir, the artist recounts the attentions of the revered William Roscoe, who showed him "everything that was of any interest" in Liverpool—including, one can only assume, the Liverpool Athenaeum.[5] As he moved from London to Paris and on to Glasgow, Harding converted letters of introduction into commissions, and took tea with the likes of Washington Irving and the Duke of Sussex. Harding's affability was reinforced by his impressive stature: he stood more than six feet tall and was said to have had such large feet and hands that his shoes and gloves were custom made. In sum, one unnamed contemporary called the artist (fig. 4.1) "the finest specimen of manly beauty" she ever saw.[6]

Like many of his patrons in Boston who would go on to establish the Athenaeum Gallery, Chester Harding approached London with the excitement of a self-styled connoisseur. But by the time he visited the famed Royal Academy exhibitions at Somerset House in 1824, his mind was focused on his own achievement. The following spring, a few of Harding's paintings were on exhibit. The annual exhibitions at Somerset House had already been running for forty years, and the shows were attracting tens of thousands of paying visitors each season. Harding's travel diary conveys the anxiety of an American artist whose canvases were to be hung among those of Thomas Lawrence and the like: "Somerset House opened this day. This is a grand display altogether. . . . My own portraits do not look as well as I thought they would: they want the broad effect so necessary in this exhibition. . . . The greatest advantage I shall derive is the opportunity of comparing myself with others. It was sickening, on first going into the room, to see some of my pictures so badly placed; but, on a little reflection, I thought I was placed as well as I deserve."[7]

The references to placement and comparison make more sense when one sees contemporary illustrations of the exhibition space at Somerset House.

FIGURE 4.1 Chester Harding self-portrait, circa 1825. (*Image courtesy of the Board of Trustees, National Gallery of Art, Washington*)

The images of finely dressed visitors filling the gallery show a dense, frame-to-frame hanging and, vertically, as high as wall space would accommodate, with the highest pictures tilting in toward the viewer (fig. 4.2). No portrait hangs in isolation, so comparison is unavoidable. And only minimal order is imposed—just a vague horizontal line separating smaller pictures from grander ones and the occasional nod toward symmetry in terms of genre and size. It is, indeed, a "broad effect," but not one that was unusual for the era.[8] From an artist's perspective, the dizzying arrangement would have required more than the "little reflection" Harding modestly allowed himself. The

FIGURE 4.2 *The Royal Academy Exhibition of 1828*, a watercolor by George Scharf. (© *Museum of London*)

saturated walls discouraged viewers from ranking artistic achievement—even though Harding's conclusion that he "was placed as well as [he] deserve[d]" insists on a clear standard. Perhaps those whose art was on display could not help but scrutinize the placement of their work. At the next Somerset House exhibition, Harding was apparently paralyzed by the vision. He "sat upon a bench for God knows how long, looking into vacancy and thinking painfully of the discouragements of the artist."[9]

Though he had studied only briefly at the Pennsylvania Academy of Fine Arts, Harding nevertheless would have been familiar with two aesthetic treatises known to many well-read Bostonians: Joshua Reynolds's *Discourses* (delivered 1769–1790) and Archibald Alison's *Essays on the Nature and Principles of Taste* (1790).[10] In 1825, Harding wrote to a friend that the "immortal" Sir Joshua had lived and died only two doors away from his own temporary London rooms: "Who knows but there may be some magic in the atmosphere around the hallowed spot?" In his seventh discourse as president of the Royal Academy, Reynolds had famously discussed the ascendancy of taste and advocated an adherence to rationality with regard to art. One passage, especially, brings to mind the American dilemma of determining the place of the fine arts in a democracy: "Whoever would reform a nation, supposing a bad taste to prevail in it, will not accomplish his purpose by going directly against the stream of his prejudice. . . . A national taste, however wrong it may be, cannot be totally changed all at once; we must yield a little to the prepossession which has taken hold on the mind, and we must bring people to adopt what would offend them, if endeavored to be introduced by violence."[11]

Other European aestheticians were more accessible to American visitors. John Locke had introduced associationism, the phenomenon of sensations linked in a series, and the Scotsman Archibald Alison helped popularize the notion. Labeled "aesthetic associationism," the process Alison described—an initial sensation setting off a train of associations—dismissed the need for history in art and validated for Americans their efforts to draw inspiration from natural abundance and other attributes of the young nation. The influence of Alison was pervasive in London and Glasgow at the time of Harding's visit.[12]

However connected to Old World theorists Chester Harding might have felt, he relished his identity as a self-made American. In spite of his exposure to Somerset House and to the society of the titled class, he seems to have embraced his particular homegrown reputation. It is clear from his memoir that he believed his success was attributable more to his "novel history," the tale of an uneducated man from "backwoods America," than to any merit he possessed as a painter. Yet he also claims for himself a genuine taste, as this excerpt from a letter to his wife suggests: "I am pretty well convinced that I have nothing to unlearn: yet there are many things I have to guard against, the most prominent of which is an artificial taste, or a kind of antiquarian madness which seems to be very contagious, judging from the number of its victims. I have met them at different exhibitions, where I have heard them praise, in the most extravagant manner, and without discrimination, the worst as well as the finest of the works of the old masters."[13] Finally, when a patron advised him to stay in England, arguing that "America is too young for the arts to flourish," Harding reaffirmed his decision to return to his wife and children in Massachusetts.[14]

Although many at the Boston Athenaeum admired the talent of the portraitist who had emerged "from the wilderness," there were some who proved immune to Harding fever. His goals were never identical to those of the nascent gallery and its organizers; a certain naive ambition characterized Harding's oeuvre. And his role as a spokesman for artists did not always fit

neatly with the program of the Athenaeum, which was beginning to prepare
for its first art exhibition when Harding reestablished himself in Boston in
1826. Artists were admitted free of charge to the Athenaeum Gallery. But as
early as 1827, Harding pleaded with the proprietors to make the institution's
small sculpture collection even more accessible to those who wanted to
sketch from it.[15] After the annual exhibitions had gained a following, Harding noticed that "foreign" artists were given preference in the Athenaeum
shows. By 1834, in fact, his own newly named "Harding's Gallery" would organize a rival exhibition in the artist's School Street studio; many of the ex-
hibitors there were local artists who shared Harding's dissatisfaction with
the Athenaeum's emphasis on older European painting. The group would
later become the Boston Artists' Association.[16]

Debates about whether galleries should show the Old Masters were common in the first decades of the nineteenth century. The British Institution,
which was founded by aristocrats in 1804—and whose gallery Harding had
visited in London[17]—routinely mixed the works of Old Masters with those
of living artists; the Boston Athenaeum, like the British Institution, also
exhibited the works of Old Masters—such as *The Meeting of Rebecca and
Abraham's Servant*, first attributed to Titian and later Murillo; paintings that
would erroneously be ascribed to Rembrandt and van Dyck; and Pieter Boel's
Fruit and Flowers. The authenticity of original masterworks was difficult to
verify in this era, so the institution often preferred to buy and exhibit known
copies.[18] In any case, the Athenaeum seemed to be privileging collectors over
working artists, whereas Harding wanted to support the artists he knew by
putting more of their work before prospective buyers. He also understood
the performative aspect of portraiture—the interplay of vanity and self-
invention. By creating a hybrid studio-gallery, he offered the public an alternative to more staid institutional venues.[19] Nevertheless, the Boston Athenaeum was a rewarding source of work for Chester Harding over the years,
and businessmen from the Athenaeum even aided him in securing a mortgage so he could purchase his studio.[20] Among other things, Harding's experiences underscore how contained the world of arts patronage was in Boston
at this time.

When Harding first arrived in Boston, the Athenaeum's permanent collection had included only seven works. In 1827 more than three hundred loaned
pieces of art helped the Athenaeum mount a debut exhibition whose success
astonished the trustees. Some 2,000 season passes were sold. In the wake of
its large book acquisitions program, the institution was slowly turning its attention to purchasing art by the early 1840s.[21]

A capsule history of the Athenaeum Gallery makes plain the drive behind
its establishment.[22] The idea for a public gallery at the Athenaeum mansion

on Pearl Street may have originated with donated statuary and a few portraits of benefactors, but the notion gained momentum in 1823, when a prospectus outlining plans for a combined lecture hall and exhibition space was circulated among prominent citizens. In 1826 a three-story brick building was erected behind the Pearl Street house. The ground floor was partitioned into administrative rooms, the second floor given over to a 500-seat lecture hall, and the top floor occupied by artists until an exhibition could be arranged. (Painters Gilbert Stuart and Washington Allston both used this area as studio space that year.)

One obvious incentive for the gallery was civic pride. The Pennsylvania Academy of Fine Arts was attracting attention, and Bostonians did not want to be outdone by their counterparts in Philadelphia. Members meant to fulfill the promise, made in the Athenaeum's founding document, to provide an "ornament for the city" through the stated goals of art exhibition and artist training. Another incentive was financial: organizers hoped that receipts from exhibitions would help cover the Athenaeum's mounting expenses.[23] Painting exhibitions defined the first dozen shows; sculpture displays were added in 1839. The Athenaeum's move to Beacon Street in 1850 disrupted the tone of the annual exhibitions but allowed interested members to rededicate their commitment to the visual arts through more purposeful layouts and sophisticated exhibits.

From the beginning, the Athenaeum Gallery was driven by patrons, not artists—a distinction that would matter to local painters, as the brief look at Chester Harding's lively career confirms. For fifty years the Athenaeum was the only museum of art in the city, and questions arise about the Bostonians in charge. How did patrons express their plans—to themselves and to the community? How did trends in taste circulate? And, perhaps most compelling, how was the gallery experienced by visitors? These questions gain wider relevance as cultural efforts engaged more popular urban audiences. Avoiding a conventional art-historical analysis of painting and sculpture, one can resurrect the life of the gallery first through promotional texts and then through building programs. Illustrative scenes relating to two distinct areas—art exhibitions and architectural design—show that the Athenaeum created new ways for men and women to view the city and themselves. What visitors saw, and *how* they saw, depended as much on the careful staging of connoisseurs and reporters as on the works of exhibiting artists. The Athenaeum now offered interested Bostonians a sense of cosmopolitanism.

"Scarcely a person passes the door-keeper who does not peep into his book or inquire the number," reported an article about the Athenaeum Gallery's ticket sales in a widely circulated newspaper. So fashionable were the exhibitions

that on a single day in May 1832, more than four hundred season tickets had
been sold before noon. The price of admission was reasonable at 25 cents;
season tickets cost 50 cents. By that year a core group of paintings owned by
the Athenaeum anchored the shows, but in the late 1820s the exhibitions' offerings had changed entirely with every season—and attendance had been
well into the thousands for season ticket-holders. In total, the Athenaeum
staged forty-six annual exhibitions over the period from 1827 through 1873,
often with accompanying fanfare in the popular press. The advent of annual
exhibitions in Boston during the second quarter of the nineteenth century
worked to stimulate artistic production, to be sure, and the shows' effect on
the growth of a viewing public proved at least equally significant.[24]

Although one finds references to a hired gallery "superintendent" named
William Harris Jones (about whom little is recorded), members of the institution's Fine Arts Committee appear to have been central to what we would
now call curatorial direction. Thomas Handasyd Perkins, the merchant and
investor whose family's periodic emergency donations had kept the Athenaeum afloat—recall the gift of the Pearl Street mansion by his brother, James
Perkins—was an important committee member. Thomas Perkins's firsthand
knowledge of European galleries shaped the space at Pearl Street. (Unfortunately, no illustration of the interior is known to exist.) Like others who took
in cultural displays abroad,[25] Perkins visited Somerset House, even making
notes with an eye to the Boston plan: "I find the Center Room is lighted, as we
propose to light our Room—this is the only room where the light is good."[26]
Martin Archer Shee, the British artist who would preside over the Royal Academy from 1830 to 1850 (and who had painted Roscoe's portrait), was a figure
well known to Perkins and other Athenaeum organizers. There is no question that the arrangement of paintings at Somerset House—conveying a sense
of abundance similar to that of a princely Kunstkammer—was admired by
the Boston elite.[27]

London exhibitions such as the ones at Somerset House were often in-
voked as models for the young gallery. A letter from one young Bostonian
woman to her friend in Paris gives some idea of the new sophistication the
Athenaeum offered the city:

> The greatest thing we have at present is the Athenaeum Exhibition of pic-
> tures. [Washington] Allston says it would do credit to Somerset House and
> certainly is far before anything which has been seen in the United States.
> There are 317 in all & perhaps not more than ten or twelve that can be called
> ordinary. It is open at all hours for two months & you seldom find fewer than
> a hundred persons in there—often two or three times that number, indeed it
> forms a most agreeable lounge & although subjected like other plans occa-
> sionally to purposes of coquetry & flirtation, & although the gentlemen get

into a corner to talk of business & news, yet I think it may do much to refine the public taste & create a love for pleasures somewhat more intellectual than have generally prevailed among us.[28]

Mention of "coquetry & flirtation" (as well as "business & news") points to the social aspect of the gallery experience. Among other priorities, the Athenaeum Gallery was conceived as a site where the sexes could mix. Of course, the fact that females did not generally venture into the Athenaeum library no doubt added to the gallery's allure for the women of Boston. An announcement dating from the spring of the first exhibition uses language crafted to welcome not only married gentlewomen but also single women to the gallery: "Visitors will find that every attention has been paid to their accommodation; and Ladies will experience no embarrassment or difficulty in visiting the gallery without the attendance of gentlemen."[29] This, too, was consistent with the London displays, at which women's involvement struck curators as both necessary and, eventually, threatening.[30]

The remnants of the Fine Arts Committee papers—exhibition catalogues and occasional gallery pamphlets—offer a glimpse into further strategies the Athenaeum used to mold its viewing public. From the earliest exhibitions, the gallery showed Old Masters alongside paintings by "Living Artists" (fig. 4.3). The second catalogue (1828) provided birth and death dates for the Old Masters, enhancing the pedagogical value of the publication. Furthermore, the listings led with the Old Masters, fostering a sense that this was a forum whose reigning taste was informed by the sights of the Grand Tour. Oddly juxtaposed to such cosmopolitanism, the catalogue recorded Americans' "Artists' Residences" on the back cover, encouraging traffic to local studios; artists "not residing in Boston" were listed separately, educating the visitor about the regional origins of American painters. Over the years, the catalogues intermittently provided more expository descriptions of the art— including biographical data on artists and other art-historical guidance.[31]

Public-loan exhibitions, which were the standard procedure at the Athenaeum, required an acknowledgment of the paintings' owners, inspiring further experimentation with the modes of the catalogue. Starting in 1831, "proprietors" of the loaned works of art were prominently showcased in print. Often, an impulse to regulate the viewing audience was obvious. In the 1839 exhibition catalogue, the owner of featured paintings, "Mr. W. Hayward," touts his connoisseurship and observes that "the collecting of so many fine examples of the great masters is the result of diligent research, liberal outlay, and extensive travel both in the United States and in England, during a period of ten years." The patron continues, quoting artists and "cognoscenti" of New York who have praised his "pictures of sterling quality"

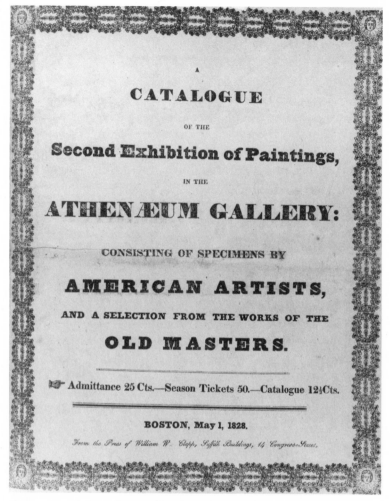

FIGURE 4.3 Cover of an early Athenaeum exhibition catalogue. (*Boston Athenaeum*)

and referred to his collection as one "whose merit is of so high a class."[32] The self-conscious quotations from puffed-up authorities ostensibly alerted the visitor to aesthetic value and authenticity. In practice, however, the aggressive catalogue text gave collectors a platform for their taste and disciplined any dissenting gaze.

Contradictory attitudes of the gallery organizers are especially apparent in pamphlets distributed during the Athenaeum's prime. "Lithographic keys"—reproductions of the principal elements of a panoramic painting—

sold for 12½ cents at the door.[33] Other guides emphasized text over illustration. One representative publication presumably distributed to gallerygoers, *Remarks upon the Athenaeum Gallery of Paintings* (1831), reflects the conflicting aims of profit-turning and arts advancement. Boasting "undisguised admiration . . . of the general multitude," the gallery was open "from 8 a.m. until 10 p.m."—certainly generous hours for viewing. (Proceeds from ticket sales went mostly to new art purchases or to a fund for future shows.) The anonymous author of *Remarks* understood the growing value of the marketplace but at the same time wanted to groom the public. This made for a chaotic blend of subject matter: deference to benefactors, acknowledgment of the visitors, apologia for the ubiquity of portraiture, cheerleading for native artists, insistence on the superiority of history painting, and, finally, defense of the precarious state of art criticism in the young nation.[34]

A range of critical responses to the Athenaeum Gallery appear in contemporary press reports, complementing comments from inside the institution. Some articles promote the annual exhibition as a means of creating a community of taste. Others go further to complain about the public's ignorance of the fine arts: "Care and attention our people, under the most favorable circumstances, are not much given to bestow. They are impetuous and bustling, and pride themselves much more on their ability to drive a good bargain, than on their taste." Still other articles reveal a profound confusion about the whole exhibition enterprise: "We have thus far hesitated to offer any criticism on the paintings because we are far from being satisfied that we could criticize them in a manner that would be of any benefit to visitors." Occasionally, a press report simply introduces visitors to the relative comforts of the gallery space or anxiously rehearses theories of art appreciation, suggesting elaborate ways to view particular works of art. "We would recommend that those who wish to feel and understand the true sentiment of [William Dunlap's *Christ Rejected*] go early in the forenoon and be prepared to sit four hours and examine it in detail," writes a reporter for the *Columbia Centinel*. "About four o'clock in the afternoon, we believe, is the best light," offers a journalist from the *Boston Courier*.[35]

The coverage vacillates from insecurity to bravado—and, as this excerpt exemplifies, the insecurity often resides *within* the bravado:

"It is amusing to lounge for an hour at the Gallery," says a writer in the *Massachusetts Journal*, "even if it offered no other attraction than the thousand contradictory criticisms one is sure to hear,"—and let me add, it is quite as amusing to read the remarks of those "self-constituted judges on the throne of taste" which appear in print after they return from the Gallery. . . . I wish people would learn (especially critics) to distinguish between the merits of a first rate historical picture and a paltry portrait or a schoolgirl's landscape.[36]

The cranky reviewer piles on criticism of critics, adding to the very noise about which he complains. This phenomenon was illustrated winningly in satirical etchings by an artist and Athenaeum exhibitor, D. C. Johnston. Speech bubbles in Johnston's witty images expand to crowd the exhibit space. In the 1830 engraving titled *Connoisseurs* (fig. 4.4), Johnston's gallerygoers make slavishly fashionable comments on the pictures, while an unsavory dealer encourages the production of quick copies.[37] In addition to graphic spoofs, the gallery inspired more earnest creative efforts. Ekphrasis, the poetic treatment of the visual arts, was popular; some gallery visitors wrote ekphrastic poems cataloguing the works stanza by stanza. Even a dramatic rendering has survived: one playlet, published on the front page of the *Boston Daily American Statesman*, is a striking example of scripted aesthetic response. The drama follows an uncle and his niece through the gallery as they comment on the Athenaeum pictures. Fictitious dialogue constitutes a training ground for proper gallery banter, with "The artist has talent, but needs practice and discipline" substituting for more thorough readings of the art.[38]

Finally, for many gallery visitors the venue afforded opportunities for casual titillation or mindless recreation. According to John Greenleaf Whittier, for example, as a youth in the late 1820s the abolitionist William Lloyd Garrison "lounged" at the Athenaeum, where he cared "not a fig for canvass faces" but relished "the fresher, and merrier, and prettier ones, all glowing with life, having the most dangerous eyes and bewitching forms."[39] By the 1830s, one young lady considered a morning's Athenaeum visit more agreeable in the absence of the regular loungers: "Pictures beautiful, some of the old masters such as never visited my dim eyes before. . . . There were not yet the usual assortment of odiosities staring from the sophas."[40] Once the exhibitions gained an audience, the line blurred somewhat between official organizers and paying visitors, some of whom seemed to appropriate the setting and claim an ownership and an authority that irritated others. Even the Athenaeum's hired gatekeeper came under criticism from stuffy, sarcastic journalists for apparently offering visitors his own reactions to the works of art on display: "The impudent puppy employed to receive the tickets at the entrance of the Athenaeum Gallery . . . should bear in mind [that] when his opinion concerning the pictures is wanted, it will be applied for."[41]

A growing sculpture collection contributed to the attractions of the Athenaeum Gallery. In 1822, Augustus Thorndike, an Athenaeum trustee, had donated a dozen casts of ancient statues—most were said to have been selected by Antonio Canova.[42] After 1835 the Boston Athenaeum became a leader in commissioning contemporary sculpture. Unlike the institution's inconsistent support of American painters, its patronage of native-born sculptors was enthusiastic. Changing exhibits were mounted almost annually, starting in 1839. "Every

FIGURE 4.4 *Connoisseurs*, an etching by D. C. Johnston, 1830. (*Courtesy, American Antiquarian Society*)

[Boston] man keeps a sculptor," wrote Clarence Cook, one of the first professional art critics in the nation.[43] The drive to make Boston "the capital of the arts" and attract "that sort of society which is principally desired," as Athenaeum member William Tudor put it, led to both financial and moral support for neoclassical sculptors.[44] As a movement, neoclassicism was a reaction against rococo. To participate, American sculptors needed to acquire skills in white marble, the preferred medium for the neoclassical style; hence, many patronized sculptors—Horatio Greenough, Shobal Vail Clevenger, John Frazee—were sent to Italy at the expense of Athenaeum members. For example, Greenough was funded by both Thomas Handasyd Perkins and George Ticknor.

Interestingly, there seems to have been little incongruity between the commissioned works and the plaster reproductions of ancient works that had launched the Athenaeum sculpture collection. Perhaps because of the neoclassical style of the commissions, an aesthetic harmony reigned. The casts served a didactic purpose and, as Alan Wallach explains, were clearly part of a widespread practice. At the Athenaeum, copies of works such as the *Apollo Belvedere*, *Venus de Medici*, *Blind Homer*, and *Ceres* were highly valued. "The study of the antique," wrote Franklin Dexter, a member of the Fine Arts Committee, "is the very alphabet of art." Even as original sculptures were being commissioned, a canon of copies grounded the exhibition space. Such reproductions signified "the height of artistic creation" and acted as "a bulwark of absolute values in a world governed by capricious and frequently changing tastes," according to Francis Haskell and Nicholas Penny.[45]

The sculpture gallery would soon set the tone for the interior of the institution. When visitors entered the ground floor of the Athenaeum's final
home on Beacon Street, their first impressions were produced by the juxtaposition of contemporary originals with reproductions of ancient figures.
Both the classical and neoclassical styles harmonized with a Unitarian emphasis on nature as a visual link between the sacred and the profane.[46]

Lillian Miller has asserted that Bostonians were not accepting of new trends
in art, and that the static taste for neoclassical sculpture and Old Masters'
paintings (often imitations, both known and forged) defined the Athenaeum
Gallery.[47] That might well have been true of the elite, who sought to recreate
a European experience for themselves. But visitors brought to the gallery expectations and criteria that differed from those of collectors. If one judges
from the variety of responses to the Athenaeum's exhibitions, any claim that
the gallery represented straightforward conservatism reflects too narrow an
understanding of the historical scene. The exhibition space started as a mon-
eymaking venture as well as a showcase for civic pride. Along the way, the
alchemy of strict Athenaeum control and visitors' appetites for urban entertainment resulted in a Boston audience that would soon demand more novelty. In an 1831 internal report the Fine Arts Committee reluctantly admitted,
"Our only resource is the curiosity of the public. It seems advisable not to
draw upon it too frequently. . . . It might receive a new impulse by a larger
interval between exhibitions." At times, the connoisseurs who organized the
shows were forced to turn their attention away from issues of lighting and
provenance and toward their increasingly fickle visitors. It became a challenge to find enough pictures that would be "a source of interest and pleasure
to the public at large, . . . public taste [becoming] more discriminating and
critical and of course more difficult to satisfy."[48] Perhaps the Athenaeum un-
derestimated Bostonians' appetite for art. The institution seemed to be in
over its head.

Through its art exhibitions, the Athenaeum became a small but powerful
cultural stage in the 1820s, '30s, and '40s. Whatever the response to Old Masters and Living Artists, the buildings inhabited by the institution mediated
the experience of gallerygoing. What role did the quest for space—the right
space—play in the story of the Athenaeum's authority? Unfortunately, little
visual evidence of the early Athenaeum sites exists. By 1822 the institution
had moved into the spacious house on Pearl Street (that site and the present
site, on Beacon Street, are its two longest-running homes, and the ones of
interest in this book). Proprietors in the early 1820s felt that a proper art gallery required space separated from the library. A first-floor plan for the Pearl
Street addition designed by Solomon Willard called for a "Room for Appara-

tus" and an "Academy of Arts" on the ground floor, indicating the intention to house tools for the advancement of science and a school for artists. There are few surviving visual documents from the Pearl Street era. Instead, we must rely on a contemporary description of the three-story building that was finally built behind the Pearl Street mansion in 1826:

> The lower story comprises four rooms [housing scientific apparatus and rented to various societies]. The second story, which is 18 feet high, consists of a lecture room conveniently arranged with circular seats on an inclined plane, and sufficiently spacious to accommodate 500 auditors. The upper story forms a single room, 60 by 60 feet square, is upwards of 20 feet high, and lighted only from the top, in a manner peculiarly adapted for the exhibition of paintings, to which purpose this room has been appropriated.[49]

John Lowell, for whom the addition was a pet project, had written a friend in 1823, when the idea for this multipurpose structure was first circulated, complaining that the plan was not attracting the interest it deserved. In his letter he argued that a lecture room surrounded with "casts," "ancient sculptures," and "fine paintings" would enhance the exploration of any topic discussed. He maintained the importance of dedicating rooms to more public cultural events—in order to "sanctify, if I may so express it," a space for the arts. "External appearances have an effect incalculable on the operations of the most cultivated and best arranged minds," he wrote.[50]

This vision of a single place that would signal cultural refinement was eventually fulfilled in even grander form when, in 1845, architects competed to satisfy the proprietors' desire for yet a different structure—this time an idiosyncratic building type, a purpose-built art museum and library to be constructed on the stylish south slope of Beacon Street. After decades at the Pearl Street site, the Athenaeum had watched the neighborhood's tranquillity decline: Irish immigrants had moved into nearby tenements, and business at a sugar refinery infringed upon the peace of the reading room. Furthermore, while painting exhibitions and, after 1839, sculpture exhibitions at the Pearl Street gallery had drawn people from throughout the region, the growing collection of casts and statuary had displaced the lecture hall and threatened to overwhelm the library building. In addition, public lectures were now commonplace in the city, and the out-of-the-way Athenaeum no longer attracted crowds for their scheduled speakers.

Of the fourteen architectural submissions of 1845, the winning design was rendered by Edward Clarke Cabot, a relatively inexperienced architect and a grandson of Thomas Handasyd Perkins. George Minot Dexter, a seasoned engineer and architect, collaborated with Cabot.[51] Stylistically, the facade of the Beacon Street building refers to Andrea Palladio, whose Palazzo da Porta Festa in Vicenza (fig. 4.5) was depicted in Ottavio Bertotti

FIGURE 4.5 Front elevation of Palazzo da Porta Festa, designed by Andrea Palladio, circa 1552. (*Boston Athenaeum*)

Scamozzi's *Le fabbriche e i disegni di Andrea Palladio* (1776), a book known to Athenaeum readers.[52] This reference to a Renaissance palace—and one of Palladio's in particular—followed a transatlantic trend. Nineteenth-century gentlemen's clubs in London introduced the notion that Italian palace architecture provided the appropriate setting for exclusive male meeting, reading, and (in the case of the British societies) dining.[53] The clubs that line Pall Mall, especially, evoke academic dignity and a harmony of proportions. This revived style was known in the United States through W. H. Leeds's books about London buildings and through architects such as Arthur Gilman, who traveled abroad and came home trumpeting the new fashion. British architect Charles Barry had designed the Travellers' Club in 1829; he followed the mode of the Palazzo Pandolfino in Florence, attributed to Raphael. (Barry went on to design the Reform Club in 1836, adapting the "simplicity, solidity, and repose" of Antonio da Sangallo's Farnese Palace in Rome. He also designed the Houses of Parliament upon their rebuilding in the 1840s and '50, after destructive fires.) In the United States, John Notman's design of the Philadelphia Athenaeum (fig. 4.6) in 1845 continued with this assumption that the style of Renaissance palaces fits the purposes of clubs and learned societies. Notman's symmetrical facade, with its sturdy rusticated ground floor and *piano nobile* (a large, elegant second floor), seems to reinforce the words of a nineteenth-century British historian: "[Italian architecture] is the most manly, firm, imposing, and on the large scale the most allied to grandeur and stateliness."[54] Notman, like Cabot, imitated Palladio. Decades earlier, features of Palladian design had been adopted by Americans such as Thomas Jefferson, who raised the University of Virginia on axial plans and triadic symmetry.[55]

The original drawings of the Beacon Street elevation made by Cabot are lost, but a photograph from 1852 (fig. 4.7) not only illustrates the completed facade but shows how placards were set up to advertise the gallery's offerings. The awkward site, overlooking the Granary Burying Ground, challenged the architect, but Cabot's plan succeeded in conveying what one commentator would later call "rich and elaborate elegance," a building "stamped at once as dedicated to literature and the fine arts." The two-level visual organization gave the structure a compact appearance. The dignified edifice would be built of gray "Little Fall" sandstone. (The special virtues of sandstone had already been touted in the Philadelphia Athenaeum design: "Rich

FIGURE 4.6 Philadelphia Athenaeum, designed by John Notman, 1845. (*Courtesy of the Athenaeum of Philadelphia*)

FIGURE 4.7 Facade of Boston Athenaeum on Beacon Street, 1852. Placards in front of the building advertise the gallery exhibitions. (*Boston Athenaeum*)

gray and brown stone from our native quarries . . . impart an air of quiet gentility to private buildings, of philosophical gravity to those of public character.") The front of the Boston Athenaeum features Corinthian pilasters flanking recessed windows on the second level and rusticated arches around windows on the first level. Inside, three floors reflect the varied uses: a first-floor sculpture gallery (fig. 4.8), a second-floor library, and a third-floor picture gallery. Two-thirds of the library was now dedicated to the visual arts, seeming to reflect an institutional shift from reading to viewing. (As men-

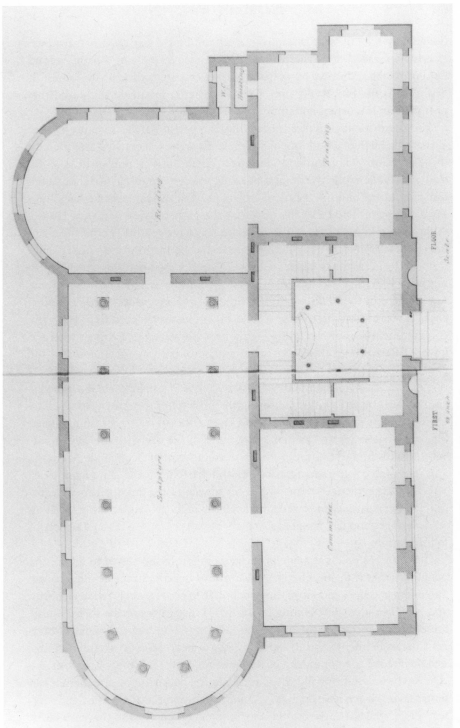

FIGURE 4.8 Athenaeum on Beacon Street, plan for the first floor, 1849. (*Boston Athenaeum*)

tioned above, book acquisitions had declined by the early 1840s as art purchases increased.) Still, the planned use of alcove shelving on the second floor provided additional book space, and, as expected, all 40,000 volumes "fit easily" into the library. In sum, Cabot's design announced the new Athenaeum as an important and imposing institution.[56]

The ritualistic laying of a cornerstone is a performance, an expression of faith in the birth of a building. As Neil Harris writes, "Focusing attention on those occasions when builders, designers, clients, critics, publicists, and officials must talk explicitly about a building's larger meaning" teaches something about the building's cultural role. On April 27, 1847, proprietors, "literary gentlemen," and other interested parties gathered near the State House, at the future home of the Athenaeum. In language reminiscent of the original circular of 1807, which had been used by the institution to attract subscribers, Josiah Quincy addressed the group. As expected, his speech summarized the story of the institution's founding and acknowledged the munificence of the Perkins family (with comparisons to the Medici of Florence). It was customary to bury a collection of historic materials beneath the cornerstone; that day the following items were placed in a copper case and lowered into the ground: "statistical annals of the time, the coins of the country, the papers of the day, with various memorials of the present condition of the city, and of the state of society, and also a silver plate, on which is engraved . . . an inscription [restating the mission of the Athenaeum]." The offering points backward and forward in an effort to construct time, reflecting, as Harris suggests, "an acute awareness of the historicity of built structures." In his remarks, Quincy emphasized institutional continuity, denying any "new fabric" in the organization and attributing the shift from Pearl Street to "convenience" alone. While the new building provided an opportunity for the Athenaeum to redefine itself through the public fanfare that attends such ceremonies, its spokespeople—not surprisingly—resisted any claim to innovation.[57]

Of course, as much as some proprietors might have wanted to ignore the possibility that it meant change, the move to Beacon Street would have repercussions. Before too long, the new building generated citywide curiosity and produced divisions among its visitors. Frequenters of the former Pearl Street library mourned the privacy of their previous resort. Assistant librarian Charles Fairbanks wrote appreciatively of Pearl Street's "awful mystery" and bemoaned the popularity of the new building: "A hundred persons use the library now for one did then; and I am left to feed upon the memory of better times, when learning was a quiet, comfortable sort of thing, and mutter secret maledictions on the revolutionary spirits who have made it otherwise."[58] Perhaps the new visitors, these "revolutionary spirits," had responded to the flurry of promotional images that appeared within a few years of the reopening. In 1852, Henry McIntyre's lavishly illustrated tourist map showcased the Athenaeum along with other noteworthy destinations in Boston. Engravings of the exterior and three interior views (figs. 4.9, 4.10, 4.11, and 4.12)—all stylized renderings—accompanied an article in the popular journal *Ballou's Pictorial Drawing-Room Companion* in 1855.[59] And small stereocards of the sculpture gallery, sold as keepsakes, encouraged private consumption of the refined settings. (Popular at the time, stereocards were designed as a parlor entertainment and viewed with the aid of an instrument called a stereopticon.)[60] Such rich visual evidence suggests that citizens embraced eagerly the sophistication represented by the Beacon Street facade. With its increasingly recognizable exterior, the Athenaeum became a part of Boston's urban identity.

One interior element seems to have been admired equally by old-line Athenaeum regulars and newer visitors. Photographs of the so-called Sumner Staircase appeared on postcards celebrating the new Athenaeum building. The architectural feature is named for Charles Sumner, a figure who would prove central to an understanding of the paradoxes that characterized cultivated society in Boston. A "Free Soiler" and United States senator whose political passions centered on abolitionism, Sumner was also a Grand Tourist; his time abroad, from 1837 to 1840, had stimulated his passionate and personal approach toward arts patronage.[61] While the Athenaeum was at Pearl Street, he had overseen the completion of *Orpheus and Cerberus*, a neoclassical sculpture by the New York-based artist Thomas Crawford, then living in Rome. Sumner staged the sculpture's exhibition in Boston so minutely that he selected and paid for the carpeting and wall colors for the display room.[62] Soon Crawford's career soared with commissions for portrait busts as well as other sculpture.

Sumner's devotion to the institution allowed him to exercise his refinement in a very public way. He had served on the commission to choose the new building's design, and in 1845, with the plans still under consideration, he wrote to his brother: "I am anxious to secure a large, generous, hospitable vestibule, hall and stairway [for the Athenaeum]. I remember the stairs (by Bernini, I think) which lead to the Vatican on the right of St. Peter's. Can you send me the measurements of these—width, height, breadth? They were stairs of such exquisite proportions that you seemed to be borne aloft on wings."[63] Sumner's experiences in the galleries and studios of Europe made him acutely aware of America's inferiority in the arts, but he was convinced that his compatriots could be trained to recognize and reward talented artists. In this, he seems to echo Joshua Reynolds's advice to be gentle with those living in a nation with "bad taste," and to introduce excellence slowly.

EXTERIOR VIEW OF THE BOSTON ATHENÆUM.

FIGURE 4.9 Exterior of the Boston Athenaeum, from a set of illustrations in *Ballou's Pictorial Drawing Room Companion*, 1855. (*Boston Athenaeum*)

FIGURE 4.10 First-floor sculpture gallery of the Athenaeum, from *Ballou's*. (*Boston Athenaeum*)

STATUARY ROOM OF THE ATHENÆUM.

LIBRARY OF THE ATHENÆUM.

FIGURE 4.11 Second-floor reading room of the Athenaeum, from *Ballou's*. (*Boston Athenaeum*)

FIGURE 4.12 Third-floor painting gallery of the Athenaeum, from *Ballou's*. (*Boston Athenaeum*)

GALLERY OF PAINTINGS AT THE ATHENÆUM.

"Americans are sheep and follow the bellwether," Sumner wrote his friend George Hillard on the subject of arts patronage.[64] Emboldened perhaps by his success with Crawford's *Orpheus*, Sumner wanted to import elegance and drama to his hometown. By inquiring about the specifications of the papal stairs, he was expressing his desire for a kind of metasouvenir. He wanted a piece of the Old World, a token of transcendence for his all-too-familiar Yankee capital. Yet, as built, the stairs have little relationship to Bernini's design.[65] Installed in 1851, the complete entry (fig. 4.13) featured a paneled rotunda and marbled staircase. Impressive as it was, the staircase could never have achieved the scale of Bernini's, and it was eventually removed to make room for the growing library. Still, nothing short of public grief describes the reaction in the Boston newspapers when, in 1889, Athenaeum visitors appealed against its "desecration" with references to Sumner and his welcoming pillared arches.[66] Perhaps like Sumner, the disappointed visitors longed to connect themselves, however remotely, to the lavish and refined styles of Europe.

For decades, the grand stairway served as the conduit to the art gallery on the third floor. With the aid of *Ballou's* idealized interior images, a virtual tour is possible. Visitors coming from the street would pass through swinging doors and enter the cool, dark hall. The first-floor sculpture gallery (fig. 4.10)—some eighty feet long—was accessible from a doorway straight ahead, opposite the front door. There, visitors were to be "delighted and instructed" by carefully placed neoclassical sculpture and plaster reproductions. A copy of Michelangelo's *Night and Day* could be seen from a long perspective, as it occupied the far "bow" gallery of the long room; Jean-Antoine Houdon's *Washington* and Robert Ball Hugh's *Bowditch* celebrated recent culture heroes.[67] From the vestibule, the visitor would be drawn to the stairs on the right and might prepare for what the *Boston Post* called the "toilsome journey upwards." The required ascent worked against the Athenaeum's accessibility but may have heightened anticipation for those visitors destined for the climactic upper level. Members with reading privileges would climb one flight of Sumner's staircase to the second-floor library (fig. 4.11), which was furnished with long tables, book alcoves, and galleries of shelving accessible by way of spiral stairs. Finally, visitors who continued to the third floor arrived at the sky-lit picture gallery (fig. 4.12), a carpeted area divided into four rooms for maximum wall space.

With the resumption of the annual exhibitions in the new gallery, changes were evident. In contrast to the gallery at Pearl Street, here a spectacle of frame-to-frame hanging does not seem to have been the goal. Each wall was only thirteen feet tall "so that no picture can be placed too high to be seen distinctly." References to "Paintings on the Staircase" and "Paintings in the

FIGURE 4.13 The Sumner Staircase, 1889. (*Boston Athenaeum*)

Gallery" appear in the catalogues dating from the 1850s, indicating that there were distinct zones for viewing. One gallery room was devoted to the work of Washington Allston, and the "North-East Room" displayed paintings predominantly by artists from Boston and New York.[68] These developments follow the practice of classifying displays according to artist and region—a trend that had begun to ritualize the museum experience by emphasizing instruction in the history of art.[69] In addition, by the 1850s a sizable permanent collection existed, and a canon of sorts had formed. Catalogues from the mid-1850s are almost identical in appearance from year to year and contain many of the same works of art with the same descriptions.[70] Apparently, the call for novelty was not satisfactorily answered. The shows, while still popular, failed to generate the same excitement as they had done at Pearl Street.[71] Yet more women would be counted among gallery visitors as the 1850s wore on. Reflecting the feminization of the gallery, one catalogue specifies that "Parasols, etc. must be left with the Doorkeeper," and the back cover of another advertises sewing machines.[72] Clearly, women of the middle

classes availed themselves of the picture gallery in increasing numbers—
even though female readers were welcome in the library only rarely.

The Beacon Street building ennobled the Boston Athenaeum's enterprise,
lending architectural coherence to a hodgepodge collection of casts and portraits and, superficially at least, expanding the institution's reach. Yet organizers of the Athenaeum, whose early skepticism about an American identity
had led to their imitation of British and Continental cultural forms, experimented quite tentatively with efforts to define their own national styles.
References to Old World models obviously continued; the transformation
from deferential anglophilia to a more stable sense of the nation's own cultural life was slow and defined by resistance. That said, well-traveled patrons
were at times baffled by the complexity of audience response. Visitors, encouraged by pamphleteers and press agents to attend the gallery, reacted to
the exhibitions in all manner of ways. The institution's majestic architectural
design inspired citizens to experience for themselves the Athenaeum cachet,
yet all the while, institution leaders anxiously maintained distance from the
same public they were courting. Robert Ferguson has written that American
identity is best considered "a jumble of available characteristics shaped into
useful combinations."[73] At midcentury, Bostonians inside and outside the
institution used the Athenaeum to mix leisure with cultivation and to min-
gle vulnerability with pride.

Part Three
CONSCIENCE

*He arose by daybreak, . . . breakfasted leisurely, gave his orders
to the servants for the day, and walked, with his head elevated
to a great height in the air, to an insurance office
or the Athenaeum.*

Mrs. Eliza [Harrison Gray] Otis
The Barclays of Boston, a novel
1854

CHAPTER FIVE

The Color of Gentility

A TYPE OF HOUSEHOLD MERCHANDISE, briefly in vogue in antebellum Boston, celebrated both abolition and British superiority: curiously decorated thimbles, pitchers, crib quilts, bookmarks, pens, watchcases, and cups (fig. 5.1) were distributed at annual bazaars organized by the women of the Boston Female Anti-Slavery Society. These items often boasted abolitionist insignia and sayings designed to keep the problem of slavery before the public eye, "and by every innocent expedient to promote perpetual discussion," according to the influential abolitionist newspaper *The Liberator*. Shoes with TRAMPLE NOT THE OPPRESSED printed on their soles were sold alongside banners that read SLAVERY ABOLISHED IN THE BRITISH WEST INDIES. Indeed, the moral leadership of Great Britain—whose government had begun emancipating its slaves in 1807—reigned at these popular Boston sales.[1] The fairs hint at the mood of the city during the 1830s and '40s, when a small segment of elite society became active in abolitionism.

Part of the elaborate network of antebellum politics, the antislavery fairs touched the Boston Athenaeum tangentially but significantly. Some of the women who attended the bazaars came from the same prominent families whose men read at the Athenaeum. Whereas these women were vocal on the subject of slavery, however, the all-male institution was relatively silent. The attitude of Athenaeum readers toward the problem of slavery is not at all clear. Unfortunately, there was no institutional consensus on abolition, and debates among Athenaeum members are difficult to reconstruct. It is this asymmetry of evidence that makes an abolitionist cup, for example, so telling: the household articles sold at female-led fund-raisers represent the most tangible evidence of organized antislavery protest among elite Bostonians.[2] In addition, these few surviving objects reveal a cultural pattern. They announce a historical phenomenon: the merging of American anglophilia with protest.

FIGURE 5.1 Abolition cup, such as those sold at antislavery fairs in New England: "Perish Slavery, Prosper Freedom." (*Courtesy, Winterthur; bequest of Henry Francis du Pont*)

The Boston Athenaeum never officially joined the antislavery movement. But by supporting the cause indirectly with a wife's (or sister's or daughter's) purchase of an antislavery teacup, a patrician no doubt assuaged his conscience somewhat. In essence, the Athenaeum at midcentury operated within a context of contradiction—sustaining an environment of benevolent authority while simultaneously taking no public stand on the question of the day. It is well known that the relationship between class and politics is complicated by the maintenance of material comforts. At the Athenaeum, the problem of slavery became a tightrope on which members precariously balanced. Even though antislavery protesters celebrated British leaders whom the Athenaeum gentlemen were themselves predisposed to admire, the institution's position on slavery remained unarticulated. Its reluctance to embrace the cause of abolitionism demonstrates that the Athenaeum did not advance the nation in all the ways that its founding documents had envisioned. The institution tried to remove itself from the "unpleasantness" of abolitionism. Meanwhile, abolitionist activities occurred throughout Boston and were occasionally attended by female relatives of Athenaeum readers. A shared sense of higher purpose was what had driven the institution's shareholders in the past, but on the matter of slavery, its leaders in the 1830s and '40s were unable to project a united ethical resolve.

The resistance to the antislavery movement among Athenaeum proprietors should not be surprising, however; such institutions did not take fixed positions on political matters. Elite Bostonians confounded moral leadership with aesthetic and scholarly leadership. And in the minds of most gentlemen readers their sponsorship of key cultural institutions compensated for any passivity regarding the growing problem of slavery. Often those Athenaeum shareholders who did speak out encountered some measure of ostracism, and the more outspoken members also tended to be newcomers to the inner circle of Bostonians—a fact that was seldom overlooked by the elite-born.

An active group, the Boston Female Anti-Slavery Society was led by educated women, largely Unitarians, who had the financial resources to stage elaborate fund-raising events. More than a few had male relatives who were readers at the Athenaeum.[3] And all were, themselves, welcome at the gallery. From 1834 to 1860 the society's fairs were a fixture in the holiday calendar. Each December the women would decorate a rented hall with evergreens and candelabras. Families would congregate around refreshment tables and at booths dispensing "antislavery handkerchiefs that operate upon many a little heart" and sewing needles that called for the buyer to "prick the conscience" of the slave master. Prizes donated by aristocratic Englishmen became the centerpiece of these events, and the audiences grew large enough to reap thousands of dollars for the antislavery effort each winter.[4] Socialite Maria Weston Chapman essentially ran the fairs with three of her five sisters. A recipient of Athenaeum borrowing privileges through a male supporter starting in 1847, Maria Chapman was an avid reader. Her anglophilic tastes appear to have been consistent with those of highbrow male abolitionists.[5] The Weston women (all but Maria were unmarried) capitalized on their own cosmopolitanism. They shopped abroad for "the most recherché articles of taste and fancy from the old world." At any given fair, they might well have arranged an English Warwick vase in front of a flag bearing the message LET THE OPPRESSED GO FREE AND BREAK EVERY YOKE.[6]

The juxtaposition of refined taste and human suffering was calculated. Unlike the evangelical women who eventually left the society, complaining of its materialistic bent, the Weston sisters and their wealthy friends used the city's appetite for fashion to attract attendees. The fairs ushered in a kind of antebellum radical chic; moral activism was linked to social fancy. This trend followed the larger abolitionist movement, as the trappings of England, in particular, gave the cause a genteel air. Abolitionist sentiment became tied to the fashions of Great Britain. Anglophilia lent credibility to the cause and added some cultural distinction to what was considered essentially a political issue. Elisa Tamarkin writes convincingly of the "sociability of antislavery," showing that many American abolitionists adopted cultural styles from England in order to inoculate themselves against charges of philistinism or naiveté.[7] (Black anglophilia was common, too. The ex-slave and activist Frederick Douglass, for example, took his surname from the rebel hero of Sir Walter Scott's *Lady of the Lake*.) By pitting prejudice against cosmopolitanism, organizers such as the Weston sisters encouraged a veritable snobbery toward racial discrimination. Boston's antislavery fairs certainly elevated the status of the abolitionist sympathizer.

Yet even in a city whose Unitarian clergymen were indistinguishable from secular scholars and whose female citizens conspicuously read serious books, the bazaars were considered unseemly by some. Most of New England's textile merchants, for example, loathed expressions of abolitionist protest in any form; their wealth depended on southern cotton, after all. Manufacturers such as Nathan Appleton and Abbott Lawrence (prominent Athenaeum members, both) had developed textile factories outside Boston that processed raw cotton. These entrepreneurs—and others like them—connected the city's shipping and investment interests to the economy of the slave states.[8] Positioning themselves as "friends of the Union," such men may have abhorred slavery, but they repeatedly assured their southern business partners that they would resist meddling in the issue. It is in studying this era in the Athenaeum's history that one recognizes it as a site not only for social and intellectual exchange but also for economic transactions.[9]

Beginning in the 1830s, abolition became an unavoidable topic in Boston. When a British abolitionist named George Thompson visited the city in 1835, thousands of "wealthy and respectable" gentlemen thronged the staircase of the hall in which "the infamous foreign scoundrel" was scheduled to speak. In a scene of "howling, stamping, and shrieking," the mob dispersed only when the event was canceled.[10] Former mayor Harrison Gray Otis, an Athenaeum regular who hosted elegant gatherings at his Beacon Hill mansion, argued that British corruption was now hiding under a veil of abolitionist sentiment. He disparaged the blueblooded women who "turned their sewing parties into abolition clubs."[11] The mix of liberal clergymen, cautious textile merchants, well-to-do intellectuals, and female abolitionists became volatile by the late 1830s. In some very real sense, Boston's elite was at war with itself. Privileged citizens on both sides of the abolition debate criticized one another in print. In a novel, Harrison Gray Otis's daughter-in-law, herself a so-called Boston Brahmin, would gently satirize the rigid morning ritual of another elite Bostonian, her fictional antihero Philip Egerton: "He arose by daybreak, . . . breakfasted leisurely, gave his orders to the servants for the day, and walked, with his head elevated to a great height in the air, to an insurance office or the Athenaeum."[12]

Amid the turmoil of antislavery rallies and angry mobs, Athenaeum readers must have battled with their consciences. Abolitionism had developed a genteel culture of its own, and the political movement affected even Boston's most proper institution of arts and letters. Throughout this period, anglophilia, which had characterized the early founding of the Athenaeum, became much more complex. (Recall the excitement about all things British among the clubbable Anthology Society members.) The array of British-inspired goods sold at antislavery fairs was one sign of the changing conditions in and around Boston. When "a set of lovely teacups contributed by Lord and Lady Morpeth" is rendered a tool of agitation, one can imagine that the cultural authority of the Boston Athenaeum itself seemed unstable.[13] The library's trustees apparently wavered on whether and how to support individual abolitionists. Lydia Maria Child, a leader in the abolitionist cause, read at the Athenaeum in the 1830s while preparing to publish an antislavery tract. And Athenaeum devotee Charles Sumner made enemies among the elite as his antislavery positions deepened in the late 1840s and '50s. The stories of Lydia Maria Child and Charles Sumner—neither born into the elite class—help elucidate the elite's connection to the slaveholding South. Through the mistreatment of these two passionate figures, the proprietors' dilemma was made plain. Episodes in the lives of both expose the strained contract between an urban cultural institution and its larger community. Trying to remain apolitical, the Athenaeum nevertheless unwittingly participated in the debate about slavery. Its limited role, played out through ostracism and the withdrawal of patronage, subtly contributed to the delay of emancipation.

Lydia Maria Child (1802–1880) was something of a misfit among the ladies of the Boston Female Anti-Slavery Society. The Weston sisters, however, adopted her on the strength of her moral conviction and literary renown. A baker's daughter, she was born Lydia Francis and reared in a family of modest means. In rural Medford, north of Boston, Child craved a fine library and a formal education, but her father did not share her enthusiasm for books. (Only reluctantly did he agree to allow a son, Convers Francis, to study at Harvard.) After her mother's death, Lydia was sent to Maine (then a province

of Massachusetts) to live with a married sister. Her brother-in-law was an attorney, and she became well versed in the legal and political debates of the
time. In 1820, at age nineteen, she accepted a teaching job in Gardiner, Massachusetts. Eventually, she moved to Watertown, a Massachusetts village
near Cambridge where her brother Convers led a Unitarian parish. There,
with the support of her well-connected brother, she wrote a novel, *Hobomok:
A Tale of Early Times* (1824), which drew upon the lore of the Native American
communities neighboring her sister's Maine home. The book earned praise
in the *North American Review* and was favorably received by the Boston literary establishment. She dedicated her second novel, *Rebels; or, Boston before the
Revolution* (1825), to the eminent Harvard professor George Ticknor, an ad-
mirer to whose rarified salon she had been welcomed.[14]

Ticknor, an early Athenaeum proprietor, was the likely sponsor of the
complimentary reading privileges that were granted to Child in 1832, when
the institution was still situated on Pearl Street. Ticknor praised "the brilliant Miss Francis" (fig. 5.2), as she was then known (she would later marry
the attorney and editor David Lee Child). She was gaining renown in Great
Britain, too. Her works had been reissued by British publishing houses, and
word of her activity in abolitionism was piquing interest among intellectuals
there.[15]

But the Athenaeum's patronage appears to have been conditional. Child
claimed that soon after the publication of her influential abolitionist tract,
An Appeal in Favor of That Class of Americans Called Africans (1833), the library
withdrew its sponsorship, as she related years later in a nostalgic letter to a
fellow abolitionist:

> I was quite surprised one day by a note from the Trustees of the Boston Ath-
> enaeum, offering me the free use of the library, the same as if I owned a share.
> I had never asked such a favor, and I am not aware that any friend of mine
> ever solicited it. My *conjecture* was that the move was made by Professor
> George Ticknor, who was at that time a very kind patron of mine. . . . About
> the time of the unexpected attention from the Trustees, Mr. Garrison came
> to Boston, and I had a talk with *him*. Consequently, the first use I made of my
> Athenaeum privilege was to take out several books on that subject, with a
> view to writing my "Appeal." A few weeks after the "Appeal" was published,
> I received another note from the Trustees informing me that at a recent meet-
> ing they had passed a vote to *take away* my privilege, lest it prove an inconve-
> nient precedent.[16]

Child's conversion to abolitionism had come with great force. William
Lloyd Garrison, the confrontational editor of *The Liberator*, impressed her
deeply when they met in 1830: "He got hold of the strings of my conscience,
and pulled me into Reforms," she later reminisced to a friend. "It was no use

FIGURE 5.2 Lydia Maria Child (née Francis) in engraving after a portrait by Francis Alexander, 1826. (*Courtesy of the Medford Historical Society*)

to imagine what might have been, if I had never met him. Old dreams vanished, old associates departed, and all things became new."[17] Thereafter, the author refocused her attention and embarked upon the ambitious project of detailing slavery's evils for an increasingly divided American public. The *Appeal* began as a way for Child to evaluate conservative objections to immediate emancipation; it soon evolved into a comprehensive analysis of American slavery. Although clearly influenced by the "Appeal" of another Bostonian—that of black agitator David Walker—Child sidestepped Walker's sometimes bitter call to militancy and insisted, in thorough argumentation, on the legitimacy of black claims to the benefits of full citizenship.[18]

In spite of the explicit summary of the situation by the author herself, the case of Lydia Maria Child and the Boston Athenaeum remains unclear. On one hand, the complaint that the Athenaeum trustees "took away" her permission to use the library is supported by other evidence. Consistent with Child's own account, in 1835 a letter sent between two Weston sisters active in the Boston Female Anti-Slavery Society tells of their sister Maria Weston Chapman's efforts to buy back Child's Athenaeum privileges: "Mrs. Child is writing a book [presumably what would become *The History of the Condition of Women*] & she can't go on with it, because the directors of the Athenaeum library have revoked the permission which they gave her some years ago to take out what books she chose." (The Athenaeum apparently did not reconsider its position, even with the offer of Mrs. Chapman's collected funds.) On the other hand, one of the Athenaeum's official histories puts the case this way: "If Mrs. Child's memory is reliable, some trustee must have said or written that her presence was no longer desired. But the privilege was to last until taken away by the Board, and the Trustees' Records contain no rescinding vote." (According to the ledgers of borrowed material kept by the institution, Child withdrew her last book on February 2, 1835.)[19] In 1939 an Athenaeum newsletter repeated the official absence of a recorded vote but added, confusingly, as if to perpetuate a sense of injustice, "The essentials of Mrs. Child's story appear, however, to be beyond question."[20]

Why should it matter that the Athenaeum equivocates about Child and her treatment? The gap in information on her status at the institution shows that the Athenaeum's role in the antislavery movement was passive at best. To judge from the reaction to Child's tract from the community at large, ambivalence among the most powerful proprietors contributed to the silence. The *Appeal* accuses the North of racial prejudice and, after a relatively mild preface, adopts a direct tone that many Americans were loath to tolerate in a woman. The publication was greeted with negative reviews. And soon a children's magazine Child had edited profitably for years was in peril because of canceled subscriptions. Just when she was heralded as a new spokesperson within abolitionist circles, Ticknor and his literary friends ostracized the author. One Athenaeum proprietor, James T. Austin, reportedly flung the *Appeal* out of his window with a pair of tongs.[21] But what was the Athenaeum's true reputation on matters of racial justice? And how does that reputation fit with the institution's mission as a cultural center?

As with most American institutions dedicated to the humanities, the fundamental source of the Athenaeum's cultural authority resided in the federal Constitution, "which assured the climate in which private individuals could create [libraries and] museums for the public good." In the United States, as one prominent museum director has maintained, cultural institutions must "be perceived consistent with . . . the Constitution and everything that flows from it."[22] Since American cultural institutions were first launched by private citizens, they were free from tight state control, yet at the same time they were made possible by a democratic system that values life, liberty, and the pursuit of happiness.[23] How these institutional origins applied to the problem of slavery and the Athenaeum is a question worth exploring. In the official histories of comparable libraries, such as the Salem Athenaeum and the Providence Athenaeum, no mention of slavery appears.[24] More digging in the archives of parallel institutions would no doubt reveal individuals' commitment or curiosity. Of course, even before the Athenaeum library was founded, learned Bostonians had been troubled by the situation of southern blacks. William Smith Shaw, writing to his former Harvard classmate William Ellery Channing in 1799, presses to learn more about the plight of slaves:

> You promise me Channing in [one] of your letters to give me some account of "the situation and character of the negroes in Virginia." This would be very interesting and desirable though I lament as much as you can their present situation and shrink back in horror at the idea of trafficking with human flesh yet I wish to know whether it is not now a *necessary evil*. Can they be liberated? Would their situation be bettered? Are they capable of governing and taking care of themselves? [These are] very important questions and . . . I would like to have your answers.[25]

In 1807 the Athenaeum mission had emphasized universal humanistic values. Deliberately but also excitedly, the founders of the institution declared their purpose in stirring phrases such as these: "The value of learning, whatever incidental evils it may produce, is admitted by all. . . . Propensity to reading and inquiry, which are capable of being diffused through . . . the community, should be regarded with interest and promoted with zeal. . . . A love of intellectual improvement . . . in a state or society enjoying freedom and affluence . . . tends to the removal of error and the discovery of truth, and has a friendly aspect upon the interests of virtue and religion."[26] The intent of this rhetoric is to elevate humanity; when the voices of abolition (and women's rights and the rights of immigrants) become audible, however, how much of humanity is still deemed worthy of elevation?[27] The imperative to "diffuse knowledge," a ubiquitous cry in early republican documents, was meant to protect against the dangers of ignorance and barbarism. By the 1840s, abolitionists would appropriate the language of early patriots and call their movement the legitimate successor to principles espoused by such Federalists as William Shaw and Josiah Quincy.[28] The Athenaeum—like all grand American institutions—would discover "the incongruity between ideological assertion and practical acceptance," to borrow Robert Ferguson's phrasing.[29]

The extent to which support for abolition varied among the cultural elite cannot be overstated. Ralph Waldo Emerson, who frequented the Athenaeum, helps illustrate this range of sentiment. Slow to join the movement, Emerson voiced aversion to and criticism of abolitionists in his early writings. His best-known statement comes from "Self-Reliance," originally written in the middle to late 1830s: "If an angry bigot assumes this bountiful cause of Abolition, and comes to me with his last news from Barbadoes, why should I not say to him . . . 'Thy love afar is spite at home.'" The trendiness of abolition, the "radical chic" that prevailed among antislavery advocates, provides an important context in which to view Emerson's ambivalence. Naturally, all Athenaeum readers were aware of the swirling controversies. Like the rest of the nation, they read and talked about slavery. A volume called *Essays on the Merchandise of Slaves and Souls of Men* went missing from the Athenaeum collection in 1825—but then so did *A Treatise on Spinning Machinery* and an edition of Cicero's *Orations* (the latter two titles epitomize the wealthy new manufacturers' preoccupations with business and eloquence). Although Emerson's antislavery convictions are unquestionable after 1855, for most proprietors of the Athenaeum the debate around abolition remained abstract.[30]

Not surprisingly, in practice the institution displayed little public sympathy for the antislavery cause. Indeed, most of the incidents involving abolition center on one man: Samuel J. May Jr., a Unitarian minister to whom Lydia Maria Child dedicated her *Appeal*. May, whose father was an Athenaeum proprietor, became quite active in the institution's affairs. In 1830, he arranged for William Lloyd Garrison to deliver a lecture at the Pearl Street site. The topic was the cruelty of slavery. Garrison described slave pens and badly beaten runaways in wrenching detail. At least two black ministers "called out hearty amens" during the speech, and the African American historian William Cooper Nell was also in attendance. Deemed a success by abolitionists, the talk worried many others. May's father allegedly warned his son to distance himself from discussions of "an evil that could be ameliorated only in the fullness of time."[31]

Subsequent lectures sponsored by the Athenaeum were mute on the subject of slavery, preserving the institution's tacit neutrality.[32] In 1854, however, the Massachusetts Anti-Slavery Society donated to the Boston Athenaeum a complete set of *The Liberator*. Again, Samuel May was behind the gesture; he and well-known Garrisonians (Edmund Quincy, Francis Jackson, Ellis Gray Loring, Samuel Sewell, and Wendell Phillips among them) signed a letter to the librarian declaring themselves "friends of the Anti-Slavery principle and movement . . . and friends also of the Boston Athenaeum and those great objects which it has done so much to promote."[33] A curious testimonial, given the Athenaeum's reluctance to embrace the cause, the letter nevertheless demonstrates the devotion of some key reformers to the institution's stated cultural mission. Perhaps the city's surging interest in the trial of a fugitive slave named Anthony Burns precipitated the *Liberator* gift.[34] (The donation was also a polite way to disseminate the antislavery message to a powerful audience.) On Christmas Eve of 1857, May continued his efforts and introduced the black abolitionist Sarah Remond to the Athenaeum—presumably leading her on a tour of the Beacon Street building.[35] Finally, the next year, May made a donation of his own to the institution: a marble bust of Wendell Phillips sculpted by John A. Jackson.[36]

Whatever contact Athenaeum members had with abolitionists was mostly limited to arenas outside the institution. It is telling that Lydia Maria Child's experience came soon after Garrison's disturbing 1830 lecture at the Pearl Street Athenaeum. As Child herself presumed, her presence in the early 1830s must have made Athenaeum leaders uncomfortable; it is likely that with the tide of abolitionist sentiment rising, the institution did withdraw sponsorship "lest it prove an inconvenient precedent." Interestingly, Maria Chapman had secured borrowing privileges through Samuel May; being a widow from a patrician family, she was perhaps more easily accommodated, and besides, Mrs. Chapman was not writing a radical abolitionist treatise. Some things could not be tolerated.

Beyond hinting at the Athenaeum's silence around antislavery, the story of Lydia Maria Child and her reading privileges points to a shift in the demands made by learned women. Child's fabled expulsion highlights the threatened— and threatening—female reader, recalling the difficulty women had in gaining access to well-stocked libraries. At the time of her admission to the Athenaeum, only Hannah Adams and a few others had truly penetrated the sacred masculinity of the library's reading room. Yet as a young girl, Child knew of Adams's allegedly bizarre behavior and wanted to differentiate herself from the "aged spinster," whom, it was said, she considered "the most notorious local embodiment of the female intellectual." Child saw Adams as "unsexed," insisting that a woman could be instead both feminine and learned.[37]

By entering into what appeared to be an equitable marriage, Child demonstrated her convictions; childless, she nevertheless wrote domestic manuals on parenting and household management, making her female identity congruent with her authorial voice. She spoke and wrote from the standpoint of domestic life—even when arguing politics. Whereas Hannah Adams had worked from within Boston's elite literary establishment, disguising her hard-earned authority in order to sustain male patronage, Lydia Maria Child risked disapproval. Publishing the *Appeal* defined her as an abolitionist, and she made the families of African Americans her focus. After 1835, especially, women were developing their voices as activists. The abolition movement afforded them new opportunities for writing, debating, and organizing—and the fairs of the Boston Female Anti-Slavery Society provided one such forum. Child repeatedly borrowed books on the history of women from the Boston Athenaeum.[38] And, admiring the camaraderie of her antislavery sisters, she attended the annual fairs when she could, noting the elegance with which Maria Weston Chapman arranged the events.[39] She learned that if institutions failed her, then friends would supply the resources with which to research and write. Child's experience gave her entrée into the alternative culture of abolitionism, a culture that was distinguished both by intellectual rigor and by a certain style of its own.

In antebellum Boston, the odd blend of gentility and political agitation attracted men as well as women. An active Boston Athenaeum proprietor, Charles Sumner (1811–1874) was also a Harvard alumnus, Grand Tourist, lawyer, orator, and eventually United States senator (from 1851 to 1874). Although accomplished in many areas, he is remembered largely for the violent attack upon his life in 1856 by a southern opponent who struck the first-term senator repeatedly, to the point of unconsciousness, after he delivered a bitter speech against slavery. His commitment to the rights of African Americans had been evident decades before the bloody personal attack, however. With his involvement in the Athenaeum and his role in the abolition movement, Sumner served as a go-between, a cultural broker who bridged two vastly different communities: the city's free blacks and Boston's "best" families. The Athenaeum depended on civility; the abolitionist movement attracted followers who had a more confrontational approach to society. How did Sumner connect the two impulses in his life, the drive toward excellence in the arts and the imperative to abolish slavery? And how can his life help explain the relationship between high culture and political conscience? To understand better how the region's most respected cultural center responded to the moral crisis of its day, one need only consider Charles Sumner. Without him, the intersection of the Athenaeum and abolitionism would remain a puzzle (even given the rumors pertaining to Lydia Maria Child's treatment). His full and complicated life includes three specific areas of interest: his enthusiasm for English society; the seeds of his political passion; and the complex bonds between Sumner and some of his fellow Athenaeum members.

Charles Sumner (fig. 5.3) was drawn to the problem of slavery from an early age. His father, an idealistic lawyer named Charles Pinckney Sumner,

FIGURE 5.3 Charles Sumner in 1846. (*Courtesy National Park Service, Long-fellow National Historic Site*)

had worked as sheriff of Suffolk County. Young Charles's sensitivity to racial injustice, originating with his family, was less a vehicle for personal rebellion than an extension of his father's beliefs. His place in the movement was distinctive. The Sumner family, though comfortable, was not as prominent as those of the few elite abolitionists. Gentlemen such as Wendell Phillips and Edmund Quincy, both scions of wealthy Bostonians, would come to symbolize another aspect of the elite's contribution to the abolitionist cause. Combining inherited wealth, first-rate education, urbane taste, and rhetorical

acumen, these men met frequently with William Lloyd Garrison, the editor
of *The Liberator*. Like Sumner, they tried to navigate between the African
Americans who lived on Beacon Hill's North Slope and the powerful Bostonians whose elegant Federalist homes dotted the South Slope. But Sumner
was, in fact, reared in modest homes on the poorer side of Beacon Hill, not
far from African American rooming houses, barbershops, and gambling
dens.[40] He knew two worlds but never satisfactorily reconciled them. After
completing his studies at Harvard Law School in 1834, Sumner felt lost and
unfulfilled. The trajectory of his life, especially his time in Boston leading up
to his election to the Senate in 1851, was characterized by a preoccupation
with both manners and morals.[41]

As with many young men, Sumner's first journey abroad, from 1837 to
1840, proved to be a pivotal experience in taste and maturation.[42] With funding provided by Supreme Court Justice Joseph Story, a law school mentor,
and Samuel Lawrence, an entrepreneur in the textile industry (and a supporter who would later prove to be at odds with his beneficiary), Sumner
sailed from New York intent on completing his education. Over the following three years he visited France, Italy, Austria, Germany, and, of course,
England. At the Louvre, he rhapsodized that it "might have furnished quarters for the army of Xerxes." The grandeur of art and architecture inspired
him to exclaim, "When you think that Mr. Sears's house was my type of a
palace, the Athenaeum Gallery of a collection of paintings, & the plaster
casts in the Athenaeum Reading Room & Felton's study, of a collection of
antiques!"[43] In Italy, Sumner read the works of Dante and visited Roman museums and art studios with American guides. Yet it was upper-class British
life that influenced the young American lawyer most.

"This London is socially a bewitching place," Sumner writes in his diary
upon arriving in the capital. Bearing many letters of introduction, he dined
with lords and ladies and with Britain's poets, historians, and politicians. Joseph Story reinforced Sumner's love of England, writing to his protégé, "You
are now exactly where I wish you to be, among the educated, the literary, the
noble, and, though last not least, the learned of England, of good old England, our motherland,—God bless her!" Sumner's attitude toward the British became even more admiring after his first year abroad. In a letter to his
law partner George Hillard, he writes guardedly,

I am almost afraid to [compare English and American society] for fear of being
misunderstood. In England, what is called society is better educated, more refined, and more civilized than what is called society in our country. You understand me to speak of society—not individuals. I know *persons* in America
who would be an ornament of any circle anywhere; but there is no *class* with

us that will in the least degree compare with that vast circle which constitutes English society. The difference of education is very much against us.

As if in a stage whisper, he goes on to cite a scholar who said that England was "further advanced in civilization"—quickly adding, "I would repeat this, if I did not fear being misunderstood."[44]

An important aspect of Sumner's anglophilia was his affection for the full range of English cultivation—and this included abolitionism. "My wonder at [Lord] Brougham rises anew," Sumner notes in his diary. "To-night he has displayed the knowledge of the artist and the gastronome. He criticized the ornaments of the drawing-room like a *connoisseur*, and discussed subtle points of cookery with the same earnestness with which he emancipated the West India slaves and abolished rotten boroughs." Sumner's wide-eyed admiration speaks to the full spectrum of civilized behavior with which many Americans associated liberal Englishmen. Refined taste, an appreciation of the exotic, the rejection of provincialism—these aspects of life were consistent with British liberalism. Like many other Americans sympathetic to the cause, the young lawyer from Boston treated abolitionism as "one more aspect of English decorum to be appropriated."[45]

When Sumner arrived home from his journey in 1840, he was changed both materially and spiritually. A friend reported that his "appearance had been improved under the hands of a London tailor." Distracted by European memories, Sumner returned very gradually to his professional life. His law practice awaited him, but he had little patience for the administrative details of legal work. At the time, William Wetmore Story, son of Joseph Story and a promising sculptor, was a law student working in the office of Hillard & Sumner. Of those days, observing Sumner, young Story remarked, "America seemed flat to him after Europe. This, however, slowly passed away, though never, to his dying day, completely." Edward Pierce, Sumner's first biographer, who was also his friend and collected material on him for decades, wrote of Sumner's behavior during this period of readjustment: "Sometimes . . . he recurred unwisely to his foreign life or letters in conversation with clients and lawyers, who knew or cared little about such things—a habit likely to repel those who were intent only on the business in hand. . . . Indeed, prudence dictated a greater reserve in this regard, with all except intimate friends, than he maintained."[46]

Prudent or not, Sumner's love of Europe affected his life at home. He spent much time at the Athenaeum.[47] And he was a more popular dinner guest than ever before, accepting invitations from older Athenaeum members such as George Ticknor, Nathan Appleton, Harrison Gray Otis, Samuel Lawrence, and Abbott Lawrence. Perhaps these men were especially intrigued by the ambitious Bostonian because he had enjoyed such a warm reception abroad. It was at this time, too—the early to mid-1840s—that Sumner experimented seriously with arts patronage. His interest in neoclassical sculpture, which had been piqued in Rome, led to his sponsorship of Americans Thomas Crawford and Horatio Greenough—both of whose Italian studios he had visited. In 1844, at Sumner's prompting, Crawford's *Orpheus and Cerberus* was exhibited at the Athenaeum on Pearl Street to much acclaim, and, as noted above when the Athenaeum was planning its move to Beacon Street in the late 1840s, he became preoccupied with the design of an imposing entryway and staircase. Further, the example of government-supported arts institutions in France had impressed Sumner. He remarked upon the fact that galleries and many lecture halls were open "gratis" to all. An ideal model for the United States, he believed, would be a combination of private and public patronage for the arts. To encourage the latter, in 1839 he had promoted Horatio Greenough's neoclassical sculpture of George Washington, the first work by a native artist to be commissioned by Congress.[48]

Perhaps his anxiety about American cultural life, so well articulated in letters and diaries, inspired Sumner to act as an informal cultural ambassador—allowing him to control, to some extent, the outside perception of his native country. Sumner regularly guided prominent European visitors through Boston. For example, he abandoned all business for a number of weeks in 1841 in order to entertain Lord Morpeth, an abolitionist who had befriended him in England. Together they climbed to the top of the statehouse, toured city hall and the courts, and met with George Ticknor, unofficial representative of Boston society.[49] Sumner would later write to Morpeth, with as much concern as conviction, "We love England; and I hope you will believe it, notwithstanding the vulgar cries to the contrary."[50] The "vulgar cries" were likely related to anti-abolitionist sentiment. Again, the implication is that gentility was the virtue to which Americans must aspire. But it was a special gentility, one linked to liberality of mind. Lord Morpeth's well-known antislavery stance enhanced his sophisticated manners, and Sumner was eager to represent the American citizenry as refined enough to recognize the moral leadership of England.

Sumner's public advocacy on behalf of African Americans had evolved slowly over the years. Before his Grand Tour, he read Lydia Maria Child's *Appeal in Favor of That Class of Americans Called Africans*. "The tone which you helped me adopt so early is most in unison with my present position," he wrote to her as his abolitionism progressed.[51] He also read the Reverend William Ellery Channing's book *Slavery* (1835), which, though more conservative than Child's, was grounded in the moral philosophy familiar to Sumner from his days as a Harvard undergraduate. (What disturbed Channing about slavery was typical of the gentlemanly Athenaeum ethos: the consignment of a whole of men to a mere animalistic existence.) The violent mob that protested the presence of British abolitionist George Thompson in 1835 had certainly influenced Charles Sumner, whose father was sheriff at the time. And Sumner's introduction to William Lloyd Garrison had led to a collaboration with former Harvard classmate Wendell Phillips. Phillips, Sumner, and Hillard each delivered a lecture at Boston's black lyceum, the Adelphic Union Society on Beacon Hill, in the winter of 1837. (Sumner's talk highlighted the constitutional right to petition.)[52] Upon his return to the United States in 1840, Sumner's abolitionist activity was still defined largely by his social life: he discussed the issues of the day with friends and colleagues and supported the work of the Boston Female Anti-Slavery Society. ("I went to the Anti-Slavery Fair, where I talked with Mrs. Loring and Mrs. Chapman about you," writes Charles Sumner to Lord Morpeth in 1841.)[53] Sumner's friend Cornelius Felton teased him about his politicking, remarking in the margins of one letter: "[Charles] subscribes to an abolitionist newspaper and frequents antislavery FAIRS!!!"[54] Yet his experiences in Europe deepened Sumner's sense of the larger community behind the cause. Specifically, the anglophilia he had absorbed abroad lent his abolitionism a transatlantic flavor, as the plea for emancipation became as much a cultural project as an ideological mission.[55] Perhaps recalling the abolitionist zeal of his elegant English hosts, he may have felt that connoisseurship and a finely tuned conscience were wholly compatible, even complementary, goals.

Soon, however, Sumner's ability to balance social fluidity with his abolitionist principles would be tested. In late 1843, George Ticknor, Sumner's frequent host (and literature professor at Harvard), made it clear to his former student that speaking publicly against slavery was dangerous. Shocked by Ticknor's adherence to the status quo, Sumner complained to a friend, "He sits in his rich library & laps himself in care & indulgence, *doing* nothing himself, treating unkindly the works of those who *do*, looking down upon all."[56] And when Boston city leaders invited Sumner to give the keynote speech at the 1845 Independence Day celebration, he risked his place in society even further by drafting an address that incorporated his thinking about the proposed annexation of Texas. Aligning himself with the antislavery wing of the Whig Party (a faction known as the Conscience Whigs), Sumner saw that Texas and the specter of a war with Mexico were grounded in the issue of slavery. When thousands gathered at Tremont Temple on July 4, 1845, Sumner disappointed all who expected a straightforward display of patriotism. In fact, according to one student of rhetoric, on that day he flouted the basic conventions of audience, occasion, and purpose. With a strong military presence in the audience, he announced, "In our age there can be no

peace that is not honorable; there can be no war that is not dishonourable."[57]
He went on to link war with slavery, maintaining that both denied the essential goodness of human nature. Sumner's performance was anathema to
Ticknor and to the conservative Whigs. But one auditor, who herself had
been the object of Ticknor's displeasure, cheered Sumner on: writing to him
years later, Lydia Maria Child remembered, "How I *did* thank you for your
noble and eloquent attack upon the absurd barbarism of war! It was worth
living to have done that, if you never do anything more. But the soul that did
that *will* do more."[58]

Sumner did do more, of course. His activities would jeopardize relationships with still other Athenaeum patrons: the textile merchants who
provided financial backing to the institution. For example, Abbott Lawrence and the brothers Nathan and Samuel Appleton—who would all die
millionaires—had perfected the power loom, streamlined production from
raw cotton to finished cloth, and established the successful mill city of Lowell. Ninety percent of the sixty-one directors of the large mills in New England held shares in the Boston Athenaeum. Samuel Appleton would donate
$25,000 to the institution in the 1850s, and his brother and Lawrence fre-
quented the reading room.[59] All three men disapproved of abolitionism and
the movement's rabble-rousing advocates.

An examination of borrowing patterns at the Athenaeum reveals that
Charles Sumner withdrew many books during the volatile 1840s. In 1844 he
was using the share of Cornelius Felton, a professor of Greek at Harvard, to
take out the novels of Daniel Defoe and Samuel Richardson (specifically,
Clarissa and *Pamela*)—in addition to the works of Sir William Jones, an
eighteenth-century British jurist and poet who held liberal views on slavery
and American independence. By 1845, Sumner had acquired his own share in
the Athenaeum and withdrew books on oratory (Cicero, Quintilian) and history (Thomas Clarkson on the slave trade, Thomas Carlyle's and Archibald
Alison's books on the French Revolution). Nathan Appleton, one of Sumner's
adversaries, also withdrew much Defoe during the same period, but Appleton's borrowings indicate a less directed reading style, as his list darts from
Emanuel Swedenborg's *Heavenly Mysteries* to a simple geological survey, with
a few travelogues in between. Under the auspices of the Athenaeum, Sumner
read alongside Cotton Whigs such as Appleton but fashioned his own "Free
Soil" curriculum.[60]

As he strengthened his political voice, Sumner spoke out frequently
against the ills of passivity and avarice. In June 1848, in a speech before the
Free Soil Convention in Worcester, Massachusetts, he again shocked the audience with his analysis of the slavery issue. Sumner, now a Free Soiler intent
on expanding the nation only if the land added was kept slave-free, saw the

crisis as the result of a conspiracy "between the lords of the lash and the lords of the loom."[61] The accusation incensed many textile merchants whose friendship Sumner had valued.[62] That August, Sumner started sharp epistolary exchanges with Nathan Appleton and Abbott Lawrence. "It is never too late to begin to do right," he writes to Nathan Appleton in response to an angry letter, and he complains of Abbott Lawrence's "desire of fraternity with slave-holding politicians, even at the cost of principle, which as a son of Massachusetts, he should have guarded to the last."[63] Many merchants had pooled their capital through an organization called the Boston Associates in order to limit their investment risk, and they began to counter abolitionist arguments with political rhetoric that smacked of southern values. In an effort to quell the intensifying debate, they emphasized gentlemanly leadership, orderly problem-solving, and the unity of the nation above all else.[64]

Judging from the Athenaeum's circulation records, one can imagine that Nathan Appleton and Abbott Lawrence yearned for an Old World setting—a society with less fluidity and fewer political demands. By 1850 these two Cotton Whigs had explored (among novels and adventure stories) books about chivalry and the British system of peerage. Sumner, from 1849 to 1850, withdrew an assortment of history, oratory, and poetry books (both German and English); he also borrowed an edition of his own speeches and a biography of the British abolitionist William Wilberforce. Again, the gentlemanly paradigm accommodated a range of antebellum political ideologies. Whereas the two industrialists were drawn to books about outward manifestations of rank, Sumner took out books that featured the deeds of historical agents—including a compendium by his former British host Henry Brougham called *Lives of Men of Letters and Science Who Flowered in the Time of George III* (1845).[65]

It pained Sumner that the same men with whom he shared a passion for literature and art—and for the Boston Athenaeum—were choosing to ignore their duty. The gulf between Sumner and wealthy industrialists would only grow wider as the Fugitive Slave Act of 1850 set off disturbances in the city. Although Sumner never made a speech under the auspices of the Athenaeum, another oration may have substituted for a more pointed reprimand of that institution's elite: in 1854, he addressed Boston's Mercantile Library Association, a group supported by employers to encourage upward mobility.[66] Only months earlier the dramatic attempt by abolitionists to restore the freedom of the escaped slave Anthony Burns had rocked the city, and Sumner's feud with local textile merchants who had cast their lot with southern plantation owners was continuing to simmer. Perhaps he chose to address clerks (aspiring businessmen) at the Mercantile Library in order to anticipate the corrupting influences that he saw affecting the likes of Appleton and Lawrence. Titled "The Positions and Duties of the Merchant," Sumner's speech offered a

SOUTHERN CHIVALRY — ARGUMENT versus CLUB'S.

FIGURE 5.4 Popular lithograph of the Sumner caning on the floor of the U.S. Senate, circa 1856. (*Courtesy, American Antiquarian Society*)

model for would-be millionaires—future Appletons and Lawrences—to imitate (the address was published as a bound volume within months). "With so many members and so many books, yours is an institution of positive power," Sumner began. The ostensible subject was Granville Sharp, a mid-eighteenth-century British merchant whose devotion to racial justice was legendary. "Perhaps among the apprentices of Boston, there may be yet a Granville Sharp," he said. "And just in proportion as the moral nature asserts its rightful supremacy here, will such a character be hailed as of higher worth than the products of all the mills of Lowell, backed by all the dividends and discounts of State Street."[67] That the wealthy manufacturers of New England had failed to support abolition disappointed Sumner greatly.

Even beyond the membership of the Athenaeum, patricians in Boston distanced themselves from the issue of slavery. But as a senator, Sumner grew fiercely attached to his cause. His dedication led to the brutal scene already noted: in 1856, after delivering a two-day speech against slavery's abuses, he was badly beaten with a cane by Preston Brooks, a nephew of a South Carolina senator, and lay unconscious in a puddle of blood on the floor of the United States Senate. Few colleagues were able to comprehend the act; many believed the senator would not survive, and only slowly, over three years, did he recover. Cartoons and lithographs depicting the incident circulated widely (fig. 5.4), and the tragic event sealed his popularity as a moral leader in the North.[68] Perhaps the more passive members of the Athenaeum disagreed with Sumner about the meaning of personal cultivation; gentility occasionally served to raise their awareness of the plight of others, but it also served to disguise apathy. The centenary history of the Athenaeum enigmatically refers to the "restless memory" of Charles Sumner. The ambiguity of the phrase (whose memory is restless, Sumner's or the Athenaeum's? and why?) befits the institution's confused attitude toward slavery and its opponents.[69] Athenaeum leaders sought to maintain its identity as a safe, neutral enclave for the intellectual elite. But the challenges posed by Sumner and Child show how readers at the Boston Athenaeum—an organization teeming with educated northern gentlemen representing all the prestigious professions—reacted to the most important national issue of the century.

CHAPTER SIX

Pamphlet War

ANY BOSTONIAN WHO HAPPENED to browse in the city's *Daily Advertiser* on March 24, 1853, would have encountered an angry article in defense of the Athenaeum. Perhaps the newspaper reader, indifferent to elite infighting, would have passed over the piece. But perhaps he or she would have proceeded with interest, curious about the fate of this important institution, as well as the future of an embryonic city library about which much fuss was being made in the local papers. City leaders were launching a public library, and many people considered the Boston Athenaeum the obvious site for this new civic resource: a library to be accessible to all the people of Boston. The newspaper article—fashioned as an "Appeal" to the proprietors of the Athenaeum and soon published in pamphlet form for wider circulation—was written by Josiah Quincy, who expressed his fear that, if subsumed under a public library, the Boston Athenaeum would be misused by the city:

> In behalf of the deceased benefactors and founders of this institution, who, I believe, could they speak, would with one voice reprobate the proposal as a desecration and perversion of their labors and bounties, I earnestly entreat and conjure every proprietor of the Athenaeum to be present on Monday next at the appointed meeting, and put down, by an overwhelming majority, every attempt to transfer this sacred trust to the city authorities.

What lay behind such heated rhetoric? And what does this dispute reveal about openness, diversity, and civic obligation in mid-nineteenth-century Boston?[1]

Historians have long viewed with suspicion the motives of elite cultural entrepreneurs, suggesting that a desire to control the lower classes led directly to the founding of grand city institutions.[2] But the controversy surrounding the fate of the Athenaeum points to a more complicated conclusion: elite supporters of both the Boston Athenaeum and the Boston Public Library defended their respective institutions in terms that were speculative and full of self-questioning. The aims of the Athenaeum, especially, became subject to a variety of interpretations. Above all, Boston cultural entrepreneurs struggled to sustain viable centers for self-education. The fact that the Athenaeum was considered outmoded—replaceable by a more accessible institution—shows the extent to which many of Boston's leaders were committed to sharing resources for the betterment of the city at large.

At the time of Quincy's article, the Boston Athenaeum, active for almost fifty years, had only recently settled into its new home, the elegant neo-Palladian building on Beacon Street. Now overextended because of building costs, the institution was financially vulnerable, and to Quincy—who identified himself as the "sole survivor of the first five subscribers to the Athenaeum"—the library and its prominent art gallery were in danger of a government takeover. He went on to argue that the Boston Athenaeum must heed the wishes of its earliest patrons; if the founders knew that the library was threatened, they might well deliver a screed, in unison, from their tombs.

In truth, after a half-century, the original aims of the Boston Athenaeum had become both remote and widely scattered; its history, like all history, spoke in myriad voices to diverse audiences—and the library's past was now recollected quite freely. In 1851, just two years before his appeal appeared, Quincy himself had compiled his celebratory volume *The History of the Boston Athenaeum, with Biographical Notices of Its Deceased Founders.* Earlier the library had inspired other gentlemanly memoirs, stories of the "Athenaeum ghost," and even a commemorative dinner plate. Institutions, Ralph Waldo Emerson would remark in another context, are the shadows of their founders, and particularly long and distorted shadows were being cast in Boston during March of 1853, when the Athenaeum found itself on the brink of democratization.[3]

The "venerable" Josiah Quincy, as so many prominent Bostonians had taken to calling the eighty-one-year-old former mayor and former Harvard University president, was clearly worried. His health had lately kept him from attending meetings at the Athenaeum, but he felt moved to send his impassioned appeal to the *Boston Daily Advertiser.* Quincy wanted to protest efforts by city officials—and by some of the Athenaeum's own 700 shareholders—to make the Boston Athenaeum the foundation for something called a *"real* Public Library." A public library was a novel scheme that meant, in the words of its promoters, *"many persons can be reading, in their homes, the same work at the same time."*[4] The Athenaeum, less interested in the shifting winds of popular literature, generally kept only one copy of each book listed in its catalogue.

The idea of a public library was, in itself, not irksome to Josiah Quincy. Like many other Bostonians, he understood the benefits of pooling bibliographical resources.[5] In the spring of 1848, the plan for a public library in

Boston had received legislative backing and generous citizen donations. Even Quincy's son Josiah Quincy Jr. supported the proposed union of the Athenaeum with the nascent city library.[6] What troubled the elder Quincy, in part, was the pressure from the city, whose officers had purchased property for their library on Somerset Street, around the corner from the Athenaeum, making the institution "easy prey" for a merger. The tone of Quincy's feverish language, with its Old Testament charges of "desecration" and "perversion," signaled the almost holy status the Athenaeum had come to hold for some of its members. The clamor for a public library—what Oliver Wendell Holmes would later call a palace for the people[7]—caused a stir among Athenaeum proprietors precisely because it forced them to articulate their attachment to a beloved institution that was *not*, strictly speaking, "for the people." Devotees of the Athenaeum would soon reinterpret the original mission and reconsider the tacit contract between their institution and the community at large. By 1853 Josiah Quincy and his opponents disagreed on how public the Athenaeum was meant to be.

Up to this point, the survival instincts of the Boston Athenaeum had impressed everyone. Much of its institutional history had already been lovingly documented. Founded in 1807 as a reading room whose proprietors bought shares of membership, by 1851 it had moved four times, weathered economic uncertainty, and grown to house some 50,000 volumes as well as substantial galleries of paintings and sculpture. Over time, the Athenaeum had become a kind of experimental site, a refuge from church and state, a place where privileged men communed with their friends and their books. It had always been simultaneously ostentatious and benevolent. And the democratic tone of its prospectus—for example, "the value of learning is admitted by all"[8]—had lent the place a sense of cohesion and shared belief. Yet all the while, vague assumptions and confusing claims lurked in the background. The values of permanence and honor—abstractions that floated within the institutional archive from decade to decade—also influenced the debate about whether the Athenaeum should be absorbed by a young city library.

So it was when, on March 28, 1853, a crowd of members gathered at the Beacon Street site to decide the Athenaeum's fate. A scene-setting lyric composed after the fact began this way:

> On Beacon, when the sun was low,
> The young, the old, the fast, the slow,
> Were rang'd in many a solemn row,
> Throughout the Sculpture Gallery.

In spite of the drama of the situation, the Athenaeum proprietors voted "by a large majority" to remain autonomous, and much-needed funds were raised through the sale of additional shares later that year. The number of shares was then capped at 1,049, although reading memberships continued to be offered for an annual fee.[9] In the end, a solution to the problem of sustaining two substantial city libraries was reached through simple fund-raising. But the forces behind the episode lead to more questions about the Athenaeum's power, its uses and abuses, its promises and compromises.

Any quick summary—such as the account given in the Athenaeum's centenary history[10]—masks the nuanced debate within the institution. In fact, the possible merger of the two libraries enjoyed considerable support among the institution's faithful readers. (Some eighty Athenaeum subscribers signed on to the plan.) It was George Ticknor's case in favor of the merger that alarmed Josiah Quincy and inspired his piece in the *Boston Daily Advertiser*. Ticknor, a self-appointed cultural gatekeeper who had befriended and then ostracized the abolitionists Lydia Maria Child and Charles Sumner, emerges as the intellectual architect of Boston's public library system. His plan illuminates the desperation about American education felt by many elite Bostonians at midcentury. An analysis of the "pamphlet war" waged by Ticknor and Quincy reveals both early ideas about public libraries and the threat the Boston Public Library posed to the Athenaeum's loyalists.

Arrogant, self-possessed, the host of an elite intellectual salon, George Ticknor would hardly have seemed a natural advocate for public libraries. One might instead have expected Josiah Quincy, whose life had been devoted to government service and education, to embrace any means by which the city could open so impressive an institution. Yet in their pamphlets these men took positions contrary to superficial expectations. Ticknor, a member of the Anthology Society as a young man, was an early proprietor of the Boston Athenaeum. He studied at the University of Göttingen and traveled throughout Europe before accepting, in 1819, a professorship in modern languages at Harvard University. Ticknor served as an Athenaeum trustee from 1823 through 1832; he was vice president of the institution for the year 1833 and would have been involved in the policymaking at the Athenaeum during the period when Lydia Maria Child's library privileges were allegedly withdrawn. Quincy, an Athenaeum trustee from 1813 through 1815 and president of the institution from 1820 to 1829, belonged to an old colonial family. Son of a revolutionary, he inherited a respect for higher education and was trained for a life in politics. (He had even served in Congress as a United States representative for eight years, from 1804 to 1812.) His son Edmund was an outspoken abolitionist. As mayor of the newly chartered city of Boston in 1823, Josiah Quincy had used his learning and good sense to enact impressive reforms—including a modernized police force and fire department, and the

establishment of a central marketplace: the granite structure designed by
Alexander Parris that bears Quincy's name. Both Quincy's son Josiah and
grandson Josiah would be elected mayor, too.[11]

But who were these men, really? George Ticknor perceived his role as that
of cultural guardian. After traveling abroad, he had wanted to demonstrate
to Americans the rewards of scholarship and culture. To him, establishing
the course of American educational institutions was paramount. He believed
that it was the duty of literary historians to pass judgment on societies.
Ticknor's scholarly disciplines—Spanish and French literature—were perfect subjects for him because he viewed Spain and France as "cultural corpses"
whose empires revealed mistakes Americans could learn from. Part of what
excited Ticknor was giving opportunities to men of natural intelligence.
American universities and libraries should be based on the grand European
precedents, he believed. But, in the words of one biographer, the histories
Ticknor wrote allowed him to show his contemporaries how to achieve a
cultural "ripeness that was not ominous"—in short, how to "arrest decay."[12]
On the other hand, Josiah Quincy, although a commanding presence, was
not erudite. In the 1820s and '30s he had worked alongside Ticknor during
periods of reform at the Athenaeum and at Harvard. But Quincy had approached those efforts with straightforward administrative expertise, not
with convictions based on comparative cultural studies. (In 1851, Quincy borrowed Ticknor's opus on Spanish literature from the Athenaeum library.
Withdrawing the second volume only after spending months with the first,
he seems to have made an effort to read it.)[13]

On the subject of abolition, too, the men's differences were sharp. Quincy
viewed slavery through the lens of southern expansionism; angry about the
Fugitive Slave Act, he sympathized with the work of Free Soilers such as
Charles Sumner. In 1856, at the age of eighty-four, Quincy would write to the
convalescing senator, confessing, "I am sometimes ashamed of myself at
finding the embers flaming [when] they ought naturally to be expiring."[14]
Ticknor, in contrast, was famously dogmatic on the fate of the "Negro" in
America. Like Daniel Webster, whom he had known well and admired,
Ticknor saw the Compromise of 1850 as an act of statesmanship, a necessary
measure to balance the interests of North and South. He believed in the
inferiority of blacks and insisted that a "war of the races" was inevitable.[15] To
twenty-first-century minds, Ticknor's passion for public libraries seems wildly
at odds with his racism.

The antebellum era—a time of national soul-searching—produced many
internal contradictions. Incongruously, if Quincy was the public servant who
put little trust in a potential government stewardship of the Athenaeum, Ticknor was the snob who aimed to destroy an elite enclave for the sake of the

public good. Their small manifestos—Ticknor's *Union of the Boston Athenaeum and the Public Library* and Quincy's *An Appeal in Behalf of the Boston Athenaeum*—both originated as letters to the *Boston Daily Advertiser* in March 1853 and were published as pamphlets that same spring. Each piece discloses anxiety about social change in addition to a personal interpretation of the Athenaeum mission. Both men restate the intentions of the Athenaeum's founders, and both speculate about how those aims were meant to serve a changing city.

At the time of the dispute, George Ticknor (fig. 6.1) was devoting much energy to the project of planning a public library for Boston. In order to weaken the Athenaeum's record of service, he begins his *Union of the Boston Athenaeum and the Public Library* with a short summary of the old institution's deficiencies (inadequate reference books and shortage of recent publications) and proceeds to record the Athenaeum's bumpy financial history. Central to his argument is the momentum a new public library is already enjoying—its prominent donors, its proposed features, and its substantial community backing. But his pamphlet hinges on the claim that the Athenaeum has always seen itself as fulfilling a public role, and thus the use of its building and books for that specified purpose would mark only a small shift in orientation: "Four-fifths of the proprietors of the Athenaeum, it is confidently believed, regard and always have regarded their interest in it *as a public rather than a private one*, and, like its other benefactors, they have contributed to it mainly because they have felt the importance of having something in Boston as near to a *Public* Library as their combined means could furnish."[16]

Ticknor's italicized text challenges any Athenaeum member to deny a commitment to the city at large. Laced throughout his methodically written fourteen-page pamphlet is the assertion that all citizens agree that an open city library should be Boston's next achievement. "If the City, therefore, needs a Public Library, it must begin it with its own means," he argues. The goal of providing "families and firesides" with "all good recent publications" makes clear the excitement Ticknor feels about changing ordinary lives. He seems to relish the experimental nature of such a plan, referring to "our citizens of all classes" who, though "few of them now know much of the Athenaeum, or are much benefited by it," will be able to consult freely the resources at the new library he proposes. As he closes, Ticknor is careful to comfort wary Athenaeum proprietors by nodding politely to the institution's long tradition of "doing good," offering evidence that in shedding its founders' original desire to house a laboratory and observatory, change had already been weathered. He concludes with a progressive sentiment about "the signs of the times," reading rooms being no "substitute for such a great Public Library as we want." The implication is that the Athenaeum is outmoded and awaits revival on a grander scale.[17]

FIGURE 6.1 George Ticknor in portrait by G. P. A. Healy, 1848. (*Hood Museum of Art, Dartmouth College; gift of Constance V. R. White, Nathaniel T. Dexter, Philip Dexter, and Mary Ann Streeter*)

By 1853, Josiah Quincy (fig. 6.2) had retired from public life, and he responded to Ticknor's proposal only because his opinion was "repeatedly requested." The opening passage of his *Appeal in Behalf of the Boston Athenaeum* dismisses, in effect, Ticknor's main premise. Instead of accepting the idea that the majority of Athenaeum proprietors have always thought of their institution as serving the public, Quincy insists that the transfer to government control would be an abuse of trust. Because the Athenaeum, he writes in his fifteen-page pamphlet, stands as a private memorial to its founders and benefactors, any change in its management would be presumptuous on the part of its present stewards. In a series of statements that blur into one another, Quincy claims that the proposal to have the proprietors sell their Athenaeum shares at market value to the city authorities would be "unjust," "unwise," and "unprincipled." In fact, he argues, relinquishing the institution to the ever changing powers of political parties would be both foolish and

FIGURE 6.2 Josiah Quincy in portrait by Gilbert Stuart, 1824. (*Museum of Fine Arts, Boston; gift of Miss Eliza Susan Quincy; photograph © Museum of Fine Arts, Boston*)

immoral. Quincy accuses the city of foul play in choosing a building lot so near the Athenaeum, claiming that the authorities wanted all along thereby to point to the redundancy of two libraries. In contrast to Ticknor's forward-looking conclusion, in which he predicts that quaint reading rooms will soon be obsolete, Quincy in the end recommends that the citizens of Boston wait and see how the new library develops. Only then, he writes, will one comfortably establish a sense of whether the public institution deserves to be given the valuable resources of the private one. Finally, Quincy closes with a defiant statement, again contradicting Ticknor by asserting that the Athenaeum is now *wholly out of debt, and wanting nothing but a fund adequate to meet the yearly occurring expenditures.*[18]

Whereas Ticknor emphasizes the goal, or end, of the merger (a truly public library for Boston), Quincy emphasizes the process, or means, of the merger (an unscrupulous abuse of deceased benefactors' trust). Ticknor's pamphlet characterizes the Athenaeum as superfluous, outdated; Quincy's pamphlet maintains that the institution continues to be vital, a living testament to its founders' vision. Their outlooks differ markedly, too. The well-traveled Ticknor approaches the issue of libraries as a cosmopolitan with a long-range perspective. He had always advocated library consolidation; behind the rhetoric of his pamphlet lies his interest in professionalizing American scholarship along the lines of German universities. Quincy's provincial worldview perhaps made him less comfortable with sweeping institutional change. Having just chronicled the story of the Boston Athenaeum (his affectionate *History* tells of the institution's circuitous path to its grand home on Beacon Street), Quincy invested much of himself in the library. Yet both men, in their vehemence and zeal, betray distress. Perhaps decades of political experience made Quincy distrust the government as a caretaker. A Federalist whose clout had diminished in his later years, he voices concern here about the precariousness of political life, which changes "with every turn of party or passion." Ticknor, for his part, seems driven by worry about the ordinary citizenry, whose need for a public library was as strong as their need for public schools.[19]

George Ticknor's pamphlet was informed by his experience as a contributor to the *North American Review*, a literary journal that had been promoting libraries for decades. Sandwiched between such articles as "Improved Portable Stove" and "Sketches of Scenery on Niagara River," pieces about the need for libraries had appeared frequently since 1815, the year of the publication's founding. Ticknor—together with William Tudor, the brothers Alexander and Edward Everett, Jared Sparks, Edward Channing, and William Prescott—attempted, in the pages of the *North American Review*, to improve American society by elevating its culture. The journal had risen, in fact, from the ashes of the short-lived *Monthly Anthology*, the publication of the Anthology Society (and the meeting ground for the founders of the Boston Athenaeum). These sons of Federalists used the *North American Review* as a forum for articulating their understanding of communal responsibility. "How far do [our public libraries] meet the wants of our community?" asks one anonymous contributor in 1837.[20]

In the early pages of the *North American Review*, a library was called "public" if it was more than a home-based collection; university libraries as well as those "generally held by shares open to subscription," such as the Athenaeum and the Boston Library Society, were included in this class. Among the variety of library types in the early nineteenth century, both the Boston Mercantile Library and the Boston Mechanic Apprentices Library were founded in 1820; such business libraries served artisans, clerks, and young merchants.[21] The *North American Review* seemed to argue for the cultivation of a more general reader. One detects an urgency, similar to that of Ticknor's pamphlet, in passages that express faith in the liberating power of books: "Books are needed, not confined to any single branch, but embracing the whole range of science and of literature, which shall supply the means of every species of research and inquiry, and which, placed within the reach of all, shall leave idleness no excuse for the lightness of its labors, and poverty no obstacles which industry may surmount. . . . What has been done . . . towards the performance of this duty?" Ticknor's perspective is also represented in this comment from another anonymous *North American Review* contributor in 1850: "Our people are and will be readers. They are generally prepared to make good use of books of a higher order than those offered to them in so cheap and attractive form by our enterprising publishers."[22]

The background to the establishment of the Boston Public Library—the planning that animated George Ticknor—is important because the public library provides a useful contrast and a sense of definition to the Boston Athenaeum. Oddly enough, it was a French ventriloquist and showman named Alexander Vattemare who first inspired enthusiasm for a public library in Boston, traveling around the United States advocating a system of book exchanges that he hoped would lead to a network of public libraries in this country.[23] City officials—including Josiah Quincy Jr.—were impressed by Vattemare, and in 1848 the Massachusetts legislature passed an act authorizing the library. Unlike the Athenaeum, which was insulated from state influence, the public library depended on a statute that guaranteed its support through taxation. An annual sum of $5,000 was allocated for its establishment and maintenance. This was the first law passed to help found an American public library.[24] The chief elements of the new institution would be a commitment to popular taste in literature, supreme flexibility in organization so as to gauge and capitalize upon the public's interest, and a pleasing setting for readers. In a series of letters, and finally in a formal report as library trustees, George Ticknor and his friend the statesman Edward Everett refined these ideas and together devised a rough theory of library service.

In one letter to Everett, Ticknor was especially zealous on the topic of the reading habits of the so-called middling classes. "That an appetite for reading, can be very widely excited is plain. . . . By a little judicious help, rather than any direct control or restraint," he insists, a general taste for books would "be carried much higher than previously thought possible."[25] His interest in acquiring and circulating popular books underscores his intellectual kinship with the Reverend Joseph Stevens Buckminster. Clearly, Ticknor identified with Buckminster, who, as an intimate of William Smith Shaw and Arthur Maynard Walter, had been an influential book agent for the earliest incarnation of the Boston Athenaeum. Much younger than the famous minister, Ticknor was nevertheless very familiar with the man and his mind: he had known Buckminster from the Anthology Society; he had written a brief memoir of the Buckminster family; and most of his contemporaries agreed that after the minister's death in 1819, the Ticknor home at 9 Park Street had "replaced [Buckminster's] Brattle Street parsonage as the gathering place for Boston's young intellectuals."[26] In 1807, Buckminster had urged Shaw to consider popular and useful books, instead of more arcane publications, for the young Athenaeum. "We must, at least for some time, think of popularity," he wrote, "and I know of no method so likely to procure it, as to keep our rooms furnished with an abundance of magazines, pamphlets, and new books."[27]

Of course, the project of launching the Athenaeum differed considerably—in scope, in motivation, in audience—from the project of launching Boston's public library. Yet Buckminster and Ticknor shared a keen sense of the attraction between a reader and his or her desired book. Despite their own erudition and specialized academic interests, both men were determined to exploit popularity. As early as 1828, Ticknor and his friend Nathaniel Bowditch had pushed for a strategic Athenaeum book purchase. The institution would not always purchase popular books in great quantity, however.[28]

Ticknor's plan of luring prospective new readers depended on the wide circulation of books. As his pamphlet so passionately articulates, multiple copies and generous circulation rules would ensure that "many persons, if they desired it, could be reading the same work at the same time." In a letter to Ticknor, Everett writes in a revelatory tone that "the extensive circulation of new and popular works is a feature of a public library which I have not hitherto much contemplated." These men were planning the American public library, step by step, and marveling at its novelty. Everett's main contribution was the conviction that "such a library would put the finishing hand to . . . public education."[29] And Ticknor reiterated the link between the public library and the public school in his portion of a report they made jointly as trustees in 1852: "[The library is] a new thing, a new step forward in general education." While the report was authored by both Ticknor and Everett, Ticknor wrote the most important section setting forth the philosophy of the Boston Public Library. One sees in it much phrasing later recycled for his pamphlet in support of the library's union with the Athenaeum.[30]

The public library, Ticknor wrote to Everett, must "carry this taste for reading as deep as possible into society." To that end, the trustees' report employs metaphors of transportation to argue against small, privately run libraries and for better ways in which knowledge can be "diffused": "The old roads, so to speak, are admitted to be no longer sufficient. Even the more modern turnpikes do not satisfy our wants. We ask for rail-cars and steamboats, in which many more persons—even multitudes—may advance together to the great end of life, and go faster, farther and better, by the means thus furnished to them, than they have ever been able to do before."[31] Modern notions of speed and size are used in conjunction with the older republican trope about the diffusion of knowledge. One can sense Ticknor's eagerness to begin this work.

Although they wanted citizens to be able to access popular literature, Ticknor and the other founders of the Boston Public Library were somewhat prescriptive in their discussion of books for the masses. The report describes the library as "satisfying the demands for healthy, nourishing reading" that people "cannot be expected to purchase . . . for themselves." A Londoner and former Bostonian named Joshua Bates, having learned of the Boston Public Library, donated $50,000 to the cause. Like Ticknor, he believed that the common reader should not be left to choose material indiscriminately: "There should be a book of directions for reading in every branch of knowledge, so that [readers] may know where to begin," he suggested.[32] Self-styled missionaries, these men approached their project in a patronizing but passionate manner.

Scholars of library history have written much about the conditions and motivations that led to American public libraries. Their work ranges from the institutional history that celebrates the growth of a central city library to the more sophisticated study that considers architecture, politics, or the microcommunities that libraries create.[33] Historians have claimed that members of the elite such as George Ticknor felt compelled to establish libraries because of desperation concerning a fast-changing society.[34] The notion of an open library as a social experiment involving the lower classes certainly occurred to the organizers of the Boston Public Library, and Ticknor's writing does reveal a good deal of anxiety about city life. In his 1849 sketch of the Buckminster family he expresses nostalgia for an era when people were "involved in each other's welfare and fate as it is impossible now, when our numbers are trebled," a time when "we were . . . a more compact, united, and kindly community than we have been since, or ever can be again."[35] The forces of immigration, poverty, and crime frightened Ticknor, but radical means of reform struck him as too violent or simply impolite. He chose instead to entice the disenfranchised with warm, well-lit library halls.[36] Yet the city library was designed to appeal to *all* Bostonians. The presence of hierarchy *within* the Boston Public Library (reference, special collections, main holdings) would complicate any simple interpretation of the newer institution as an instrument of control.

Ticknor's roles as an Athenaeum proprietor and early Anthology Society participant further illuminate the novel design of his public library. If implemented, his recommendations would have stripped the Boston Athenaeum of its exclusivity, for he advocated on behalf of the Boston Public Library *as against* the Athenaeum and other such subscription libraries. Given what he saw as a necessary choice between a well-established public library and the preservation of the elite Athenaeum, he preferred the former. Furthermore, even if patrons such as Ticknor were trying to practice social control, there were no clear alternatives for the formation of public libraries; only gentlemen of means had the authority necessary for the task. For Ticknor— who, as a young man, had embarked upon a life of letters (neither the law nor business interested him)—books became tools for solving urban problems. In privileging the Boston Public Library over the Boston Athenaeum, he chose to sacrifice a comfortable, gentlemanly retreat for the sake of his larger community. But his fellow proprietors proved unyielding.

The dispute over whether to merge with the city's library in 1853 certainly jarred many of the Athenaeum's members. Yet discomfort about access to their institution—and about the evolving public library—was nothing new. For example, in 1847 a letter to the editor of one newspaper had suggested that the Athenaeum reduce its subscription price so that it could "become what it ought to be, a Public Library." The newspaper added the comment that "a good public library more generally accessible than any we have is certainly to be desired. In this respect, we are far behind many European cities, inferior to our own [in] population."[37] The next year a scheme for opening up the institution was floated: A printed circular dated October 1848 announced a special meeting of the proprietors "to consider the expediency of admitting the citizens of Boston to the use of the Library of the Athenaeum."

The suggested terms, though no doubt radical to the shareholders, would have preserved special status: proprietors would have sole access to the reading room, while "citizens" would be confined to the library. (Since the Beacon Street building was not yet completed, it is unclear which physical spaces were implied by these distinctions.) Furthermore, an elaborate method of compensation from the city was laid out—a payment of $50,000 to the Athenaeum, followed by five annual payments of $5,000—and, finally, a stipulation that six of ten "Library Directors" would be chosen by Athenaeum trustees. Not surprisingly, given the ornate nature of the plan, the proprietors resisted any shift in policy. "Having been discussed by several gentlemen," the record reads, "it was voted that the whole subject be indefinitely postponed."[38]

In the waning years of the 1840s, proprietors sensed a change in the way the city perceived the Athenaeum. Notes from their annual meeting of 1849 refer to a "feeling of anxious interest which has lately been awakened as to the future prospects of this valuable Institution."[39] If the newfangled public library was considered a threat to the Athenaeum, what exactly was threatened? The Athenaeum had always functioned as a network of families. In his short study of the institution, Ronald Story observes that five distinct family groups filled most of the administrative roles of the Athenaeum from 1807 to 1860, and that the idea of inherited privilege was strengthened with the passing down of shares to a son (or very occasionally to a daughter) at a formal occasion.[40] The notion of the Athenaeum's library as a protected space, apart from the world, had contributed to the safety and pleasure of its readers. During its years on Pearl Street, the dignity of the Perkins mansion and the enforcement of the institution's rules invited shareholders to become members of a special community. The Athenaeum's well-known gallery rendered the institution a hybrid of fine books and fine art. Notwithstanding the claim in George Ticknor's pamphlet that "four-fifths" of its proprietors regarded their interest in the Athenaeum as public rather than private, the place was, of course, relatively exclusive. The fee of $300 a share was prohibitive to many, and proprietors always maintained a limit on the number of shares outstanding.

The complicated structure of Athenaeum membership allowed for at least four levels of use. Proprietors paid $300 for the privilege of using the reading room and for access to the bookshelves. Life subscribers, for a fee of $100, held a kind of midlevel status: they were not share holders and, therefore, were not permitted to vote on institutional matters. So-called annual subscribers, also known as reading-room members, paid $10 (later $12) each calendar year but could not always access the shelves. "Strangers" (people living outside a five-mile radius) were permitted to visit only after a proprietor introduced them. There were also guests and "ticketholders," nonmembers for whom temporary borrowing privileges were granted by proprietors.[41]

Complaints about the inaccessibility of the Athenaeum appear throughout the historical record. A glance backward shows that this unease started early. In an 1817 letter to librarian William Smith Shaw (while the Athenaeum was still located on Tremont Street), a young scholar, John Everett, holds forth on what he sees as the confused identity of the institution:

> You tell me that a Proprietor, the only one who can use the upper rooms, pays $300. Now I venture to say that there are not ten young men here who just finished an expensive publick education who can afford to pay this sum, and even if they could they would act more judiciously to send to Göttingen and London and procure, for it, 500 valuable volumes, which will always bring them a decent interest on their money when convenient to dispose of them. . . . If the other supposition is true, namely that this Establishment is meant as the exclusive privilege of the few whose property it is, they have miserably mistaken the means of attaining any object we can suppose they had in view.[42]

Everett's remonstrations are the earliest surviving comment on the Athenaeum's exclusionary practices. It was his rebuffed attempt to gain affordable access to the "upper rooms" that inspired him to articulate his views on library service. His sentiments were echoed in 1826, when a scathing letter to the editor appeared in a Boston newspaper:

> What literary advantages have the mass of our citizens derived from the Athenaeum? Who gets a peep within its lofty walls without a ten dollar bill? . . . When the poor are favoured with admission to study the neatly fitted up shelves of books which adorn the Athenaeum, we shall be convinced of the necessity as well as the worth of it, and not before. . . . We hope there will be an end to libraries, which are the gift of the public, if the same public must be compelled to pay as much for looking at their known property as they would for gazing at a dancing bear.[43]

Again, the possible levels of use are left unarticulated.[44] Calling the Athenaeum's restrictions "preposterous" and "abominable," the anonymous letter-writer argues that all Bostonians deserve access to books, anticipating the debate that would rage between Ticknor and Quincy almost thirty years later.

Throughout the Athenaeum's history, the term "public" remained slippery and changeable. John Everett's letter defines "Publick Library" as "an establishment for the general benefit of the persons of literary taste in the vicinity." Contributors to the *North American Review* initially recognized "public library" to mean any collection of books not based in a home and, therefore, accessible to a larger constituency. The Boston Athenaeum was the focus of a baffling array of characterizations. For example, in 1816 Josiah Quincy, in an oxymoronic flourish, called it "exclusively publick," meaning that the library was not the property of a private individual collector.[45] That description would seem to align Quincy with his eventual adversary George Ticknor, whose assertion about the public spirit of the proprietors was central to his 1853 pamphlet. Thirty-five years after Quincy's comment, Charles Jewett, librarian of the Smithsonian Institution in 1851, identified the Athenaeum in similar terms: "The library is hardly surpassed, either in size or in value, by any other in the country; and its regulations are framed with the design that it shall answer the highest purposes of a public library. Practically it is such."[46] Yet the practices of the institution (no direct access to the shelves without a costly membership or a personal introduction) opposed these claims.[47] And when the pressure to "go public" was truly applied, the Athenaeum retreated.

So how can one understand the survival of the Boston Athenaeum in the dawning era of the great American public library? How could one city accommodate both the Athenaeum and the Boston Public Library? Haynes McMullen points to the staggering variety of library types that proliferated up to the late nineteenth century. Sometimes, as his data show, redundancy did not deter prospective patrons from enthusiastically supporting all kinds of libraries.[48] Consolidation was not the universal goal. The city's competing membership library, the Boston Library Society, survived as an independent entity until 1939; even the Boston Mercantile Library persisted until 1952, long after the founding of the Boston Public Library.[49] In the case of the Athenaeum and the public library, there was much overlap in their missions, their benefactors, and their supporters; yet each institution attracted its own constituency. Was this an instance of "cultural coding," the invisible labeling of "high" and "low" for two opposing sets of consumers? In Lawrence Levine's controversial book *Highbrow/Lowbrow: The Emergence of Cultural Hierarchy in America*, he writes that "accessibility . . . becomes a key to cultural categorization." (By "cultural categorization," he means that certain places and practices become "highbrow" in the public consciousness.) Levine argues that a deliberate "sacralization" of cultural forums in the latter part of the nineteenth century reinforced class distinctions beneficial to elites. He constructs his claims around audience expectations and behavior at performances of Shakespearean plays and symphonic music before and after a significant mid-nineteenth-century shift. But his argument does not explain the phenomenon of the Boston Athenaeum, whose "highbrow" qualities antedate Levine's watershed time period. *Highbrow/Lowbrow* steadfastly avoids any prolonged discussion of literary culture.[50]

In their "pamphlet war," both Ticknor and Quincy use the language of cultural categorization in order to appeal to educated parties. But their arguments

fail to reinforce a definitive high-low division between a "sacralized" Athenaeum and a more mainstream Boston Public Library.[51] Nor is *access* a definitive key to cultural hierarchy. Ticknor advocated the circulation of popular
books and the availability of reference material for more specialized study;
the Boston Public Library was to have both—even though the former was
more central to his plan. It should be emphasized that the cultural authority
of study, as opposed to reading, was something Ticknor's library not only
accommodated but encouraged.[52] Another potent category that appears in
the pamphlets is that of gender, but the result is not a reductive division between high and low libraries. In Ticknor's plan, "women as well as men"
would enjoy the privilege of withdrawing and consulting books; the holdings, he maintained, could be exported to "our families and firesides." Quincy
uses the equivalent of a schoolyard taunt to conclude his pamphlet, urging
Athenaeum sympathizers to shake off "unmanly fears" and cease to put their
"fingers in their eyes and whine about 'difficulties.'"[53] His implication is simply that the Athenaeum should have the strength to withstand hardship and
assert its independence. Women had been allowed to own proprietary shares
as early as 1829, and, through the various levels of use, some women (most of
them from the upper echelons of Boston society) had been able to withdraw
circulating books after 1826.[54]

Part of the exceptional nature of libraries is that their cultural work shut-
tles between public and private life seamlessly. In his Boston Public Library
plan, Ticknor wanted to continue to attract private money from "public-
spirited individuals," suggesting that such benefactors donate to the reference department, whose books would not circulate.[55] And at the Athenaeum
a feeling of civic pride accompanied the purchase of a life subscription or proprietary share. In various ways both libraries exploited the notions of public
and private, inclusive and exclusive, to achieve their ends.

Cultural historians have suggested that a public site for books should include "an *experience* of democracy," not just an abstract consideration of it. By
that standard the Boston Athenaeum is decidedly private and self-contained.
Certainly the Athenaeum struggled to retain its preferred membership, especially in the 1840s and 1850s. There was always some apprehension about
welcoming the citizenry into rooms carefully arranged with fine books and
works of art. A close-knit group, the Athenaeum's readers were accustomed
to one another and comforted by familiarity in the reading room. The institution was launched in the decades after the American Revolution, a time
when people worried about stable civic foundations. The Athenaeum's original aim to become "the fountain, at which all, who choose, may gratify their
thirst for knowledge" would sound insincere, for the implications of such a

mission proved unpalatable to many elite Bostonians. Just as anxiety contributed to the Athenaeum's founding, so anxiety explains its survival.[56]

Although a number of Athenaeum leaders were active in the public library movement, the crisis of threatened "publicness" triggered by the Boston Public Library forced the Athenaeum to look inward and cultivate pride in its distinct but admittedly shrunken role. A remark by the Committee of the Library in 1855 reveals a newfound comfort with its settled, if marginal, place in the city: "While the City Library is fulfilling to so gratifying an extent the anticipations of its warmest friends, by supplying the demand for popular literature, it is hoped that the Athenaeum may supply to its proprietors, and to men of letters and science generally, a constantly improving collection of works of intrinsic value and permanent importance."[57]

A hierarchy is underscored, to be sure. But a redefined purpose is also detectible. No longer does the institutional mission soar uncontrollably, as it did in 1807. Instead of advancing a catalogue of lofty goals, the proprietors are content to "supply" readers with a "constantly improving collection" of worthy, enduring books.[58] The dispute between George Ticknor and Josiah Quincy allowed buried assumptions to surface. Ultimately, the city accommodated, and would sustain, a wide range of library experiences. That the Boston Athenaeum does not represent a mere phase in the evolution of the public library, as Ticknor predicted it would, is part of its rich and complicated history. It became, in effect, a cultural cul-de-sac—a resilient institution that continued to attract substantial funding in spite of its limited reach and discreet image.

CONCLUSION
Ex Libris

In *The American Scene*, Henry James noted, with heartbreak, how "snubbed" the Boston Athenaeum had looked to him upon returning to Beacon Street in 1904. Its facade overshadowed by taller buildings, the poor Athenaeum showed James "how much one's own sense of the small city of the earlier time had been dependent on that institution." Beside the "brute ugliness" of newer buildings, the Athenaeum looked "hopelessly down in the world."[1] These brief observations occur in the larger context of *The American Scene*, where James bemoans the direction of his native country. What he longs for is almost ineffable. He misses what the Athenaeum and similarly "exquisite" places had offered. Privacy and leisure, perhaps. In a word, distinction.

The distinction that the Boston Athenaeum held is a quality that inheres in the notion of high culture. One could never fix a single definition of American culture, but it is possible to elucidate variations on the general theme. The amorphous idea of high culture has emerged in these chapters as a collection of personal and political forces. In the first half of the nineteenth century, versions of culture began to proliferate around the Boston Athenaeum. With the Anthology Society, we perceived culture as civility, the attempt of a worried and self-conscious group of anglophilic readers to ennoble their nation through a purposeful institution. But we also saw culture as identity, culture as commercialism, and culture as radical protest—all within the framework of one ambitious community.[2] For example, Hannah Adams both used and was used by the Athenaeum; her identity as a female historian answered both parties' needs. With the advent of the public gallery and other civic gestures, the Athenaeum's "product" had become somewhat commercialized by the 1830s; the institution's audience broadened after exhibition notices appeared, and a new cultural realm emerged, defined in part by the marketplace and the press. The agitation of Boston abolitionists spawned yet another kind of culture. The patrician prototype of the noble institution blended with the radicalism of antislavery to generate a version of culture in which British curios signified both protest *and* style.

What began as a small reading room, founded by friends, was transformed over the decades into an institution with a distinguished public face. The act of inviting the public in—through the art gallery after 1827 and, piecemeal, through selected expansion of membership—caused a shift in the Athenaeum's character. By the late 1840s and '50s it was challenged by its larger role in the urban community. Indeed, much of the controversy around it concerned public access. For reasons argued above, however, the Athenaeum is more than a display of power. It started not as an instrument of social control but rather as a niche where gentlemen could relieve anxieties about their place in the world. The institution's own historiography projects an image of polite society, learnedness, and patronage of the arts. These goals ran parallel to more personal goals of companionship and comfort. Self-published institutional newsletters, pamphlets, and exhibition catalogs—even the speeches delivered at inaugural events—avoid the Athenaeum's private past, presenting the work of William Shaw and others as merely administrative. Over time, twentieth-century guardians and visitors who partook of the quiet glory of the place reinforced its neutral cultural authority.

The early history of the Boston Athenaeum tells us about the pressures of cities and the stresses of individual men and women. Of course the challenges of the Athenaeum continued well beyond the mid-nineteenth century. The successful Boston Public Library lured readers from all walks of life. And when the Museum of Fine Arts opened its first building in 1876, the Athenaeum lent its best works of art to that nascent Boston institution. Consequently, many of the gallerygoers who had been attracted to the Athenaeum no longer visited, and the institution became less important to the public at large. A proposed move to Arlington Street was voted down by the Athenaeum proprietors in 1906, and in 1913 the building was refurbished with fireproof materials and the addition of an elegant fifth-floor reading room. It was declared a National Historic Landmark in 1966. Now, in the early twenty-first century, the Athenaeum has experienced an afterlife. Computer catalogues arrived in 1997. And in the autumn of 2002 the extensively renovated premises on Beacon Street were unveiled: expansion into the neighboring space of 14 Beacon, a children's library, a new gallery, and a conference room are just a few of the alterations. With climate-control systems and stricter regulations for members, the place immediately announces itself as a more secure, less idiosyncratic home for books and art. Gone are the cozy window seats in the ladies' lounge and the pipe smokers on the second floor. Indeed, a research fellowship program for scholars and a state-of-the-art conservation facility greatly enhance the institution's national profile. In 2007 the Athenaeum celebrated its bicentennial with much fanfare. The following year the new strategic plan called for a program on "civic discourse."

The stated purpose of the Athenaeum is echoed in libraries and museums today. The democratic credo "to collect, preserve, and present" has been the shared goal of many lasting American institutions. Yet the claim of institutional leaders to endorse an ideal that transcends sex, race, and class is as false as it is ubiquitous. Since there are no ministers of culture in the United States, authoritative arts advocacy falls largely to politicized bodies such as the National Endowment for the Humanities or to corporations and corporate-driven foundations. Visual arts, literature, music, theater—these are essential to any democracy. Sadly, many men and women who wield power fear the free expression of artists and authors. Exhibitions that include provocative imagery or that criticize national agendas draw disapproval from conservative Americans. Indeed, culture has become a "wedge issue," a term used by political analysts to describe an emotional, controversial topic that divides a large electorate. In the first half of the nineteenth century, culture was less overtly politicized than it is today. (Without computer blogs and television spin doctors, politics proceeded rather differently.) Neither abolitionist values nor women's rights were embraced by the Athenaeum; still, incremental change was evident. The reach of radical forces interests me, for there is no such thing as apolitical culture. Institutions considered to be prime cultural sites are generally conservative in origin, yet subtly and in arbitrary ways, they are penetrated by the disenfranchised groups whom these same institutions ostensibly served from the beginning. Eventually, elite culture adopts elements of both the avant-garde and the underground. Such is the mystery of democracy. Cultural authority circulates with strange abandon.[3]

Throughout these chapters I have maintained that dividing culture into rigid categories of high and low has distracted prominent scholars. It has reduced the complexity of hegemonic society into binary oppositions: us versus them. The story of the Boston Athenaeum, as I have tried to tell it, is the story of how certain gentlemen sought safety and dignity as Americans. It is the story of the sometimes elegant, sometimes awkward posturing they found necessary in order to right their relationship with the Old World and with themselves. It is also the story of the cultural enthusiasm contained in one uncommon institution.

This study of the Boston Athenaeum leads to two observations. The first is that as an effort to consolidate the intelligentsia in the nineteenth century, the Athenaeum obviously failed: that is, the institution's narrow audience and almost familial atmosphere limited its national influence—even as many members enjoyed "performing knowledge," reading and debating books and art, on the semipublic stage it afforded them. As cultural authority became fragmented, the sense of purpose shared by early Athenaeum readers disintegrated. A second observation is more uplifting. The American experience of public life is increasingly defined by solitary acts—exercising to packaged music on i-Pods, downloading digital texts from home, listening to audiobooks—and the Boston Athenaeum provides an alternative model. The best public libraries have evolved to resemble a version of the multipurpose athenaeum: libraries now routinely organize reading groups, sponsor book talks, host art exhibits, and function as vibrant microcommunities. The simple dedication to gather for aesthetic, intellectual, and social refreshment is perhaps the Athenaeum's greatest legacy. However troubling, the institution's history speaks to the drive for an invented American culture, the resolve to erect a kind of scaffolding for the national imagination. It is a project replicated across the United States—sometimes with prejudice, but more often with promise.

ACKNOWLEDGMENTS

Libraries are extraordinary places. They are central to the experience of reading, to the satisfaction of literary curiosity and appetite. And, as I now know, libraries point to assumptions about culture: definitions of identity (class, race, gender), hierarchies of disciplines and genres, establishment of professions, and shifting boundaries between edification and pleasure. I first became interested in the history of the Boston Athenaeum in 1989, when I took the position of editor at the denominational headquarters of the Unitarian Universalists on Beacon Hill. Down the street from my office, I read and wrote in the Athenaeum rooms, often wondering how such a singular library came to be—but never imagining that years later I would make it the topic of a book.

From the first day that I began researching that topic in 2002, the director and staff of the Boston Athenaeum assisted me with grace and professionalism. Specifically, I owe much to Pat Boulos, Stanley Cushing, Barbara Adams Hebard, Hina Hirayama, Stephen Nonack, Sally Pierce, Catharina Slautterback, Lisa Starzyk, Mary Warnement, and Richard Wendorf. The special collections staffs at the Boston Public Library and the Massachusetts Historical Society also helped tremendously. And very special thanks are due to those who discussed the project with me at an early stage: David Hall, Jill Lepore, Lance Morrow, and (once again) Richard Wendorf. I was honored to have one long, relaxed conversation with the late Michael Wentworth in May 2002; I have often reviewed my notes from our talk, and I remember him with fondness.

It is my pleasure to thank Bruce Redford, whose intelligence guided me through the project; I always left his office energized and with the resolve to think more deeply and write more clearly. His scholarship and remarkable gift for expression continue to inspire me. Keith Morgan read drafts with great care and offered advice in the warm spirit of collegiality. (It should be said, of course, that any shortcomings in this study are entirely my responsibility.) I am also grateful to Anita Patterson for agreeing to join other readers at the eleventh hour. My many other intellectual debts are acknowledged in notes throughout. At the University of Massachusetts Press, Clark Dougan was an understanding editor who helped in more ways than he knows. Comments from two anonymous scholars strengthened the manuscript in important areas. Patricia Sterling did the hard work of copyediting, and Carol Betsch shepherded the manuscript through production expertly.

On a personal note, I express my gratitude to Elif Armbruster, who read and reacted to chapters as they first appeared. Other friends eased the process with kindness and good counsel—patiently enduring my progress reports. Thank you Yvonne Abraham, Daren Bascome, Margaret Beck, Deborah Benjamin, Amanda Calobrisi, Philippa Gilmore, Aimee Good, Peter Guthrie, Stephen Heuser, Marcia Karp, Debra Klein, Amy Koenigbauer, Emily Liman, Linda Lowenthal, Kate Neave, Cheryl Nicholas, Marsha Pomerantz, Rebecca Sargent, J. Sybylla Smith, Jack Trumpbour, and Molly Watkins. I am lucky, also, to have had the backing of the extended D'Amato family and of my siblings, Alexander Wolff and Stephanie Wolff, and their families. This study would not have been possible without significant encouragement from my mother and late father, Mary and Nikolaus Wolff. Throughout this project, as through all the projects of my life, they enthusiastically supported me. I dedicate this work to them.

Finally, my husband and best friend, Stephen D'Amato, saw me through countless hours of writing. His help ran the gamut from returning heavy knapsacks of library volumes to listening to me talk about the Athenaeum's cast of characters. I can never thank him enough. The long gestation of this book ran parallel to another gestation: we welcomed twin daughters into the world at roughly the time that I had first intended to finish the study. Delays can sometimes turn out to be happy things, and I am deeply grateful for Phoebe and Julia—whose own love of libraries is well under way.

BIOGRAPHIES

HANNAH ADAMS (1755–1831) · *historian*

Reared in rural Massachusetts by her bookish father, Adams was a serious reader from an early age. When she was still a girl, she was tutored by divinity students who boarded at her father's house. As a young woman, she compiled *An Alphabetical Compendium of the Various Sects* (1784) in order to make sense of the practices of competing styles of Christianity. Like this first work, several subsequent books—*A Summary History of New-England* (1799), *A View of Religions* (1801), *The History of the Jews* (1812), and *Letters on the Gospels* (1824)—took the form of historical summaries. Adams was purported to be distantly related to President John Adams. Her interactions with the gentlemen of the Boston Athenaeum were always cordial; many supported her financially after she sparred with fellow historian Jedidiah Morse and unscrupulous printers. [Hannah Adams, *A Memoir of Miss Hannah Adams, Written By Herself with Additional Notices by a Friend* (Boston: Gray and Bowen, 1832); Gary D. Schmidt, *A Passionate Usefulness: The Life and Literary Labors of Hannah Adams* (Charlottesville: University of Virginia Press, 2004); Mrs. Sarah Josepha Hale, ed., "Mrs. Hannah Adams," *Ladies' Magazine*, July 1828, 309–313; Olive M. Tilden, "Hannah Adams," *Dedham Historical Register* 7 (July 1896): 83–100; and Alma Lutz, "Hannah Adams: An American Bluestocking," *New-England Galaxy* 12 (Spring 1971): 29–33.]

JOSEPH STEVENS BUCKMINSTER (1784–1812) · *minister and scholar*

An intimate of both William Smith Shaw and Arthur Maynard Walter from their Harvard days, Joseph Buckminster was a member of the Anthology Society. He was also a famous minister who popularized sermon-writing and energized biblical scholarship. A Unitarian, he came to believe that the Bible was a vehicle for God's word but not the express work of God. This stance provoked his father, who was a more orthodox minister. Buckminster traveled to Europe in order to treat his worsening epilepsy. In England he operated as a "book scout" for Shaw and the young Athenaeum. Back in Boston, as pastor of the Brattle Street Church, he regularly welcomed guests to the parsonage library to discuss art, literature, and science. He was especially kind to Hannah Adams, the most public beneficiary of his patronage. Buckminster was widely eulogized after his early death. [Andrews

Norton, "Character of the Rev. Joseph Stevens Buckminster" (1812), in *The Works of Joseph Stevens Buckminster* (Boston: James Monroe, 1839); Eliza Buckminster Lee, *Memoirs of Rev. Joseph Buckminster, D.D., and His Son, Rev. Joseph Stevens Buckminster, D.D.* (Boston: Wm. Crosby and H. P. Nichols, 1849); Joseph Stevens Buckminster, "The Dangers and Duties of Men of Letters," Phi Beta Kappa Society address, Harvard University, 31 August 1809, *Monthly Anthology and Boston Review* 7 (September 1809): 146–153; Lawrence Buell, "Joseph Stevens Buckminster: The Making of a New England Saint," *Canadian Review of American Studies* 10 (Spring 1979): 1–29.]

LYDIA MARIA CHILD (1802–1880) • *author and abolitionist*

Child was born Lydia Francis in Medford, a village outside of Boston. Through her brother-in-law and her husband, attorney and editor David Lee Child, she was introduced to well-stocked libraries. In her early twenties she wrote novels. After meeting the abolitionist William Lloyd Garrison, Child focused her attention on the cause of antislavery, insisting in *An Appeal in Favor of That Class of Americans Called Africans* (1833) that African Americans should be granted all the benefits of United States citizenship. The Boston Athenaeum allowed Child access to its library for a time; her abolitionist activities, however, seem to have jeopardized her Athenaeum privileges. Child also wrote popular domestic manuals on parenting and household management. [*Lydia Maria Child: Selected Letters, 1817–1880* (Amherst: University of Massachusetts Press, 1982); Lydia Maria Child, *An Appeal in Favor of That Class of Americans Called Africans*, ed. Carolyn L. Karcher (Amherst: University of Massachusetts Press, 1996); Carolyn L. Karcher, *The First Woman of the Republic: A Cultural Biography of Lydia Maria Child* (Durham, N.C.: Duke University Press, 1994); Deborah Pickman Clifford, *Crusader for Freedom: A Life of Lydia Maria Child* (Boston: Beacon Press, 1992).]

CHESTER HARDING (1792–1866) • *painter*

Chester Harding came to Boston via Kentucky and Pittsburgh, where he had worked as a sign painter. Largely self-taught, he traveled to London and Glasgow in the 1820s before launching a profitable portraiture studio among the Boston elite. Harding was never comfortable with the Athenaeum Gallery's emphasis on collecting and exhibiting the works of Old Masters. Acting as a spokesman for his fellow artists, he eventually established a rival to the Athenaeum's exhibitions at his own studio. Still, having sampled the paintings at the Royal Academy in London firsthand, Harding had much in common with the self-styled connoisseurs at the Boston Athenaeum. He benefited considerably from the patronage of admiring Athenaeum members—through commissions and timely loans. [Chester Harding, *A Sketch of Chester Harding, Artist, Drawn by His Own Hand* (Boston: Houghton Mifflin, 1929: published privately in 1866; a second edition, supplemented with material gathered by one of his daughters, Margaret White, appeared in 1890; yet another edition includes an introduction by the artist's grandson W. P. G. Harding and was published in 1929); Leah Lipton, *A Truthful Likeness: Chester Harding and His Portraits* (Washington, D.C.: Smithsonian Institution, 1985).]

JEDIDIAH MORSE (1761–1826) • *minister, geographer, and historian*

Stubborn and highly ambitious, Morse was minister of the First Church of Charlestown, a Congregationalist parish near Boston. He was known as a contentious critic of those who dissented from orthodox Trinitarian theology. Having profited greatly from his best-selling *Geography Made Easy* (1784), he published his *Compendious History of New England* in 1804. Hannah Adams had published her *Summary History of New-England* in 1799, and by 1805 a controversy about competing abridgments ensued. Throughout his professional life, Morse felt threatened by the gradual secularization of the New England clergy. He launched *The Panoplist*, a periodical designed to combat the Unitarian "menace." In 1819, however, Morse's own parish dismissed him in favor of a more liberal pastor. One of Morse's sons, Samuel F. B. Morse, would become a highly regarded artist and the inventor of the telegraph. [Richard J. Moss, *The Life of Jedidiah Morse: A Station of Peculiar Exposure* (Knoxville: University of Tennessee Press, 1995); Conrad Wright, "The Controversial Career of Jedidiah Morse," *Harvard Library Bulletin* 31 (1983): 64–87; Peter S. Field, *The Crisis of the Standing Order: Clerical Intellectuals and Cultural Authority in Massachusetts, 1780–1833* (Amherst: University of Massachusetts Press, 1998).]

JAMES PERKINS (1761–1822) • *merchant*

A devoted Athenaeum benefactor, James Perkins made his fortune in the lucrative China trade. His Federal-style Pearl Street house, which had more than a dozen rooms on three floors, became the institution's penultimate home. According to the deed he gave to the Athenaeum, Perkins's gift was a true charitable impulse inspired by his appreciation of libraries. A bookish man (he sought out reading material even in the remote locales to which his business took him), Perkins wanted to promote the growth of public libraries and reading rooms. Samuel Johnson's *Lives of the Poets* was a favorite book of his. From a business trip in the West Indies, he brought home a freed slave, a man he called Moose, who was reportedly loved by all generations of the Perkins family. Perkins died of pneumonia soon after the transfer of the Pearl Street property. His brother and business partner, Thomas Handasyd Perkins, was active in the Athenaeum's Fine Arts Committee. ["Memoir of James Perkins," *Proceedings of the Massachusetts Historical Society* 1 (April 1823): 353–368; Michael Wentworth, with Elizabeth Lamb Clark, *The Boston Library Society, 1794–1994: An Exhibition of Portraits, Views, and Materials Related to the Foundation of the Society and Some of Its Early Members* (Boston: Boston Athenaeum, 1995).]

JOSIAH QUINCY (1772–1864) · *administrator and politician*

Having been mayor of Boston and president of Harvard University, Quincy was a master at administration. He belonged to an old colonial family and was the son of a revolutionary. From 1804 until 1812 he served as a Federalist congressman in the United States House of Representatives before abandoning the national stage. Known as the Great Mayor, Quincy modernized the Boston police force and fire department. He also established a central marketplace—the granite structure now called Quincy Market. (Both Quincy's son Josiah and grandson Josiah would be elected mayor, too.) Quincy served as an Athenaeum trustee from 1813 through 1815 and was president of the institution from 1820 to 1829. His *History of the Boston Athenaeum, with Biographical Notices of Its Deceased Founders* (1851) narrates the events leading up to the groundbreaking ceremony at the site of the Athenaeum's final home on Beacon Street. In a dispute with George Ticknor, Quincy wrote passionately about the legacy of the Athenaeum founders and their original intent. [Edmund Quincy, *Life of Josiah Quincy*, 6th ed. (Boston: Little, Brown, 1874); Robert A. McCaughey, *Josiah Quincy, 1772–1864: The Last Federalist* (Cambridge, Mass.: Harvard University Press, 1974).]

WILLIAM ROSCOE (1753–1831) · *politician, banker, and author*

Englishman William Roscoe was a founder of the Liverpool Athenaeum, one of the chief inspirations for the Boston Athenaeum. He was a liberal Whig Member of Parliament, a critic of the slave trade, and an early proponent of prison reform; in addition, he was an avid book collector, an amateur botanist, a poet for children, and the author of two Renaissance biographies: the lives of Lorenzo de' Medici and, later, Pope Leo X. For decades starting around the turn of the century, Roscoe received enthusiastic praise from the Boston gentlemen who founded the Boston Athenaeum. A visit to Allerton Hall, Roscoe's country house outside Liverpool, was de rigueur for elite Bostonians traveling abroad. Roscoe declared bankruptcy toward the end of his life and was forced to sell his estate—including his beloved library. [Washington Irving, "Roscoe," in *The Sketchbook of Geoffrey Crayon, Gentleman*, 2nd ed. (London: John Murray, 1820); Henry Roscoe, *The Life of William Roscoe*, 2 vols. (London: T. Cadell, 1833); George Chandler, *William Roscoe of Liverpool, 1753–1831* (London: B. T. Batsford, 1853); George Chandler, *Liverpool* (London: B. T. Batsford, 1857).]

WILLIAM SMITH SHAW (1778–1826) · *lawyer and book collector*

The nephew of President John Adams, Shaw served as private secretary to his uncle during the Adams one-term presidency. In 1800, Shaw returned to Boston and trained as a lawyer. He had a delicate constitution, according to an early biographer; he suffered from "dangerous coughs" and was "more like the sensitive plant than the young oak." Shaw and his friend Arthur Maynard Walter helped form a reading club called the Anthology Society, which published a monthly review of literature and the arts. Following Walter's death in 1807, the Anthology Society's reading room became the Boston Athenaeum. Shaw led the effort to collect books and pamphlets for the institution, and the Boston Athenaeum soon became his sole object. [Joseph B. Felt, *Memorials of William Smith Shaw* (Boston: S. K. Whipple, 1852); Josiah Quincy, "Biographical Notices," in *The History of the Boston Athenaeum, with Biographical Notices of Its Deceased Founders* (Boston: Boston Athenaeum, 1851), 22–44 (the "Biographical Notices" are repaginated at the back of the volume); Lewis P. Simpson, ed., *The Federalist Literary Mind: Selections from "The Monthly Anthology and Boston Review," 1803–1811, Including Documents Relating to the Boston Athenaeum* (Baton Rouge: Louisiana State University Press, 1962).]

CHARLES SUMNER (1811–1874) • *lawyer, abolitionist, and politician*

A United States senator whose political passions centered on abolitionism, Sumner was also an active Boston Athenaeum proprietor. He is often remembered for surviving a brutal assault by a southern opponent on the floor of the United States Senate: in 1856, as a first-term senator, Sumner was caned to the point of unconsciousness after delivering a speech against slavery. Following his recovery, he continued to serve as a senator until his death, most memorably as chairman of the Committee on Foreign Affairs. With his involvement in the Athenaeum and his role in the abolition movement, Sumner acted as a go-between, a cultural broker who bridged two vastly different communities—the city's free blacks and Boston's wealthiest families. [*Memoir and Letters of Charles Sumner*, ed. Edward L. Pierce, 4 vols. (Boston: Roberts Brothers, 1893); *The Selected Letters of Charles Sumner*, ed. Beverly Wilson Palmer (Boston: Northeastern University Press, 1990); David Donald, *Charles Sumner and the Coming of the Civil War* (New York: Knopf, 1960); Anne-Marie Taylor, *Young Charles Sumner and the Legacy of the American Enlightenment, 1811–1851* (Amherst: University of Massachusetts Press, 2001).]

GEORGE TICKNOR (1791–1871) • *scholar*

A member of the Anthology Society as a young man, Ticknor was an early proprietor of the Boston Athenaeum. He studied at the University of Göttingen and traveled throughout Europe before accepting, in 1819, a professorship in modern languages at Harvard University. He served as an Athenaeum trustee from 1823 through 1832 and was vice president of the institution for the year 1833. His private book collection drew admiring guests to his home at 9 Park Street. Both learned and gregarious, Ticknor was considered a formidable social power. He was involved in the policymaking at the Athenaeum during the period when Lydia Maria Child's library privileges were allegedly withdrawn, and his disagreement with Charles Sumner over abolitionism led him to ostracize the young politician. Ticknor was a passionate advocate for the establishment of the Boston Public Library. [*Life, Letters, and Journals of George Ticknor*, ed. George S. Hillard, 2 vols. (Boston:

Houghton Mifflin, 1909); David B. Tyack, *George Ticknor and the Boston Brahmins* (Cambridge, Mass.: Harvard University Press, 1967).]

Arthur Maynard Walter (1780–1807) · *lawyer*

The son of a Loyalist rector whose Anglican views caused the family to flee to Nova Scotia some years after the Revolution, young Walter, upon his return, studied at Harvard University, where he met William Smith Shaw and Joseph Stevens Buckminster. Together, these men were among a small group who wanted desperately to elevate American society by encouraging literary pursuits. Their club, the Anthology Society, soon launched a monthly publication. Rejecting a career in the clergy, Walter chose instead to study law and travel abroad. He wrote essays and letters, corresponding faithfully with Shaw. His hope was to establish an American counterpart to the Johnsonian circle of late eighteenth-century London. Walter died of consumption at age twenty-six. [Josiah Quincy, "Biographical Notices," in *The History of the Boston Athenaeum, with Biographical Notices of Its Deceased Founders* (Boston: Boston Athenaeum, 1851), 13–21 (the "Biographical Notices" are repaginated at the back of the volume); Lewis P. Simpson, ed., *The Federalist Literary Mind: Selections from "The Monthly Anthology and Boston Review," 1803–1811, Including Documents Relating to the Boston Athenaeum* (Baton Rouge: Louisiana State University Press, 1962), 233.]

NOTES

PREFACE

1. Raymond Williams charts the complicated history of the word and shows how "culture"—elusive, malleable, and multifaceted—embraced a range of attitudes over time. The Latin *colere* means to protect, honor, inhabit, and cultivate; *culter* refers to a plowshare, a tool used to tend crops. Metaphors of growth and development continued to inhere in the word. *Culture* controlled *nature*, arguably its antithesis (though now even the idea of nature is perceived as a cultural byproduct). The word "culture" became more controversial in the late nineteenth century. Matthew Arnold sharpened it with a contrast to "anarchy" and provided a gloss: "the best that has been thought and said in the world." The word also connotes civility, an understanding of polite behavior and social order. Of course, anthropologists came to use "culture" in a less normative, more descriptive sense, to mean a people's particular way of life. Terry Eagleton attempts to unravel the entwined meanings, concluding that "culture is not only what we live by" but also, in great measure, "what we live for." See Raymond Williams, *Keywords: A Vocabulary of Culture and Society* (New York: Oxford University Press, 1976), 76–82; Matthew Arnold, *Culture and Anarchy* (New Haven, Conn.: Yale University Press, 1994 [1869]); and Terry Eagleton, *The Idea of Culture* (Oxford: Blackwell, 2000), 1–31, 131.

2. David D. Hall, manuscript chapter on "learned culture" for the ongoing *A History of the Book in America*, vol. 3., *The Industrial Book, 1840–1880* (Chapel Hill: University of North Carolina Press/American Antiquarian Society, 2007). Hall makes this point: "In 1800 no one in the English-speaking world used 'culture' in the sense that was becoming commonplace when Thomas Wentworth Higginson published 'A Plea for Culture' in *The Atlantic Monthly* in 1867. In this and parallel essays Higginson insisted on the importance of the artist and of the arts, literary and visual, for a society that was overly materialistic, too accepting of 'mediocrity,' and obsessed with money-making." I thank Professor Hall for sharing his work-in-progress years ago.

3. Pierre Bourdieu, *Distinction: A Social Critique of the Judgement of Taste*, trans. Richard Nice (Cambridge, Mass.: Harvard University Press, 1984), esp. 53–54.

4. For two general discussions of cultural authority, see T. J. Jackson Lears, "The Concept of Cultural Hegemony: Problems and Possibilities," *American Quarterly* 90 (June 1985): 567–593; and Michael Schudson, "Paper Tigers: A Sociologist Follows Cultural Studies into the Wilderness," *Lingua Franca* (August 1997): 49–56.

5. Richard L. Bushman, *The Refinement of America: Persons, Houses, Cities* (New York: Random House, 1992), 409; and Bushman, "American High-Style and Vernacular Cultures," in *Colonial British America: Essays in the New History of the Early Modern Era* ed. Jack P. Greene and J. R. Pole (Baltimore: Johns Hopkins University Press, 1984), 309. Bushman also writes persuasively of the alchemy of capitalism and refinement that resulted in consumer culture.

6. Alan Wallach, *Exhibiting Contradiction: Essays on the Art Museum in the United States* (Amherst: University of Massachusetts Press, 1998), esp. 15.

7. Lawrence W. Levine, *Highbrow/Lowbrow: The Emergence of Cultural Hierarchy in America* (Cambridge, Mass.: Harvard University Press, 1988); Paul DiMaggio, "Cultural Entrepreneurship

in Nineteenth-Century Boston," pts. 1 and 2, in *Media, Culture, and Society: A Critical Reader*, ed. Richard Collins et al. (London: Sage Publications, 1986), 194–211, 303–322.

8. Again, for alternative approaches to similar material, see DiMaggio's "Cultural Entrepreneurship" and Levine's *Highbrow/Lowbrow*. See also Lillian Miller, *Patrons and Patriotism: The Encouragement of the Fine Arts in the United States, 1790–1860* (Chicago: University of Chicago Press, 1966); and Ronald Story, "Class and Culture in Boston: The Athenaeum, 1807–1860," *American Quarterly* 27 (May 1975): 178–199. I am indebted to Professor Story's article for helping me refine my own thesis.

9. In "Class and Culture in Boston," Ronald Story emphasizes only one use: class consolidation.

10. The launching of the Boston Athenaeum features a remarkably close cast of characters, so a number of men and women reappear throughout the text. For example, George Ticknor appears as a minor name in Chapter 1 but plays a much larger role in Chapter 6. And Joseph Buckminster is integral to Chapters 1, 2, and 3.

INTRODUCTION

1. Russel Blaine Nye, *The Cultural Life of the New Nation: 1776–1830* (New York: Harper, 1960). See also Howard Mumford Jones and Bessie Zaban Jones, eds., *The Many Voices of Boston: A Historical Anthology, 1630–1975* (Boston: Little, Brown / Atlantic Monthly Press, 1975).

2. I found the catchphrase of self-definition and the number of volumes in the Athenaeum's holdings on the institution's website, www.bostonathenaeum.org. Richard Wendorf, Athenaeum director, provided an endowment figure of $80 million in 2008.

3. This description is attributed to poet and former Athenaeum trustee David McCord (1897–1997).

4. Samuel Eliot Morison, *Harrison Gray Otis, 1765–1848: The Urbane Federalist* (Boston: Houghton Mifflin, 1969), quoted in Jones and Jones, *Many Voices*, 146.

5. Harold Kirker and James Kirker, *Bulfinch's Boston: 1787–1817* (New York: Oxford University Press, 1964), 16–24. The Kirkers suggest that these North Shore merchants, who were also patriots, had fought the Revolution to secure commercial, not personal, freedom from Great Britain.

6. John Adams to Abigail Adams, 12 May 1780, cited in Anne-Marie Taylor, *Young Charles Sumner and the Legacy of the American Enlightenment, 1811–1851* (Amherst: University of Massachusetts Press, 2001), 11.

7. Tamara Plakins Thornton, *Cultivating Gentlemen: The Meaning of Country Life among the Boston Elite, 1785–1860* (New Haven, Conn.: Yale University Press, 1989), 16.

8. Since the term "elite" is anachronistic for the antebellum decades, I apply the expression with caution and in a general sense only. Any citizen of great learning was usually awarded status comparable but not identical to the status awarded a wealthy citizen. (A holder of a university degree or any practicing minister was almost always accorded elite status.) Boston's elite, then, exerted the most overt power and influence—though the complicated motivations of the elite are a central problem discussed in this book.

9. Ronald Story, *The Forging of an Aristocracy: Harvard and the Boston Upper Class, 1800–1870* (Middletown, Conn.: Wesleyan University Press, 1980), 41–88. In the 1820s, a controversy between Harvard faculty and Harvard administrators illustrates some of the misgivings that the more established Bostonians had about arrivistes who wanted to manage the college as a business. Many of the individuals who led Harvard's new administrative initiatives were leaders at the Athenaeum, too. See also Thornton, *Cultivating Gentlemen*, 82.

10. See Thornton, *Cultivating Gentlemen*, 141–145; and Story, *Forging of an Aristocracy*, 5–6. Ronald Story, reporting on the composition of the Athenaeum leadership very exactly (14 and n. 45), identifies five distinct "clans" that populated the power base of the institution in its heyday after 1830: Quincy-Adams-Shaw; Perkins-Cary-Forbes-Cushing; Lowell-Jackson-Lee-Higginson-Cabot; Gray; and Appleton.

11. Robert A. McCaughey, *Josiah Quincy, 1772–1864: The Last Federalist* (Cambridge, Mass.: Harvard University Press, 1974), 2; David Tyack, *George Ticknor and the Boston Brahmins* (Cambridge, Mass.: Harvard University Press, 1967), 17.

12. Thornton's eloquent study of gentlemen farmers, *Cultivating Gentlemen*, probes the symbolic power of rural pursuits for Boston elites during this period.

13. Charging Records, vol. 1 (1827–1834); vol. 2 (1835–1843); vol. 3 (1844–1849), vol. 4 (1849–1850), and vol. 5 (1851), Boston Athenaeum (hereafter BA). Some of the readers whose habits I discuss had large personal libraries, so the Charging Records merely suggest a larger trend. In addition, one must remember that withdrawing books is not the same as reading books; one can imagine that some of the books taken out by Athenaeum shareholders were read only by their family members or by friends or by no one at all. Still, the fact that the books were selected and handled by the proprietor indicates more than a passing interest.

14. BA Proprietors' Records, 23 January 1823 and 4 February 1828. Ticknor and Bowditch's subcommittee recommended that the proprietors continue to pay a five-dollar annual assessment for the privilege of taking out books. The subcommittee cited the necessity of the added income for future purchases: "It cannot be forgotten that the value of . . . a library is generally in proportion to the number of volumes it contains." Furthermore, the subcommittee recommended that only the trustees—and not the entire group of proprietors—be granted the authority to withhold certain rare and costly books from circulation; they deemed any scrutiny from the larger group to be "impractical." According to the minutes, these recommendations provoked "considerable debate." After a vote was taken, 43 proprietors did not endorse these individuals (who were also running for board positions) or their agenda; 107 proprietors stood with the reformers.

15. These conclusions are based on a comparison of the library inventory in 1824 with a chart of purchases dated 1828. Unfortunately, the categories in these two records are not identical, so comparisons must remain broad. "Report of the Standing Committee to the Proprietors," January 1824, BA Letters; and BA Proprietors' Records, 5 January 1829.

16. Stray notes about acquisitions appear the next year, too, urging the purchase of works "on the subject of railroads" and the completion of all "imperfect sets" as soon as possible. BA Trustees' Records, 12 May 1829.

17. Many of the same men—Quincy, Bowditch, Gray, and Ward—would soon move on to reform Harvard University in the 1830s. Again, see Story, *Forging of an Aristocracy*, 41–56. In a sense, this team of intellects/businessmen rehearsed their ensemble management style at the Athenaeum before transferring it to Harvard. Story notes the strong presence of a "Salem element" and the pejorative tone that older elites attached to it. Bowditch, Gray, and Ward had all moved to Boston from Salem in the early nineteenth century, and for that reason they were initially viewed as overreaching arrivistes.

18. Stanley Cushing and David Dearinger, eds. *Acquired Tastes: 200 Years of Collecting for the Boston Athenaeum* (Boston: Boston Athenaeum, 2006), 17–18.

19. For the parallel Harvard ethos, see Story, *Forging of an Aristocracy*, 77 and passim.

20. To eminent Bostonians, self-discipline (in both church and state) was the watchword. Internal disagreements among Unitarians—specifically, arguments about how radical the emerging Transcendental movement was—amounted to what one scholar calls a family quarrel. See Lawrence Buell, *New England Literary Culture: From Revolution through Renaissance* (Cambridge: Cambridge University Press, 1986), 46–47.

21. After visiting the United States, Dickens published his *American Notes* in 1842. He is quoted in Eugene P. Moehring, *Urban America and the Foreign Traveler, 1815–1855* (New York: Arno Press, 1974), 25. Tocqueville made his comments after visiting Boston in September 1831. See Alexis de Tocqueville, *Journey to America*, trans. George Lawrence, ed. J. P. Mayer (New Haven, Conn.: Yale University Press, 1960), 202–203. The phrase "Athens of America" originated with William Tudor, a Boston Athenaeum founder who, according to *Bacon's Dictionary of Boston* (1886), in 1819 wrote to a friend in Philadelphia, "This town is perhaps the most perfect and certainly the best regulated democracy that ever existed. There is something so

imposing in the immortal flame of Athens that the name makes everything modern shrink from comparison; but since the days of that glorious city, I know of none that has approached so near in some points, distant as it may still be from that illustrious model."

22. Everett quoted in Dorothy C. Broaddus, *Genteel Rhetoric: Writing High Culture in Nineteenth-Century Boston* (Columbia: University of South Carolina Press, 1999), 3.

23. Thomas H. O'Connor, *The Athens of America: Boston, 1825–1845* (Amherst: University of Massachusetts Press, 2006), 91–125.

24. Richard Wendorf, "Athenaeum Origins," in Wendorf, ed., *The Boston Athenaeum: Bicentennial Essays* (Boston: Boston Athenaeum, 2009). I am grateful to Maria Tymoczko for helping me consider these buried assumptions about "the new Athens."

25. Clifford S. Griffin, *Their Brothers' Keepers: Moral Stewardship in the United States, 1800–1865* (New Brunswick, N.J.: Rutgers University Press, 1960), xii.

26. "Boston Athenaeum," in *Monthly Anthology and Boston Review* 4 (November 1807): 601 (author unidentified, probably William Shaw), quoted in Lewis P. Simpson, *The Man of Letters in New England and the South: Essays on the History of the Literary Vocation in America* (Baton Rouge: Louisiana State University Press, 1973), 57–58.

27. See Edwin Harrison Cady, *The Gentleman in America: A Literary Study in American Culture* (Syracuse, N.Y.: Syracuse University Press, 1949); John F. Kasson, *Rudeness and Civility: Manners in Nineteenth-Century Urban America* (New York: Hill and Wang, 1990), 34–35. In 1827, "life subscriber" William Lyman twice withdrew Brackenridge's *Modern Chivalry* (1792–1797, revised 1805); see BA Charging Records, vol. 1.

28. Cady, *Gentleman in America*, 14. For a cogent revision of Story's analysis of Harvard, see Richard D. Brown, "Who Should Rule at Home? The Establishment of the Brahmin Upper Class," *Reviews in American History*, March 1981, 55–61.

29. Cady, *Gentleman in America*, 13–14. Thomas Ward took out Chesterfield's book in the late 1820s (BA Charging Records, vol. 1); after thirty editions, an Americanized version of his etiquette manual appeared in 1827: Karen Haltunnen, *Confidence Men and Painted Women: A Study of Middle-Class Culture in America, 1830–1870* (New Haven, Conn.: Yale University Press, 1982), 94. The Richardson novel referred to is *The History of Sir Charles Grandison* (1753–1754). John Locke's *Some Thoughts concerning Education* (1693) was a popular conduct book at the Athenaeum, and George Washington's "Rules of Civility & Decent Behavior" was influential. See also Arthur M. Schlesinger, *Learning To Behave: A Historical Study of American Etiquette Books* (New York: Macmillan, 1946).

30. Tyack, *Ticknor*, 145; BA Charging Records, vols. 1–3. A sure sign of popularity, volumes of the Waverly series often went missing from the shelves; see library inventory reports in BA Proprietors' Records, 1835–1838.

31. See Story, *Forging of an Aristocracy*, 110. Again (65), the cultural practices of Harvard and the Athenaeum often overlapped; one-third of men appointed to Harvard professorships in the antebellum era were officers at the Boston Athenaeum.

32. William Atkinson, *A Letter to a Young Man Who Has Just Entered College, from an Older One Who Has Been Through* (Boston: Crosby and Nichols, 1849), 37, 29 (for Atkinson's borrowing habits, see BA Charging Records, vol. 2); Daniel Walker Howe, *The Political Culture of the American Whigs* (Chicago: University of Chicago, 1979), 31; and Howe, *The Unitarian Conscience: Harvard Moral Philosophy* (Cambridge, Mass.: Harvard University Press, 1970).

33. Broaddus, *Genteel Rhetoric*, 8, 23–24, 82; "Professor Channing and His Lectures," *North American Review*, January 1857, 34–48; Edward T. Channing, "The Abuses of Political Discussion," *North-American Review and Miscellaneous Journal*, January 1817; 192–201; William Ellery Channing, *Slavery* (Boston: J. Munroe, 1835).

34. *The Essays of Ralph Waldo Emerson*, ed. Alfred R. Ferguson and Jean Ferguson Carr (Cambridge, Mass.: Harvard University Press/Belknap, 2006 [1841, 1844]), 73, 77, 85, 87. According to records at Harvard's Houghton Library, a version of "Manners" may have been delivered as a lecture as early as February 1837. A similar lecture (called "Natural Aristocracy") possibly originated in the late 1840s but appeared only posthumously. Emerson's eclec-

tic borrowings at the Athenaeum are noted in the BA Charging Records; for a complete record, see Kenneth Walter Cameron, *Ralph Waldo Emerson's Reading: A Guide for Source-Hunters and Scholars* (Raleigh, N.C.: Thistle Press, 1941).

35. I borrowed this list of reasons from Cady, *Gentleman in America*, 27. Taken together, they suggest an "Athenaeum sensibility." See Daniel Wickberg, "What Is the History of Sensibilities? On Cultural Histories Old and New," *American Historical Review*, June 2007, 1–27. Wickberg defines "sensibility" as "a pattern of moral and emotional understanding."

36. Richard Eddy Sykes, "Massachusetts Unitarianism and Social Change: A Religious Social System in Transition, 1780–1870" (Ph.D. diss., University of Minnesota, 1966), 283. For two fine examples that cover, respectively, geographical and emotional territory, see the environmental history by Norman B. Leventhal, Alex Krieger, and David Cobb, *Mapping Boston* (Cambridge, Mass.: MIT Press, 1999); and the sociopolitical history by J. Anthony Lukas, *Common Ground: A Turbulent Decade in the Lives of Three American Families* (New York: Vintage Books, 1986). The latter, a profound group portrait, touches on class and race but moves beyond both.

37. Elizabeth Hardwick, "Boston," in *A View of My Own: Essays in Literature and Society* (New York: Farrar, Straus and Cudahy, 1962), 146.

CHAPTER ONE

1. William Smith Shaw, Washington, to Arthur Maynard Walter, Boston, 16 December 1800, Shaw Papers, BA. Unless otherwise noted, citations for the Shaw-Walter correspondence refer to this Boston Athenaeum collection, and when possible the locations of both correspondents are cited.

2. Stanley Cushing and David Dearinger, eds. *Acquired Tastes: 200 Years of Collecting for the Boston Athenaeum* (Boston: Boston Athenaeum, 2006), 16. The sartorial detail is from William Tudor, one of Shaw's contemporaries.

3. Samuel Cary to Shaw, undated, Shaw Papers, BA; Josiah Quincy, *The History of the Boston Athenaeum, with Biographical Notices of Its Deceased Founders* (Boston: Boston Athenaeum, 1851), 64 (the "Biographical Notices" are repaginated at the back of the volume), hereafter cited as Quincy, *History*. See also Charles Knowles Bolton, *The Athenaeum Centenary: The Influence and History of the Boston Athenaeum from 1807 to 1907 with a Record of Its Officers and Benefactors and a Complete List of Proprietors* (Boston: Boston Athenaeum, 1907), 26. Samuel Cary was the assistant minister at King's Chapel in Boston after 1809. Organized first as an Anglican (1686) and later as a Unitarian (1789) church, King's Chapel is still home to an active congregation.

4. Much has been written on the anxieties inherent in the early republic: see, e.g., Robert A. Ferguson, *The American Enlightenment: 1750–1820* (Cambridge, Mass.: Harvard University Press, 1997); Gordon S. Wood, ed., *The Rising Glory of America, 1760–1820*, rev. ed. (Boston: Northeastern University Press, 1990); and Henry May, *The Enlightenment in America* (New York: Oxford University Press, 1976). On the interconnectedness of literature and the law, see Robert A. Ferguson, *Law and Letters in American Culture* (Cambridge: Harvard University Press, 1984).

5. For more on Shaw, see Joseph B. Felt, *Memorials of William Smith Shaw* (Boston: S. K. Whipple, 1852); Quincy, "Biographical Notices," in *History*, 22–44; and Lewis P. Simpson, ed., *The Federalist Literary Mind: Selections from "The Monthly Anthology and Boston Review," 1803–1811, including Documents Relating to the Boston Athenaeum* (Baton Rouge: Louisiana State University Press, 1962), 232.

6. Anthony Mann argues persuasively that the Federalists' reputation for anglomania is too crudely characterized in most historiography; contrary to many scholars, Mann claims that it was to the provincial bourgeoisie (merchants, mostly), not to the landed aristocracy, that these men turned for models of social and economic institutions—and even then, their views were more critical than has been generally believed. Anthony Mann, "'A Nation First

in All the Arts of Civilization': Boston's Post-Revolutionary Elites View Great Britain," *American Nineteenth-Century History* 2 (Summer 2001): 1–34.

7. Young Walter spent his early childhood in Halifax, but his family returned to Boston in 1791. For more on Walter, see Quincy, "Biographical Notices," in *History*, 13–21; and Simpson, *Federalist Literary Mind*, 233.

8. Walter, Boston, to Shaw, Quincy, 12 October 1798, Shaw Papers. Addison's play *Cato* (1713) was popular throughout the eighteenth century. In his *Life of Samuel Johnson* (1791) Boswell wants to "enable mankind" to see Johnson live, "and to 'live o'er each scene' with him." Boswell, *Life of Johnson* (Oxford: Oxford University Press, 1953), 22.

9. Walter, New York, to Shaw, Philadelphia, 29 March 1799, Shaw Papers. The "Literary Club" founded in London in 1764 included author Samuel Johnson (1709–1784), portraitist Sir Joshua Reynolds (1723–1792), editor and lawyer Edmund Malone (1741–1812), and political philosopher Edmund Burke (1729–1797), among others. *The Pursuits of Literature* was a satire by T. J. Mathias (1754–1835), published in parts from 1792 to 1798. "Sinclair" was probably Sir John Sinclair (1754–1835), a Scottish writer on finance and agriculture. Topham Beauclerk (1739–1780) was a man about London and a younger friend of Samuel Johnson.

10. On the Anthology Society, see Quincy, *History*, 1–11; M. A. DeWolfe Howe, ed., *Journal of the Proceedings of the Society Which Conducts the Monthly Anthology and Boston Review, October 3, 1805, to July 2, 1811* (Boston: Boston Athenaeum, 1910); and Simpson, *Federalist Literary Mind*, 3–41. For helpful analysis of the periodical's content and purpose, I relied on Simpson and on Catherine O'Donnell Kaplan, " 'We Have Joys They Do Not Know': Letters, Federalism, and Sentiment in the New Nation, 1790–1812" (Ph.D. diss., University of Michigan, 1998).

11. David S. Shields, *Civil Tongues and Polite Letters in British America* (Chapel Hill: University of North Carolina Press, 1997); Peter Clark, *British Clubs and Societies, 1580–1800: The Origins of an Associational World* (New York: Oxford University Press, 2000).

12. Howe, *Journal of the Proceedings of the Society*, 238.

13. Simpson, *Federalist Literary Mind*, 19; Howe, *Journal of the Proceedings of the Society*, 243, 120, 128.

14. Felt, *Memorials*, 213–214.

15. "Reminiscences of Robert Hallowell Gardiner," BA, Anthology Society Records. (Dated 1861, this source appears as eight typed pages, clearly assembled from older originals.) Since the Anthologists intended their reading room to operate on the basis of subscriptions, the word "public" might ring false to us. Even if one accepts its anachronistic use, the statement that there was at the time "no public reading room" is misleading. The subscription-based Boston Library Society, founded in 1794, predated the Anthology Society—and could also claim female founders, in contrast to the Anthology Society's (and Athenaeum's) all-male origins. In 1939 the Library Society was absorbed by the Athenaeum. Michael Wentworth, with Elizabeth Lamb Clark, *The Boston Library Society, 1794–1994: An Exhibition of Portraits, Views, and Materials Related to the Foundation of the Society and Some of Its Early Members* (Boston: Boston Athenaeum, 1995).

16. Felt, *Memorials*, 213–214; "Reminiscences of Robert Hallowell Gardiner."

17. Howe, *Journal of the Proceedings of the Society*, 114; Quincy, "Biographical Notices," in *History*, 38, 63–64; and Felt, *Memorials*, 328.

18. Arthur Maynard Walter, London Journals, 1803–1804, 29 December 1804, Walter Papers, BA; Samuel Knapp, *Extracts from the Journal of Marshal Soult, Addressed to a Friend: How Obtained, and By Whom Translated, Is Not a Subject of Enquiry* (Newburyport, Mass.: William E. Allen, 1817), 15–16 (this is a satirical description of life in Boston by the fictional Marshal Soult; Knapp [1783–1838], writer and lawyer, served as a biographer to his contemporaries).

19. William Tudor (1779–1830), remarks on William Smith Shaw attached to a treatise titled "Observations upon the State of Our Jurisprudence, Or a Collection of a Series of Papers upon That Subject," published originally in the *Citoyen Français*, undated, BA The remarks about Shaw appear to have been copied down by Shaw himself, as they are introduced by these words in the same handwriting: "Tudor wrote these observations & when he returned

from Paris presented them to me—saying with good natured sarcasm. . . ." Shaw seems to have relished his own odd reputation.

20. Boston minister Joseph Stevens Buckminster, as Lawrence Buell writes, "is a pivotal but elusive figure in New England intellectual history." Now credited with giving the sermon form a more essayistic style, he was eulogized as a tragic genius after his early death from epilepsy. Buell, "Joseph Stevens Buckminster: The Making of a New England Saint," *Canadian Review of American Studies* 10 (Spring 1979): 1–29. His close relationship with Walter and Shaw is evident from the correspondence.

21. What Bruce Redford calls "epistolary performance" in *The Converse of the Pen: Acts of Intimacy in the Eighteenth-Century Familiar Letter* (Chicago: University of Chicago Press, 1986) informs my examination of the Shaw-Walter letters; Redford argues that the eighteenth-century letter, like the eighteenth-century conversation, depended on the idea of performance. Letter-writers, according to Redford, found substitutes for the devices of an actor such as gesture, impersonation, inflection.

22. Walter, Boston, to Shaw, Quincy, 12 October 1798, Shaw Papers.

23. Ronald J. Zboray, *A Fictive People: Antebellum Economic Development and the American Reading Public* (New York: Oxford University Press, 1993), 114.

24. "No, Shaw, I boast not of writing letters like Chesterfield or Pope," Walter writes self-consciously, from Boston, to Shaw, 24 October 1798. On self-conscious letter-writing, see Richard L. Bushman, *The Refinement of America: Persons, Houses, Cities* (New York: Vintage Books, 1992), 90–92. Though not wealthy, Walter and Shaw were members of the elite and had ties to the axes of power in Boston, New York, and Philadelphia; they were aware of their positions in the hierarchy of American men. In *Converse of the Pen*, 9, Bruce Redford suggests criteria by which to judge letter-writing: autonomy (the ability of a writer to create his or her own microcosmic context on the page), fertility (consistency of output), and versatility (talent in tailoring the work to the particular recipient); Walter shows some mastery in all areas, but Shaw does not demonstrate extraordinary epistolary talent.

25. E. Anthony Rotundo, *American Manhood: Transformations in Masculinity from the Revolution to the Modern Era* (New York: Basic Books, 1993), 82–91. The categories "homosexual" and "heterosexual" were nonexistent in the eighteenth (and much of the nineteenth) century. For more on same-sex intimacy, see Carol Smith-Rosenberg's landmark essay, "The Female World of Love and Ritual: Relations between Women in Nineteenth-Century America," *Signs* 1 (Autumn 1975); and Christopher Looby, " 'Innocent Homosexuality': The Fiedler Thesis in Retrospect," in *Mark Twain, "Adventures of Huckleberry Finn": A Case Study in Critical Controversy* (Boston: Bedford Books, 1995). Walter and Shaw socialized with women but fretted about marriage. For example, Shaw writes to Walter, "I am quite lonely. I have spent but two evenings out of the house here since I left you. One of those was to see a couple swing by Hymen's noose, from the gallows of celibacy into the eternity of matrimony. Horrid dull, horrid dull!" Shaw, Atkinson, N.H., to Walter, Boston, 23 January 1798.

26. Walter, New York, to Shaw, 11 March 1799; Walter to Shaw, Haverhill, Mass., 27 June 1798; Shaw, Philadelphia, to Walter, New York, 12 December 1798; Walter, New York, to Shaw, Philadelphia, 19 December 1798; Shaw, Quincy, to Walter, Boston, 31 October 1798. William Ellery Channing (1780–1842) became a celebrated Unitarian minister.

27. Benevolus, "On Friendship," *Monthly Anthology and Boston Review* 1 (June 1804): 354.

28. Walter, Boston, to Shaw, Atkinson, N.H., 29 January 1798; Shaw, Quincy, to Walter, 26 April 1799, quoted in Kaplan, "We Have Joys," 29. For an exploration of another circle of American men for whom sympathy mattered, see Caleb Crain, *American Sympathy: Men, Friendship, and Literature in the New Nation* (New Haven: Yale University Press, 2001).

29. Daniel Walker Howe, *The Unitarian Conscience: Harvard Moral Philosophy, 1805–1861* (Cambridge, Mass.: Harvard University Press, 1970), 63–64, 95–97.

30. Walter, London Journals, 1803–1804, 20 November 1803.

31. Hugh Blair, (1718–1800), *An Abridgment of Lectures on Rhetorick*, ed. J. L. Blake, 5th ed. (Concord, N.H.: Jacob B. Moore, 1825), 11; Dorothy C. Broaddus, *Genteel Rhetoric: Writing High*

Culture in Nineteenth-Century Boston (Columbia: University of South Carolina Press, 1999), 9, 28. Broaddus claims that the Harvard men who were taught by professor of rhetoric Edward Everett in the 1820s (and Edward T. Channing from 1819 through 1851) absorbed a potent blend of rhetorical principles derived from Cicero, Scottish Enlightenment philosophy, and the Christian story—and went on to position themselves as prophets of high culture. Everett matriculated at Harvard a few years after Shaw and Walter had left; nevertheless, the intellectual atmosphere was undoubtedly similar for all three men.

32. William Shaw, scraps of a diary, October 1802, Shaw Papers; Walter, New York, to Shaw, 29 March 1799.

33. Shaw, Atkinson, N.H., to Walter, Boston, 6 January 1798.

34. Shaw, Quincy, to Walter, Boston, 7 July 1800; Walter, Boston, to Shaw, Quincy, 12 October 1798. On "the progress of the arts," see Simpson, *Federalist Literary Mind*, 31–41; see also Chapter 2 of this book.

35. Walter, Boston, to Shaw, 3 October 1799. Reminiscent of Cyrano de Bergerac's exploits as later rendered by Edmond Rostand, Walter's offer to aid Shaw with a love letter is the stuff of romantic drama.

36. Walter, Boston, to Shaw, Philadelphia, 27 March 1800; Walter, Philadelphia, to Shaw, Boston, 16 October 1802; Walter, Boston, to Shaw, Philadelphia, 2 April 1800.

37. See Lewis P. Simpson, *The Man of Letters in New England and the South: Essays on the History of the Literary Vocation in America* (Baton Rouge: Louisiana State University Press, 1973), 32–61, esp. 58. Walter, Boston, to Shaw, 12 October 1798; Walter, Boston, to Shaw, 12 October 1798; Walter, New York, to Shaw, Quincy, 1 June 1799. Shaw's father, though dead by this time, was still a strong memory. For more on the Federalists' insistence on amateurism, see William Charvat, *The Profession of Authorship in America, 1800–1870*, ed. Matthew J. Bruccoli (Athens: Ohio State University Press, 1968), 283–297. For a compelling discussion of professions in this era, see Bryan Waterman, *The Republic of Intellect: The Friendly Club and the Making of American Literature* (Baltimore, Md.: Johns Hopkins University Press, 2007).

38. Shaw, Washington, to Walter, 16 January 1800; Shaw, Washington, to Walter, 11 December 1800; Shaw, Boston, to Walter, London, July 1803; Shaw, Boston, to Walter, London, 4 February 1803.

39. Quincy, "Biographical Notices," in *History*, 18.

40. Joseph Buckminster, London, to Shaw, Boston, 22 February 1807, quoted in Eliza Buckminster Lee, *Memoirs of Rev. Joseph Buckminster, D.D., and His Son, Rev. Joseph Stevens Buckminster, D.D.* (Boston: Wm. Crosby and H. P. Nichols, 1849), 304–305; Shaw, Boston, to Buckminster, 13 May 1807, quoted in Quincy, "Biographical Notices," in *History*, 19; Josiah Quincy, Washington, to Shaw, Boston, 10 February 1807, quoted in Felt, *Memorials*, 237.

41. Family of Arthur Maynard Walter to William Smith Shaw, 14 January 1807, Shaw Papers.

42. Blair, *Abridgment of Lectures*, 236; Broaddus, *Genteel Rhetoric*, 8–9. See also George Kennedy, *Classical Rhetoric and Its Christian and Secular Tradition* (Chapel Hill: University of North Carolina Press, 1980).

43. Wood, *Rising Glory of America*, 6.

44. See Mark Mitchell and David Leavitt, eds., *Pages Passed from Hand to Hand: The Hidden Tradition of Homosexual Literature in English from 1748–1914* (Boston: Houghton Mifflin, 1997).

45. BA Trustees' Records, 2 July 1810, 7 January and 1 July 1811. A salary of $300 a year was agreed upon by the trustees as compensation for the combined duties of librarian and secretary; however, Shaw apparently never accepted payment for his services: Felt, *Memorials*, 292; BA Trustees' Records, 7 April 1808; Quincy, "Biographical Notices," in *History*, 41.

46. See Simpson, *Man of Letters*. See also Timothy Patrick Duffy, "The Gender of Letters: The Man of Letters and Intellectual Authority in Nineteenth-Century Boston" (Ph.D. diss., University of Virginia, 1993).

47. Joseph Stevens Buckminster, "The Dangers and Duties of Men of Letters," Phi Beta Kappa Society address, Harvard University, 31 August 1809, quoted in Simpson, *Federalist Literary Mind*, 102.

48. Simpson, *Federalist Literary Mind*, 78, and Kaplan, "We Have Joys," 13.

49. Jean Baudrillard, "The System of Collecting," in *The Cultures of Collecting*, ed. John Elsner and Roger Cardinal (Cambridge, Mass.: Harvard University Press, 1994), 11 (translated by Roger Cardinal; italics appear in the original).

50. Shaw to Eliza Sargent, no year, Shaw Papers.

51. Peale and Shaw died within a year of each other (Wood, *Rising Glory of America*, 17, 117). For a time, Shaw had directed the Linnaean Society, an association dedicated to natural science that was housed with the Athenaeum.

52. "Duties to Be Performed at the Boston Athenaeum," undated manuscript, BA. See also Bolton, *Athenaeum Centenary*, 27.

53. John Thornton Kirkland, *Memoir of the Boston Athenaeum* (1807), in Quincy, *History*, 30, 36.

54. Elizabeth Shaw Peabody to William Smith Shaw, 25 August 1812, quoted in Felt, *Memorials*, 293.

55. Shaw, Washington, to Walter, 11 December 1800.

56. Buckminster confessed a similar prejudice for exclusivity when he warned Shaw about the Anthology Society: "Be careful, I beseech you, about admitting new members. I am very much afraid that, during my absence, you will metamorphose it from a club of friends into a club of editors." No date. Quoted in Lee, *Memoirs*, 236.

57. For an introduction to the history of emotions, see Peter N. Stearns and Jan Lewis, eds., *An Emotional History of the United States* (New York: New York University Press, 1998).

58. The ambiguity of institutional missions is often troubling. James Smithson's bequest for what became the Smithsonian specified funds for "the increase and diffusion of knowledge." Various interpretations of that language resulted in conflicting goals. Wilcomb E. Washburn, "Joseph Henry's Conception of the Purpose of the Smithsonian Institution," in Walter Muir Whitehill, ed., *A Cabinet of Curiosities: Five Episodes in the Evolution of American Art Museums* (Charlottesville: University of Virginia Press, 1967), 106–166. The late editor of that volume, a celebrated director and librarian of the Boston Athenaeum, no doubt witnessed at close hand the Athenaeum's own discontinuous evolution—though that story is not told.

59. Shields, *Civil Tongues*, 318.

60. Samuel Goodenow to William Smith Shaw, 19 November 1810, quoted in Felt, *Memorials*, 285; Shaw, Boston, to Thaddeus Harris, London, 13 November 1810; William Sumner, Philadelphia, to Shaw, Boston, 25 January 1808; Quincy, *History*, 66. At the January 1819 trustees' meeting, the tally of volumes came to 11,958 owned by the Athenaeum, with another 7,500 on loan from the American Academy of Arts and Sciences and individual lenders (BA Trustees' Records).

Chapter Two

1. The original *Memoir of the Boston Athenaeum*, 1807 (John Thornton Kirkland, in Quincy, *History*), states, under the Act of Incorporation, *"Be it further enacted,* That it shall and may be lawful for the said corporation to have a common seal for their use and benefit." After considering an earlier design overcrowded with Homeric references, the trustees welcomed a simpler, more elegant seal. See John Davis, 11 April 1812, in BA, *Athenaeum Letters*. See also *Athenaeum Items* 1 (March 1934). Figure 2.1 is the current seal, which is virtually identical to the prototype that was approved in 1814. The Athenaeum's device is, strictly speaking, a hybrid of seal and emblem; seals were used as official stamps, to furnish marks on contracts, whereas emblems were moralistic and fanciful—what one scholar calls a "curious knot that ties man to his world" (John Manning, *The Emblem* (London: Reaktion Books, 2002). Since the accepted design was adapted from one that originated in an Italian emblem book, I focus on that tradition in my brief interpretation; however, I use the three terms—seal, device, and emblem—interchangeably to refer to the Athenaeum's symbol. I am grateful to my late father, Nikolaus Wolff, for his help in translating the preface to the Italian folio of emblems by

Michelangelo de La Chausse (1660–1738): *Le gemme antiche: Figurate di Michelangelo Causeo de La Chausse, Parigino; Consagrate all' eminentissimo e reverendissimo principe Il Signor Cardinale Cesare Destrees* (Rome, 1700), in which the emblem in question appears on page 34.

2. Manning, *Emblem*, 186. For this analysis, I drew from a perceptive discussion of the Charleston Library Society's seal. See James Raven, *London Booksellers and American Customers: Transatlantic Literary Community and the Charleston Library Society, 1748–1811* (Columbia: University of South Carolina Press, 2002), 43. I also borrow the useful phrase "visual manifesto" from Raven. Sadly, though it is known that a man named John Skey Eustace (1760–1805) owned the Athenaeum copy of the original Italian emblem book, any written communication between the trustees and those who fashioned the Athenaeum emblem appears to be lost.

3. Joseph B. Felt, *Memorials of William Smith Shaw* (Boston: S. K. Whipple, 1852), chap. 1. Shaw was considered to have a fragile constitution. On page 33 of his tribute, Felt makes note of Shaw's frequent "dangerous coughs" and calls him "more like the sensitive plant than the young oak."

4. Quoted in M. A. DeWolfe Howe, ed., *Journal of the Proceedings of the Society Which Conducts the Monthly Anthology and Boston Review, October 3, 1805, to July 2, 1811* (Boston: Boston Athenaeum, 1910), 19.

5. Much as the official emblem follows a design crafted by an Italian subject eager for his prince's approval, in some very real sense the Boston gentlemen sought the approval of their own self-appointed patrons-in-kind: Europeans who championed human reason over blind authority, natural rights over royal prerogatives.

6. Quoted in Lewis P. Simpson, ed., *The Federalist Literary Mind: Selections from "The Monthly Anthology and Boston Review," 1803–1811, including Documents Relating to the Boston Athenaeum* (Baton Rouge: Louisiana State University Press, 1962), 31–41.

7. Gordon S. Wood, ed., *The Rising Glory of America, 1760–1820*, rev. ed. (Boston: Northeastern University Press, 1990), 8.

8. Ronald Story, "Class and Culture in Boston: The Athenaeum, 1807–1860," *American Quarterly* 27 (May 1975): 178–199.

9. Anthony Mann, "'A Nation First in All the Arts of Civilization': Boston's Post-Revolutionary Elites View Great Britain," *American Nineteenth-Century History* 2 (Summer 2001): 23.

10. Even when the Athenaeum collection was relatively small, the library kept two copies of Roscoe's *Life of Lorenzo de' Medici*, as well as numerous other Roscoe works, presumably to meet the demand; see *Catalogue of Books in the Boston Athenaeum* (Boston: William L. Lewis, 1827). The circulation records reveal that Nathan Appleton withdrew *The Life of William Roscoe*, by Henry Roscoe, in 1833, and Thomas W. Ward withdrew Roscoe's *Leo X* in the mid-1830s. Charles Jackson, Edward G. Davis, Josiah Quincy Jr., Ebenezer Francis, and others also withdrew books by or about Roscoe. See BA Charging Records, vols. 1–2. According to Roscoe's son, the orator Edward Everett and the biographer Jared Sparks (both Athenaeum readers) also corresponded with William Roscoe regularly.

11. The new work was Roscoe's biography of Leo X. Walter's meeting, if it happened, is apparently not documented. Arthur Maynard Walter, Boston, to William Smith Shaw, Washington, 29 January 1800; Walter, Liverpool, to Shaw, Boston, 22 December 1802, Shaw Papers, BA.

12. Francis Parkman, "Diary 1811–1813," 22 April 1812, quoted in Mann, "A Nation First," 25.

13. Story, "Class and Culture," 185.

14. George Ticknor, *Life, Letters, and Journals*, ed. George S. Hillard, 2 vols. (Boston: Houghton Mifflin, 1909 [1875]), 1:51.

15. Henry Roscoe, *The Life of William Roscoe*, 2 vols. (London: T. Cadell, 1833), 2:103–118; Ticknor, *Life, Letters, and Journals*, 1:298.

16. Andrew B. Myers, *The Worlds of Washington Irving, 1783–1859* (Tarrytown, N.Y.: Sleepy Hollow Restorations / New York Public Library, 1974), 36. In 1822, Ralph Waldo Emerson, a

famous Athenaeum reader, refers to Irving's "fine Sketchbook style" in a letter to a friend; see *The Letters of Ralph Waldo Emerson*, ed. Ralph L. Rusk, 6 vols. (New York: Columbia University Press, 1939), 1:122. An 1820 copy of the *Sketchbook* was passed down from Athenaeum reader Charles Eliot to Henry Wadsworth Longfellow in 1837, and then from Longfellow to Eliot's son, Samuel, in 1872; see current online catalogue of Boston Athenaeum for details of the provenance: www.bostonathenaeum.org.

17. Ernst Robert Curtius, *European Literature and the Latin Middle Ages*, trans. Willard R. Trask (Princeton, N.J.: Princeton University Press / Bollingen Paperbacks, 1983 [1953]), 160.

18. Washington Irving, *The Sketchbook of Geoffrey Crayon, Gentleman*, 2nd ed. (London: John Murray, 1820), 7, 23–24.

19. Story, "Class and Culture," 187–188. Martin Archer Shee (1769–1850) was president of the Royal Academy of Arts from 1830 to 1850. For more on Shee, see *The Life of Sir Martin Archer Shee, President of the Royal Academy, by His Son, Martin Archer Shee*, 2 vols. (London: Longman, 1860). Gilbert Stuart (1755–1828) produced more than a thousand portraits of his socially and politically prominent sitters; he died in Boston, where he had lived his last years.

20. Irving, *Sketchbook*, 25–26, 32, 33, 36. Roscoe's songs and poetry "swept the country" in the late eighteenth and early nineteenth centuries, according to one historian. His children's verses were especially popular. See George Chandler, *Liverpool* (London: B. T. Batsford, 1857), 435; and, Chandler, *William Roscoe of Liverpool, 1753–1831* (London: B. T. Batsford, 1853).

21. Jeffrey Rubin-Dorsky, "Washington Irving: Sketches of Anxiety," *American Literature* 58 (December 1986): 499–522, points to an intriguing paradox relevant to the project of founding American cultural institutions, as well: "American anxiety and solicitude to establish a national literature made it impossible for [American] critics to recognize that the source from which literature would emanate was that anxiety itself" (509). Irving's sketch also stands within the context of the literary celebrity that was developing at the time; nineteenth-century Americans were beginning to exhibit curiosity about authors' homes. Literary pilgrimages (to Litchfield, England, the birthplace of Samuel Johnson, for example) were not uncommon (see Mann, "A Nation First," 17). Presumably, visiting an author's home allowed one to recreate, more directly, his or her manner of living and thus to judge the author's ethical and aesthetic codes with greater precision. In the case of Roscoe, the change of home (and status) instructed readers to look more closely at his constancy of character.

22. Michael Wentworth, introduction to *Fifty Books in the Collection of the Boston Athenaeum: An Exhibition Catalogue* (Boston: Boston Athenaeum, 1994), 15; Story, "Class and Culture," 181.

23. Roscoe, *Life of William Roscoe*, 2:53–56. See also Tamara Plakins Thornton, *Cultivating Gentlemen: The Meaning of Country Life among the Boston Elite, 1785–1860* (New Haven, Conn.: Yale University Press, 1989), 36–37; Mann, "A Nation First," 26.

24. Adrian Johns, *The Nature of the Book: Print and Knowledge in the Making* (Chicago: University of Chicago Press, 1998), 373, argues persuasively that only with the iteration (and, often, the manipulation) of personal character and reputation did the printed word gain credibility in early modern Europe. Johns's thesis serves as a corrective to Elizabeth Eisenstein's *The Printing Press as an Agent of Change: Communications and Cultural Transformations in Early Modern Europe* (Cambridge: Cambridge University Press, 1979), which treats the advent of "print culture" as the result of a revolution driven primarily by the technology of the press. Johns's work addresses issues of civility and credit that are integral to this study of the Athenaeum.

25. Jacques Ravel, "The Uses of Civility," in Roger Chartier, ed., *A History of Private Life: Passions of the Renaissance* (Cambridge Harvard University Press / Belknap Press, 1989), 3:173.

26. Thornton, *Cultivating Gentlemen*, 36.

27. Walter, Liverpool, to Shaw, Boston, 22 December 1802; Kirkland *Memoir of the Boston Athenaeum*, 37; Shaw, Boston, to Joseph Buckminster, London, 13 December 1806; N. Lawrence, Boston, to William Shepherd, near Liverpool, late summer or early fall 1808.

28. Two studies of etiquette discuss American uses of civility in this era. See John F. Kasson, *Rudeness and Civility: Manners in Nineteenth-Century Urban America* (New York: Hill and Wang, 1990); and Karen Haltunnen, *Confidence Men and Painted Women: A Study of Middle-Class Culture*

in America, 1830–1870 (New Haven, Conn.: Yale University Press, 1982). Both studies show that by the mid-nineteenth century, the self had become the most important unit (as opposed to family or church or even nation).

29. Paul Goodman, "Ethics and Enterprise: The Values of a Boston Elite, 1800–1860," *American Quarterly* 18 (August 1966): 448.

30. Roscoe, *Life of William Roscoe*, 2:53–54; Thomas Frognall Dibdin, *The Bibliomania; or, Book-Madness: Containing Some Account of the History, Symptoms, and Cure of This Fatal Disease* (London: Longman, Hurst, Rees, and Orme, 1809); Nicholas Basbanes, *A Gentle Madness: Bibliophiles, Bibliomanes, and the Eternal Passion for Books* (New York: Henry Holt, 1995), 25.

31. Anna Cabot Lowell to Anne Grant, Boston, 23 July 1810, quoted in Mann, "A Nation First," 16. Lowell anticipates the famous Scottish taunt from Sydney Smith: "Who reads an American book? Or goes to an American play? Or looks at an American statue?" (*Edinburgh Review,* January 1820).

32. Quoted in Quincy, "Biographical Notices," in *History*, 15. The two "gigantic" names that might seem less than gigantic to us now were, presumably, John Cudworth (1656–1726), who wrote on the early doctrine of the Church of England, and John Selden (1584–1654), the author of *Table Talk*, a posthumously published collection of essays.

33. Alain Corbain, "The Secret of the Individual," in ed. Michelle Perrot, *A History of Private Life: From the Fires of Revolution to the Great War* (Cambridge: Harvard University Press / Belknap Press, 1990), 4:545. See also Werner L. Muensterberger, *Collecting: An Unruly Passion* (Princeton, N.J.: Princeton University Press, 1993); John Elsner and Roger Cardinal, eds., *The Cultures of Collecting* (Cambridge: Harvard University Press, 1994); and Basbanes, *Gentle Madness*.

34. According to Richard Bushman, responses to the problem of America's status as a "cultural province of Great Britain" varied; he describes two extremes: a "renewed boosterism," in which Americans are moved to claim sophistication on their behalf, and the insistence on a "noble" and "simplistic" native style. On the whole, early Athenaeum advocates fall into the first camp. Richard L. Bushman, "American High-Style and Vernacular Cultures," in *Colonial British America: Essays in the New History of the Early Modern Era*, eds. Jack P. Greene and J. R. Pole (Baltimore: Johns Hopkins University Press, 1984), 309.

35. Simpson, *Federalist Literary Mind*, 31.

36. For more on Buckminster, see Andrews Norton, "Character of the Rev. Joseph Stevens Buckminster (1812), in *The Works of Joseph Stevens Buckminster, with Memoirs of His Life* (Boston: James Monroe, 1839); Eliza Buckminster Lee, *Memoirs of Rev. Joseph Buckminster, D.D., and His Son, Rev. Joseph Stevens Buckminster, D.D.* (Boston: Wm. Crosby and H. P. Nichols, 1849); Lawrence Buell, "Joseph Stevens Buckminster: The Making of a New England Saint," *Canadian Review of American Studies* 10 (Spring 1979): 1–29; and Lewis P. Simpson, *The Man of Letters in New England and the South: Essays on the History of the Literary Vocation in America* (Baton Rouge: Louisiana State University Press, 1973), 3–31.

37. Raven, *London Booksellers*, 7; David D. Hall, comments on "learned culture" for the ongoing *A History of the Book in America*, vol. 3, *The Industrial Book, 1840–1880* (Chapel Hill: University of North Carolina Press / American Antiquarian Society, 2007). I am grateful to Professor Hall for sharing his work-in-progress years ago.

38. William Smith Shaw, Boston, to Joseph Stevens Buckminster, London, 1 December 1806.

39. Shaw, Boston, to Buckminster, London, 13 December 1806. Shaw considered any Athenaeum member who was traveling abroad as a potential "book scout" for the institution. The Athenaeum would be chartered by the state legislature on February 13, 1807: see Simpson, *Federalist Literary Mind*, 29; Quincy, *History*, 18–22.

40. A paraphrase of that letter (July 16, 1806) is given in Felt, *Memorials*, 215. The original appears to be missing from the Shaw Papers at the Athenaeum.

41. Shaw, Boston, to Buckminster, London, 13 May 1807, quoted in Felt, *Memorials*, 243; Shaw, Boston, to Buckminster, London, 13 December 1806.

42. "Reflections on the Literary Delinquency of America," *North-American Review and Miscellaneous Journal*, November 1815, 37, 39–43.

43. Benjamin Franklin, *The Autobiography and Other Writings*, ed. Kenneth Silverman (New York: Viking/Penguin Books, 1986 [1771]), 77.

44. See Cathy N. Davidson, *Revolution and the Word: The Rise of the Novel in America* (New York: Oxford University Press, 1986), 27–30; David Kaser, *A Book for a Sixpence: The Circulating Library in America* (Pittsburgh: Beta Phi Mu, 1980); and Paul Kaufman, "The Community Library," in *Libraries and Their Users: Collected Papers in Library History* (London: Library Association, 1969).

45. Richard Brown, "Communications and Commerce: Information Diffusion in Northern Ports from the 1760s to the 1790s," in his *Knowledge Is Power: The Diffusion of Information in Early America, 1700–1865* (New York: Oxford University Press, 1989); Michael Wentworth, with Elizabeth Lamb Clark, *The Boston Library Society, 1794–1994: An Exhibition of Portraits, Views, and Materials Related to the Foundation of the Society and Some of Its Early Members* (Boston: Boston Athenaeum, 1995); Samuel S. Shaw, *The Boston Library Society: Historical Sketch* (Boston, 1895); Peter Dobkin Hall, "'To make us bold and learn to read—to be friends to each other and friends to the world': Libraries and the Origins of Civil Society in the United States," *Libraries & Culture* 31 (Winter 1996): 14–35.

46. The *North American Review* would again serve as a forum for these discussions. A book about its editors and contributors suggests that that journal was the most influential voice for cultural issues at the time. See Marshall Foletta, *Coming to Terms with Democracy: Federalist Intellectuals and the Shaping of American Culture* (Charlottesville: University Press of Virginia, 2001).

47. Nathan Hale, "Boston Athenaeum," *North American Review* 23 (June 1826): 206; Buckminster to Shaw, 3 April 1807, quoted in Simpson, *Federalist Literary Mind*, 30. Shaw had apparently requested from Buckminster only the dry transactions of various English learned societies.

48. Seth Bass had been the "keeper" of the East India Marine Society's Museum, in Salem; he was also a shareholder of the Salem Athenaeum. The Boston Athenaeum made a financial investment in professionalism by increasing its expenditure for a librarian from a mere $562 in 1825 (a year before Bass's tenure began) to $2,375 in 1839. Bass continued as head librarian until 1846, at which point Charles Folsom was hired from Harvard, and Bass became assistant librarian. See BA Proprietors' Records, 2 January 1826 and 6 January 1840; BA Trustees' Records, 28 January 1825.

49. A harmonious tone had pervaded the Anthology Society, too; assumptions about a shared audience and a shared purpose were common to both the original society and the Athenaeum. See Catherine O'Donnell Kaplan, "'We Have Joys They Do Not Know': Letters, Federalism, and Sentiment in the New Nation, 1790–1812" (Ph.D. diss., University of Michigan, 1998), 174; Johns, *Nature of the Book*, 379.

50. Catharina Slautterback, *Designing the Boston Athenaeum: 10½ at 150* (Boston: Boston Athenaeum, 1999), 11–15. The American architect Charles Bulfinch (1763–1844) designed many of the homes on Beacon Hill—as well as numerous institutions in the Boston area. He was influenced by the work of William Chambers and Robert Adam. His style is characterized by symmetrical flat brick facades, flared lintels, recessed arches, and decorative ironwork on the *piano nobile*.

51. "Memoir of James Perkins," *Proceedings of the Massachusetts Historical Society* 1 (April 1823): 361 (he also owned an estate called Pine Bank, on Jamaica Pond near Brookline, for use during the summer months); Quincy, *History* 70; see also Wentworth and Clark, *Boston Library Society*, 50.

52. *Aguecheek* (Boston: Shepard, Clark, and Brown, 1859), 116; these memories appear in a digression embedded within a travel piece about Paris. *Aguecheek*, published anonymously as a collection of sketches, was almost certainly written by Charles Bullard Fairbanks, who served with Athenaeum assistant librarian Seth Bass from 1847 to 1853. I am grateful for

Michael Wentworth's posthumously published *Look Again: Essays on the Boston Athenaeum's Art Collections* (Boston: Boston Athenaeum, 2003), in which Fairbanks's curious career is discussed.

53. Joseph Stevens Buckminster, "Literary Institutions in Liverpool," *Monthly Anthology and Boston Review* 4 (November 1807): 597–599.

54. Kirkland, *Memoir of the Boston Athenaeum*, 31, 32–34; Robert A. Ferguson, "The Literature of Public Documents," in *The American Enlightenment: 1750–1820* (Cambridge, Mass.: Harvard University Press, 1997), xi, 124–125. The elements of repetition, syllogistic reasoning, and explicitly addressed beginnings—all singled out by Ferguson as characteristic of American founding documents—feature prominently in the analogous documents of early American cultural institutions, as my examples demonstrate.

55. Francis Lieber, *A Lecture on the History and Uses of Athenaeums* (Columbia, S.C.: Columbia Athenaeum, 1856). Lieber (1800–1872) was a close associate of the abolitionist, U.S. senator, and Boston Athenaeum reader Charles Sumner, as well (see Chapter 5).

56. Kirkland, *Memoir of the Boston Athenaeum*, 27–28, 30. I borrow the expression "ostentatious and benevolent" from Catherine O'Donnell Kaplan.

57. In *Imagined Communities: Reflections on the Origin and Spread of Nationalism* (London: Verso, 1983), Benedict Anderson uses the term "imagined community" to define nationalism. He sees nations as constructions in the imagination, made possible by print media. The Boston Athenaeum—though obviously much smaller in scope—originally functioned on this level, creating a horizontal sense of community through shared aims and values articulated in printed documents.

58. Quincy, "Biographical Notices," in *History*, 66; Ferguson, "Literature of Public Documents," 147.

59. Both Robert Darnton and Roger Chartier emphasize the importance of examining reading practices and settings as part of a matrix of book-historical concerns that include attention to bibliographic details and textual criticism. See Darnton, "First Steps toward a History of Reading," in *The Kiss of Lamourette: Reflections in Cultural History* (New York: Norton, 1990); and Chartier, "Communities of Readers," in *The Order of Books: Readers, Authors, and Libraries in Europe between the Fourteenth and Eighteenth Centuries*, trans. Lydia G. Cochrane (Stanford, Calif.: Stanford University Press, 1994).

60. BA Trustees' Records, 1 January 1810 (at this time the Athenaeum was open every day except Sunday, from eight o'clock in the morning until nine at night); 21 March 1814; 2 April 1821; 14 October 1822.

61. BA Letters Collection, 31 May 1827.

62. [Fairbanks], *Aguecheek*, 116–117.

63. Seth Bass to the Trustees, 11 July 1825. This letter accompanied a report of the BA Examining Committee.

64. Charles Bullard Fairbanks, Diary, 2 September 1847, BA. Again, I credit Michael Wentworth's *Look Again* for leading me to the Fairbanks material, a valuable primary source.

65. For an example of how cultural space can be interpreted, see Carol Duncan and Alan Wallach. "The Universal Survey Museum," *Art History* 3 (December 1980): 448–469; drawing on concepts common to anthropology, the authors analyze museum installation and show how installations "shape the average visitor's experience."

66. The payment allocated by the Athenaeum was $300. See Quincy, *History*, 79.

67. George C. Mason, *The Life and Works of Gilbert Stuart* (New York: Scribner, 1879), 238.

68. William T. Whitley, *Gilbert Stuart* (Cambridge, Mass.: Harvard University Press, 1932), 81. An Irishman, Shee met Stuart in Dublin when the latter was living in Ireland during the years 1787 to 1793.

69. For more insight into the range of Roscoe's interests, see Donald A. Macnaughton, *Roscoe of Liverpool: His Life, Writings, and Treasures, 1753–1831* (Birkenhead, U.K.: Countyvise, 1996). The portrait was commissioned by Roscoe's friend T. W. Coke, of Holkham, the first

Earl of Leicester. Coke also bought much of Roscoe's library after Allerton Hall was sold. See Chandler, *William Roscoe of Liverpool*. For details pertaining to the portrait's attributes, I am grateful to Audrey Hall, of the Walker Gallery in Liverpool, who alerted me to one of the gallery's publications: *Merseyside: Painters, People, and Places—Catalogue of Oil Paintings* (Liverpool: Merseyside County Council, 1978), 190–193. Charles James Fox (1749–1806) was a Whig Member of Parliament off and on from 1768; a colorful gentleman, he was a great orator but gambled incessantly.

70. Dorinda Evans, *The Genius of Gilbert Stuart* (Princeton, N.J.: Princeton University Press, 1999), 90–92. Two other Stuart portraits share the tone and attributes of the Perkins portrait—Thomas Jefferson in the so-called Bowdoin portrait of 1805, and James Monroe in a portrait completed in 1821–1822—yet neither of those includes a home library in the background. See also Richard McLanathan, *Gilbert Stuart* (New York: Harry N. Abrams / National Museum of American Art, Smithsonian Institution, 1986).

71. Quincy, *History*, 84; Wentworth and Clark, *Boston Library Society*, 48–52. Evans, *Genius of Gilbert Stuart*, 50.

72. Ralph Waldo Emerson, Boston, to John Boynton Hill, Boston, 3 July 1822, in Emerson, *Letters*, 1:119–120.

73. Peter A. Thacher to Trustees, 3 January 1825; and Seth Bass to Trustees, 11 July 1825, letters accompanying two respective reports of the BA Examining Committee. A scrap of paper, dated tentatively ("June 1825"), assigns inventory tasks to various members; apparently, each examiner belonged to a small team that had responsibility for an area. For example, George Ticknor, Theodore Lyman, and Francis Parkman were assigned "2nd Story, West Rooms, 3, 4, and 5"—which coincided with theology, metaphysics, and belles-lettres; these assignments suggest which members were perceived as experts in, or at least interested students of, which subjects.

74. See Goodman, "Ethics and Enterprise," 437–451; and Thornton, *Cultivating Gentlemen*.

75. William Appleton, diary entry, January 1835, in *Selections from the Diaries of William Appleton, 1786–1862*, ed. Susan M. Loring (Boston: privately printed, 1922), in the Massachusetts Historical Society.

76. Kirkland, *Memoir of the Boston Athenaeum*, 36. Guides such as George Hillard's *The Dangers and Duties of the Mercantile Profession* (Boston: Ticknor, Reeds and Fields, 1850) would later tutor merchants on conduct befitting a man of business.

77. BA Charging Records, vol. 1.

78. See BA Charging Records, vols. 1–3. For a helpful research note on meeting the challenges of finding "real" readers, see Emily B. Todd, "Antebellum Libraries in Richmond and New Orleans and the Search for the Practices and Preferences of 'Real' Readers," in *Libraries as Agencies of Culture*, ed. Thomas Augst and Wayne Wiegand (Madison: University of Wisconsin Press, 2001).

79. Fairbanks Diary, 2 September 1847 and 25 January 1848.

80. Raven, *London Booksellers*, 228.

81. I have benefited from an anthropological perspective provided in, among other works, Eric Hobsbawn and Terence Ranger, eds., *The Invention of Tradition* (Cambridge: Cambridge University Press, 1983).

82. *Quinquennial Catalogue of Harvard*. John Everett (1801–1826) addressed his fellow students in 1818: see *Oration on the Prospects of the Young Men of America* (Boston: Wells and Lilly, 1818). If this identification is correct, Everett would have been only sixteen years old when he petitioned Shaw. I am indebted to Lisa Starzyk, former Boston Athenaeum archivist, for this spadework.

83. John Everett to William Smith Shaw, Boston, 28 December 1817, Shaw Papers. Later, other protests erupted in the press: "What literary advantages have the mass of our citizens derived from the Athenaeum? Who gets a peep within the walls without a ten dollar bill?" *Bowen's Boston News-Letter* (February 25, 1826), 116, quoted in Wentworth et al., *Fifty Books*.

Chapter Three

1. Chester Harding's portrait, oil on canvas, was completed in 1827; it appears to be the only surviving original image of Adams. A copy by Francis Alexander, now hanging at the American Antiquarian Society in Worcester, Mass., was painted as early as a year later; a popular lithograph soon followed from the copy. (For more on Harding, see Leah Lipton's *A Truthful Likeness: Chester Harding and His Portraits* [Washington, D.C.: Smithsonian Institution, 1985].) There is also mention in the Athenaeum's records of a miniature portrait of Adams painted by an unnamed artist at the request of a friend, Catharine Hay; no other evidence of the miniature has been found.

2. M.B., "First of Our Women to Earn a Living with the Pen," *New York Times*, c. 1887. This published article, signed only with initials, resides in a folder of newspaper clippings at the Boston Athenaeum. A photocopy now separated from the original issue, it includes no page numbers and is labeled with conflicting dates (1885 and 1887). I am grateful to Linda J. Docherty for her discussion of Chester Harding's portrait of Hannah Adams in "Women as Readers: Visual Interpretations," *Proceedings of the American Antiquarian Society* 107 (1998): 335–388. Docherty surveys portraits that feature American women with books; she identifies six pictorial categories, or types, of represented female readers in an effort to reveal ideological patterns.

3. See Gene Gleason, "Hannah Adams," *American Heritage*, December 1972, 80–84.

4. In 1832, Elizabeth Peabody and Lydia Maria Child were allowed to withdraw books from the Athenaeum without paying the customary fee. After her *Appeal in Favor of That Class of Americans Called Africans* was published in 1833, however, Child became unpopular with certain members of the Athenaeum; whether that disapproval led to a retraction of her reading privileges is disputed to this day. See chapter 5 of this book; see also Charles Knowles Bolton, *The Athenaeum Centenary* (Boston: Boston Athenaeum, 1907), 40–41; and Barbara Adams Hebard's essay in *The Boston Athenaeum: Bicentennial Essays*, ed. Richard Wendorf (Boston: Boston Athenaeum, 2009). Hebard's research on women at the Athenaeum was especially helpful to me. She notes that the word "free" in accounts of Hannah Adams's Athenaeum privileges is ambiguous; it is unclear whether the privileges were simply given at no cost or whether they involved free, unfettered access to the library. Hebard also reports that at least two women owned shares of proprietorship early on: Helen Ruthren in 1829 and Anna P. Jones in 1839. In addition, female family members were given access to the library's holdings all along (the Athenaeum by-laws allowed for this).

5. John Adams added, in a comment that says much about the infancy of American identity, "A line of virtuous, independent New England farmers . . . [is] a better foundation than a descent through royal or titled scoundrels since the flood"; quoted in Elizabeth Porter Gould, "Hannah Adams," *New England Magazine* 10 (May 1894): 369.

6. For more on the social anxieties that such a woman both caused and experienced, see Susan Phinney Conrad, *Perish the Thought: Intellectual Women in Romantic America, 1830–1860* (New York: Oxford University Press, 1976).

7. Biographical sources beyond Hannah Adams's papers and her memoir include Gary D. Schmidt, *A Passionate Usefulness: The Life and Literary Labors of Hannah Adams* (Charlottesville: University Press of Virginia, 2004); Mrs. Sarah Josepha Hale, ed., "Mrs. Hannah Adams," *Ladies' Magazine*, July 1828, 309–313; Olive M. Tilden, "Hannah Adams," *Dedham Historical Register* 7 (July 1896): 83–100; and Alma Lutz, "Hannah Adams: An American Bluestocking," *New-England Galaxy* 12 (Spring 1971): 29–33.

8. Hannah Adams, *A Memoir of Miss Hannah Adams, Written by Herself with Additional Notices by a Friend* (Boston: Gray and Bowen, 1832), 9, 52. The friend is not identified in the published memoir but is named as "Mrs. G. S. Lee" in Oscar Fay Adams, "Hannah Adams," *Christian Register*, 29 August 1912, 827–829.

9. My thoughts about autobiography, and the complicated motivations behind women's narratives especially, were influenced by Ann Fabian, *The Unvarnished Truth: Personal Narratives in Nineteenth-Century America* (Berkeley: University of California Press, 2000); and Jill Ker

Conway, *When Memory Speaks: Reflections on Autobiography* (New York: Knopf, 1998). Fabian traces a handful of rhetorical tropes that show how authenticity and authority were granted through the publication of sensationalized life stories. According to Conway, women autobiographers historically appear as passive receptors of divine will, as opposed to the male paradigm of the epic hero in search of truth or treasure. The case of Hannah Adams fits neatly into neither scholar's canon, but both studies have informed my reading of her memoir.

10. Adams, *Memoir*, 22, 37–42; Conway, *When Memory Speaks*, 15–16.

11. On the former, see Lincoln B. Faller, *The Forms and Functions of English Criminal Biography* (Cambridge: Cambridge University Press, 1987). On the latter, see Karen Haltunnen, *Confidence Men and Painted Women: A Study of Middle-Class Culture in America, 1830–1870* (New Haven, Conn.: Yale University Press, 1982); and John F. Kasson, *Rudeness and Civility: Manners in Nineteenth-Century Urban America* (New York: Hill and Wang, 1990).

12. Adams, *Memoir*, 4, 9.

13. For examples, see Benjamin Rush, "Thoughts upon Female Education" (1787); Judith Sargent Murray, *The Gleaner* (1798); and Lydia Maria Child, *The Mother's Book* (1831).

14. Adams, *Memoir*, 10–11. The influential book was Thomas Broughton's *An Historical Dictionary of All Religions from the Creation of the World to This Present Time* (1742).

15. For biographical material I have relied upon Richard J. Moss, *The Life of Jedidiah Morse: A Station of Peculiar Exposure* (Knoxville: University of Tennessee Press, 1995); and Conrad Wright, "The Controversial Career of Jedidiah Morse," *Harvard Library Bulletin* 31 (1983): 64–87. (Morse was the father of Samuel F. B. Morse, painter and inventor of the Morse Code.) Extensive background on Adams's legal battle with Morse and its aftermath is contained in these pamphlets: Jedidiah Morse and Elijah Parish, *An Appeal to the Public, on the Controversy respecting the Revolution in Harvard College, and the Events Which Have Followed It, Occasioned by the Use Which Has Been Made of Certain Complaints and Accusations of Miss Hannah Adams, against the Authors* (Charlestown, Mass.: printed for the author, 1814); Hannah Adams, *A Narrative of the Controversy between the Rev. Jedidiah Morse, D.D., and the Author* (Boston: Cummings and Hilliard, 1814); and Sidney Edwards Morse, *Remarks on the Controversy between Doctor Morse and Miss Adams* (Boston: Armstrong, 1814).

16. The Bavanan Illuminati was a loose organization of Republican free thinkers whose tenets were often associated with those of free masons; founded in enlightenment era Germany, the secret society attracted some American followers in the late eighteenth century. The "Standing Order" was the traditional term adopted by Congregational ministers in the colonial era to denote the authority wielded at a time when church and state were not entirely distinguishable, a time before the Congregationalists split into revealed (orthodox) religion and rational (Unitarian) religion. See Peter S. Field, *The Crisis of the Standing Order: Clerical Intellectuals and Cultural Authority in Massachusetts, 1780–1833* (Amherst: University of Massachusetts Press, 1998). Field (108) mistakenly refers to Adams as a widow; however, he provides helpful background on how shifts in the theological landscape affected other cultural spheres. For example, Morse opposed the election of a Unitarian, Henry Ware, as Hollis Professor at Harvard University, and he launched *The Panoplist*, a periodical designed to combat the Unitarian "menace."

17. Morse and Parish, *Appeal*, 8–9.

18. Given the animosity of some members toward him, it is a very odd fact that Jedidiah Morse is listed as a "life subscriber" at the Boston Athenaeum (Bolton, *Athenaeum Centenary*, 213.) Life subscriptions cost only one-third of a share ($100 versus $300), so gentlemen of standing could afford to support the institution in this way. Also, it is true that the Athenaeum did not speak with one voice and that many leading Boston gentlemen took pride in recognizing alternative views, if such views came from distinguished people. The rift between Morse and liberal theologians (and their sympathizers) became much more pronounced after 1808, when Morse's litigiousness was full-blown.

19. M.B., "First of Our Women to Earn a Living with the Pen." Only scant evidence has been found as to the extent of the financial support provided to Adams by the Athenaeum

membership. For example, a letter from a Mr. Boott's secretary to William Shaw reads: "Mr. Shaw will find inclosed Mr. Boott's subscription of fifteen Dollars for Miss H. Adams—." Boott to Shaw, 8 March 1816, Shaw Papers. See also Schmidt, *Passionate Usefulness*, 411, n. 3.

20. Adams, *Memoir*, 30. Adams does continue for three more shadowy sentences, but they only serve to distance her further from the affair.

21. S. Hale, "Mrs. Hannah Adams," 311; *Christian Examiner*, September 1832, 130; M.B., "First of Our Women to Earn a Living with the Pen"; Fabian, *Unvarnished Truth*, 4.

22. S. Hale, "Mrs. Hannah Adams," 311–312; William Charvat, *Literary Publishing in America, 1790–1850* (Amherst: University of Massachusetts Press, 1993 [1959]), 74. History's cachet, writes Charvat, was also attributable to its methods, thought to be in accord with Scottish Common Sense philosophy, which "celebrated actuality and denigrated possibility." In the memoir's postscript (Adams, *Memoir*, 85), the author's friend refers to fiction's dangers and the coming of Scott: "Had the Waverly novels made their appearance in her youthful days, they would probably have rendered harmless the greater part of [the fiction] which fell into her hand." On the post-Revolutionary novel as a successfully subversive genre, see Cathy N. Davidson, *Revolution and the Word: The Rise of the Novel in America* (New York: Oxford University Press, 1986).

23. For leading me to valuable primary and secondary sources that elucidate Adams's gifts, I owe much to Michael W. Vella's "Theology, Genre, and Gender: The Precarious Place of Hannah Adams in American Literary History," *Early American Literature* 28 (1993): 21–41. Vella details the achievements of Hannah Adams as a protofeminist theologian, a woman whose unique contributions depended on both her faith and her gender. He examines what he calls "transpersonal cultural factors"—the historically contingent attitudes toward gender, genre, and theology—that were provoked by Adams's work and by her ensuing controversy with Morse.

24. *North American Review* 19 (1818): 86–92, quoted in Vella, "Theology, Genre, and Gender," n 1, 27–28; Sharon M. Harris, ed., *Women's Early American Historical Narratives* (New York: Penguin Classics, 2003), 94.

25. Apparently, the passage originally appeared in a biography of a "Mrs. Charlotte Smith," but Adams adapted it for her own use: Hannah Adams to William Smith Shaw, 28 August 1805, quoted in Joseph B. Felt, *Memorials of William Smith Shaw* (Boston: S. K. Whipple, 1852), 200. See also Adams, *Memoir*, 34–35.

26. Felt, *Memorials*, 194; Morse and Parish, *Appeal*, 8–9.

27. Adams, *Narrative of the Controversy*, vii–viii.

28. Arthur Maynard Walter, New York, to William Smith Shaw, Philadelphia, 8 January 1799, Shaw Papers.

29. Hannah Adams to William Smith Shaw, n.d., n.p. Quoted in Vella, "Theology, Genre, and Gender," 33.

30. Felt, *Memorials*, 200.

31. It might be interesting to compare Morse's notion with that of the historian Ann Douglas, who, in *The Feminization of American Culture* (New York: Farrar Straus Giroux / Noonday Press, 1998 [1976]), argues that liberal clergy collaborated with the disenfranchised female middle class to conserve a cultural status quo. Lawrence Buell, too, has noted odd alliances and describes a kind of "Unitarian orthodoxy" in Boston, where the elite assumed its "self-appointed role as arbiters of virtue and taste": *New England Literary Culture: From Revolution through Renaissance* (Cambridge: Cambridge University Press, 1986), 44, 93–94.

32. Wright, "Controversial Career," 87.

33. S. Morse, *Remarks on the Controversy* , 17, 25, 27.

34. Adams, *Narrative of the Controversy*, vii–viii.

35. *Monthly Anthology and Boston Review* 2 (July 1805): 538, 541–542, quoted in Vella, "Theology, Genre, and Gender," 29.

36. Alan Wallach, "Thomas Cole and the Aristocracy," in *Reading American Art*, ed. Marianne Doezema and Elizabeth Milroy (New Haven: Yale University Press, 1998), 100. Wallach

makes his general points about patronage within an argument about the painter Thomas Cole's differences with his patrons.

37. Samuel F. B. Morse (1791–1872) revered his father, who from all accounts was a powerful patriarch, a stern master of his family. See Paul J. Staiti, *Samuel F. B. Morse* (Cambridge: Cambridge University Press, 1989), 1–7 and 11 for details of the Morse portrait. See also William Kloss, *Samuel F. B. Morse* (New York: Harry N. Abrams / National Museum of Art, Smithsonian Institution, 1988), 12. I am grateful to Keith Morgan, whose curiosity prompted the portrait comparison; he suggests that, paradoxically, the Adams portrait is more in keeping with portraits of Congregationalists and the Morse portrait more reminiscent of portraits of leading Unitarians.

38. See Adams, *Memoir*, 48; Gould, "Hannah Adams," 367, 368; and M.B., "First of Our Women to Earn a Living with the Pen."

39. See Paul Goodman, "Ethics and Enterprise: The Values of a Boston Elite, 1800–1860," *American Quarterly* 18 (August 1966): 437–451; and Tamara Plakins Thornton, *Cultivating Gentlemen: The Meaning of Country Life among the Boston Elite, 1785–1860* (New Haven, Conn.: Yale University Press, 1989).

40. Quoted in Gordon Wood, ed., *The Rising Glory of America, 1760–1820*, rev. ed. (Boston: Northeastern University Press, 1990 [1971]), 22.

41. Marshall Foletta, *Coming to Terms with Democracy: Federalist Intellectuals and the Shaping of American Culture* (Charlottesville: University Press of Virginia, 2001), 45. Buckminster kept a low profile with respect to the Unitarian-Trinitarian controversy.

42. Adams, *Memoir*, iv, 89, and 77–79. For an insightful reading of how Ralph Waldo Emerson was reinvented by lyceum audiences in the Midwest, see Mary Kupiec Cayton, "The Making of an American Prophet: Emerson, His Audiences, and the Rise of the Culture Industry in Nineteenth-Century America," *American Historical Review* 92 (June 1987): 587–620. Toward the end of her article (from 615), Cayton uses reception theory (a field of literary study that emphasizes readers' cultural backgrounds) to show how audiences invent themselves, too, through reviews in the press.

43. See Catherine O'Donnell Kaplan, "'We Have Joys They Do Not Know': Letters, Federalism, and Sentiment in the New Nation, 1790–1812" (Ph.D. diss., University of Michigan, 1998), 84–101, for a cogent overview of gender roles in the early republic.

44. Lutz, "Hannah Adams"; Gleason, "Hannah Adams," 82.

45. Adams was not "the first tenant of Mount Auburn," as the inscription on her gravestone claims, but hers was the first *monument* erected at the Boston-area cemetery (in 1832). The obelisk-like neoclassical marble form is inscribed, "This monument is erected by her female friends." Subscriptions for the tribute were raised by women supporters, and an iron fence (installed for $35, donated by the Massachusetts Horticultural Society) once protected the site. The monument also reads, "Historian of the Jews" and "Reviewer of Christian Sects," reinforcing Adams's identity as an author: Schmidt, *Passionate Usefulness*, 8. See also Blanche Linden-Ward, *Silent City on a Hill: Landscapes of Memory and Boston's Mount Auburn Cemetery* (Columbus: Ohio State University Press, 1989), 217–218.

46. See, for example, Linda K. Kerber, *Women of the Republic: Intellect and Ideology in Revolutionary America* (Chapel Hill: University of North Carolina Press, 1980).

47. Anthology Society Minutes, 24 October 1809, quoted in Kaplan, "We Have Joys," 90–91.

48. Kaplan, "We Have Joys," 84.

49. Adams, *Memoir*, 74. See also M.B., "First of Our Women to Earn a Living with the Pen"; and Gleason, "Hannah Adams," 82.

50. T. J. Jackson Lears, in "The Concept of Cultural Hegemony: Problems and Possibilities," *American Quarterly* 90 (June 1985): 567–593, reflects upon Antonio Gramsci's work, explaining that Gramsci deepened Marxism by thinking in terms of "historical blocs," not rigid social classes; even groups that challenge the dominant culture often identify with it internally, and for sound reasons. Further, in "Paper Tigers: A Sociologist Follows Cultural Studies into the Wilderness," *Lingua Franca*, August 1997, 49–56—a complaint about simplistic cultural

studies—Michael Schudson concludes, "If culture is only the discursive shaping and serving of power, there is no place for the radical assertion that power is designed and valued to serve culture."

51. Adams *Memoir*, 43.

52. Marcia Pointon, *Hanging the Head: Portraiture and Social Formation in Eighteenth-Century England* (New Haven, Conn.: Yale University Press, 1993), 85.

CHAPTER FOUR

1. From an undated letter written by Miss E. S. Quincy of Quincy, Mass., quoted in Chester Harding, *A Sketch of Chester Harding, Artist, Drawn By His Own Hand* (Boston: Houghton Mifflin, 1929), 140. The autobiography, which Harding called his "egotistography," was published privately in 1866; a second edition, supplemented with material gathered by one of his daughters, Margaret White, appeared in 1890; yet another edition includes an introduction by the artist's grandson W. P. G. Harding, and was published in 1929. It is this last edition that I cite. All unattributed material on Harding is drawn from this memoir (hereafter Harding, *Sketch*).

2. "Gallery of Portraits," *Boston Lyceum* 1 (January–June 1827): 218–219.

3. Harding arrived in Boston in 1823 and departed for Europe in August of that same year (Harding, *Sketch*, 4, 34, 36); *Boston Daily Evening Transcript*, 5 May 1831. The report went on to describe the artist as "a noble-looking fellow, very large and muscular, with an agreeable and gentlemanly address."

4. "Gallery of Portraits."

5. En route for a later trip, Harding reported seeing icebergs "as large as the State House" (Harding, *Sketch*, 42, 166, 128–129).

6. Leah Lipton, *A Truthful Likeness: Chester Harding and His Portraits* (Washington, D.C.: Smithsonian Institution, 1985), 8; Harding, *Sketch*, xix.

7. Harding, *Sketch*, 75–76. Among his works on display at Somerset House that spring was a portrait of Robert Owen, the Welsh-born social reformer whose theories were adopted at cotton mills in New Lanark, Scotland (59, 82). The same year as the exhibition (1824), Owen traveled to the United States to start an ill-fated utopian community in Indiana.

8. Europeans from the late sixteenth to the early twentieth century would have been accustomed to such a style of gallery hanging; as art historian David Solkin has explained, any "pure" aesthetic response was intentionally frustrated by the tradition of crowding framed images together. The result was a simultaneous multiplicity of perspectives and a more subjective experience of the paintings. See David H. Solkin, ed., *Art on the Line: The Royal Academy Exhibitions at Somerset House, 1780–1836* (New Haven, Conn.: Yale University Press, 2001), 1–8, "This Great Mart of Genius," Solkin's introduction to this collection of essays.

9. Harding, *Sketch*, 122–123, from a diary entry dated April 7, 1825.

10. For Harding's devotion to Reynolds, see ibid., 112. Archibald Alison's son and namesake was the author of a popular ten-volume history of France. Harding found himself painting the historian's portrait on a second journey to England, in 1846. By that time, the ideas of the senior Alison had circulated widely in the United States. Among other Athenaeum members, George Ticknor and Henry Higginson withdrew works by Reynolds, and Nathan Appleton took out Alison's essays on taste; see BA Charging Records, vols. 1 and 2. For Harding's encounter with historian Archibald Alison, see his *Sketch*, 168.

11. Joshua Reynolds, *Discourses*, ed. Pat Rogers (London: Penguin Classics [1797] 1992), 201.

12. Archibald Alison, *Essays on the Nature and Principles of Taste* (Hartford, Conn.: George Goodwin, 1821). See also Robert E. Streeter, "Association Psychology and Literary Nationalism in the *North American Review*, 1815–1825," *American Literature* 17 (November 1945): 243–254.

13. Chester Harding, London, to Caroline Harding, Northampton, 4 November 1823, in *Sketch*, 57.

14. Harding, *Sketch*, 83, 103.

15. "Artists, it is known, are admitted gratuitously to these [Athenaeum] exhibitions": *Columbia Centinel*, 11 July 1829; BA Proprietors' Records, 1 January 1827.

16. William H. Gerdts, "The American 'Discourses': A Survey of Lectures and Writings on American Art, 1770–1858," *American Art Journal*, Summer 1983, 68. Leah Lipton, "The Boston Artists' Association, 1841–1851," *American Art Journal*, Autumn 1983, 47. At least one newspaper reporter expressed relief after the 1834 show opened at Harding's Gallery, claiming that the rival exhibition caused "no injury to the *permanent* gallery" (*Boston Daily Evening Transcript*, 23 April 1834; emphasis added). Despite differences in outlook, the Boston Artists' Association would eventually collaborate with the Athenaeum on exhibitions.

17. Harding, *Sketch*, 72.

18. Jonathan P. Harding, "The Painting Gallery," in *A Climate for Art: The History of the Boston Athenaeum Gallery, 1827–1973* (Boston: Boston Athenaeum, 1980), 9–10, 14, 22. In *The Ephemeral Museum: Old Master Paintings and the Rise of the Art Exhibition* (New Haven, Conn.: Yale University Press, 2000), Francis Haskell addresses the phenomenon of exhibiting the Old Masters—a term he defines as European artists "who had lived before the French Revolution" (4); for the practices of the British Institution, see 88–99.

19. Marcia Pointon recovers the "social performances" that occurred in portrait studios such as Joshua Reynolds's; see her *Hanging the Head: Portraiture and Social Formation in Eighteenth-Century England* (New Haven, Conn.: Yale University Press, 1993), 42–43. See also Richard Wendorf's fascinating *Sir Joshua Reynolds: The Painter in Society* (Cambridge, Mass.: Harvard University Press, 1996); Wendorf explores the many transactions (both social and professional) that pass between artist and subject.

20. In addition to the portrait of Hannah Adams, Harding painted a full-size portrait of Daniel Webster for several subscribers from the Athenaeum in 1828; his portrait of John Marshall, painted in 1830, was purchased by the Athenaeum; and his works were regularly displayed in Athenaeum exhibitions. Abbott Lawrence spearheaded the effort to help Harding. See Samuel L. Gerry, "The Old Masters of Boston," *New England Magazine*, n.s. 3, no. 6 (February 1891): 684. A mortgage deed at the Boston Athenaeum lists Thomas Handasyd Perkins, S. G. Perkins, and W. H. Gardiner as lenders: cited in Lipton, *Truthful Likeness*, 33.

21. Whereas annual subscribers increased over the 1830s and 1840s, book purchases had dropped by 1839. After the $12,000 shopping spree made possible by the Perkins family and other donors, the Athenaeum seems to have bought roughly $1,000 worth of books annually until the early 1840s, when book purchases hovered around $300 to $400 per year. See BA Proprietors' Records, 1825–1848.

22. For background on the gallery, I have referred to the plentiful assortment of Athenaeum publications: Mabel Munson Swan, *The Athenaeum Gallery, 1827–1873: The Boston Athenaeum as an Early Patron of Art* (Boston: Boston Athenaeum, 1940); Jane S. Knowles, *Change and Continuity: A Pictorial History of the Boston Athenaeum* (Boston: Boston Athenaeum, 1976); Pamela Hoyle, Jonathan P. Harding, and Rosemary Booth, *A Climate for Art: The History of the Boston Athenaeum Gallery, 1827–1973* (Boston: Boston Athenaeum, 1980); Catharina Slautterback, *Designing the Boston Athenaeum: 10½ at 150* (Boston: Boston Athenaeum, 1999); Michael Wentworth, *Look Again: Essays on the Boston Athenaeum's Art Collections* (Boston: Boston Athenaeum, 2003); and Stanley Cushing and David Dearinger, eds. *Acquired Tastes: 200 Years of Collecting for the Boston Athenaeum* (Boston: Boston Athenaeum, 2006). In addition, the broader institutional histories—Quincy, *History*; and Charles Knowles Bolton, *The Athenaeum Centenary* (Boston: Boston Athenaeum, 1907)—were indispensable. One caveat: although Swan's volume is frequently relied upon, its primary sources are not all identifiable by Athenaeum staff; I have, where possible, worked to verify any material drawn solely from that account.

23. Kirkland, *Memoir of the Boston Athenaeum*, in Quincy, *History*, 30, 35, 37; circulars dated March 6, 1823, soliciting subscriptions for an arts facility, claimed that such a space would "contribute directly to [the institution's] prosperity and wealth, . . . increase the value of our real estate, and materially enlarge our own personal sources of enjoyment. . . . It will probably increase the value of the Shares." BA Letters Collection.

24. *Boston Daily Evening Transcript*, 17 May 1832; "In the ten days the Exhibition has been open, about 2600 season tickets have been sold," according to the *Boston Weekly Messenger* of May 24, 1827; "The interesting Exhibition of Paintings in the Gallery of the Athenaeum closed last evening—Nearly twelve thousand visitors have viewed it," the *Columbia Centinel* announced on July 11, 1827.

25. Arthur Maynard Walter and Nathan Appleton also visited Somerset House and were wowed by the spectacle; on a trip to Paris in 1811, Francis Parkman found the Louvre's exhibitions worthy of serious study, "more than an hour's amusement." For these reactions and a better understanding of Bostonians' subtly critical interpretations of British life, see Anthony Mann, " 'A Nation First in All the Arts of Civilization': Boston's Post-Revolutionary Elites View Great Britain," *American Nineteenth-Century History* 2 (Summer 2001): 16.

26. Thomas Handasyd Perkins (1764–1854) and his bookish brother James were partners in a lucrative China trade. As Michael Wentworth explains, Thomas was more interested in the Athenaeum's Fine Arts Committee than in the institution's literary holdings; Michael Wentworth, with Elizabeth Lamb Clark, *The Boston Library Society, 1794–1994: An Exhibition of Portraits, Views, and Materials Related to the Foundation of the Society and Some of Its Early Members* (Boston: Boston Athenaeum, 1995), 48–51; Diary of Thomas Handasyd Perkins, 9 May 1826, Massachusetts Historical Society, quoted in Swan, *Athenaeum Gallery*, 19. Perkins was in Great Britain in the years 1795, 1812, and 1820, as well.

27. Andrew McClellan, *Inventing the Louvre: Art, Politics, and the Origins of the Modern Museum in Eighteenth-Century Paris* (Cambridge: Cambridge University Press, 1994), includes an overview of the shift from sumptuous decorative displays of the Renaissance era to careful classifications into national schools and the historical evolution of artists. The Somerset House exhibitions owed much to the former.

28. Susan Tyng, Boston, to Sarah Jarvis, Paris, 24 May 1827. Jarvis Papers (2:12), Connecticut State Library, quoted in typescript of the letter, page 6, BA Collections File, Art Department. Susan Tyng was the daughter of jurist Dudley Tyng. The "317" refers to the number of catalogued pieces on display. Washington Allston (1779–1843) traveled through Europe and studied in London with Benjamin West (1738–1820). He was known as an ambitious romantic; his most famous work, the historical *Feast of Belshazzar*, never satisfied him.

29. Typed and dated May 12, 1827, presumably from a draft of a public notice. BA Collections File, Art Department.

30. K. Dian Kriz, " 'Stare Cases': Engendering the Public's Two Bodies at the Royal Academy of the Arts," in *Art on the Line*, 55–63.

31. Exhibition Catalogues, vol. 1 (1827–1828), BA Art Department.

32. Exhibition Catalogue, 1839. BA Art Department.

33. *Columbia Centinel*, 28 July 1827 and 15 September 1830.

34. *Remarks upon the Athenaeum Gallery of Paintings* (Boston: L. R. Butts, 1831), in Boston Athenaeum Collection.

35. *Columbia Centinel*, 2 October and 2 June 1830; *Boston Courier*, 8 August 1839. For a good sense of American art criticism of the time, see the introduction to David B. Dearinger, *Rave Reviews: American Art and Its Critics, 1826–1925* (New York: National Academy of Design, 2000).

36. *Columbia Centinel*, 16 May 1829.

37. See David Tatham, "D.C. Johnston's Satiric Views of Art in Boston, 1825–1850," in *Art & Commerce: American Prints of the Nineteenth Century* (Charlottesville: University Press of Virginia, 1975), 9–24. Through parody, Johnston (1798–1865) mused publicly about the place of the fine arts in the United States. In figure 4.4, the second man from the left tells a forger, "I have sold your Guido—go to work again, but be sure to make nothing distinct otherwise it will be condemned as modern daub in spite of the smoked canvas." The husband at the center tells his wife, "My dear you are perfectly right but the boy's nat'rl taste will be ruined if his attention is allowed to dwell on modern pictures. I have just bought a Guido for him to

study." And the lone man to the far right says to himself, "What useful things these tubes are when a body wants to see just the gildin' without nothin' else."

38. *Boston Daily American Statesman*, 16 May 1827; *Columbia Centinel*, 16 May 1827; *Boston Daily American Statesman*, 21 May 1827.

39. John Greenleaf Whittier to Edwin Harriman, 18 May 1829, quoted in Henry Mayer, *All on Fire: William Lloyd Garrison and the Abolition of Slavery* (New York: St. Martin's Press, 1998), 59–61.

40. Transcribed from the diary of Anna Cabot Lowell Quincy, entry dated 27 May 1833, courtesy Mr. M. A. DeWolfe Howe. BA Collections File, Art Department.

41. *Boston Daily Evening Transcript*, 5 October 1839.

42. "The Boston Athenaeum," in *Norton's Literary Almanac* (1852), 29–30. See also Rosemary Booth, "A Taste for Sculpture," in *A Climate for Art*, 23–35. Antonio Canova (1757–1822) was an internationally famous artist who sculpted in white marble.

43. For detailed background on the patronage of sculpture in nineteenth-century Boston, see David B. Dearinger, "American Neoclassical Sculptors and Their Private Patrons in Boston" (Ph.D. diss., City University of New York, 1993). On May 6, 2004, Dearinger, then Curator of Art at the Boston Athenaeum, delivered a talk called "Boston's Marmoreal Love Affair," in which he quoted the comment by the critic Clarence Cook, who was born in 1828; it reflects the fashion of sculpture patronage that raged by midcentury. By the time Hiram Powers's controversial *The Greek Slave* stopped in Boston on its East Coast tour in 1847, the city had been under the spell of neoclassical sculpture for a decade.

44. William Tudor to Harrison Gray Otis, 2 September 1815, in Samuel Eliot Morison, *Harrison Gray Otis, 1765–1848: The Urbane Federalist* (Boston: Houghton Mifflin, 1969), quoted in Lillian Miller, *Patrons and Patriotism: The Encouragement of the Fine Arts in the United States, 1790–1860* (Chicago: University of Chicago Press, 1966), 114.

45. Alan Wallach, "The American Cast Museum: An Episode in the History of the Institutional Definition of Art," in his *Exhibiting Contradiction: Essays on the Art Museum in the United States* (Amherst: University of Massachusetts Press, 1998); Dexter quoted in Swan, *Athenaeum Gallery*, 139; Francis Haskell and Nicholas Penny, *Taste and the Antique* (New Haven, Conn.: Yale University Press, 1981), xiii, quoted in Wallach, *Exhibiting Contradiction*, 48.

46. Neoclassical statuary, commissioned by the same Athenaeum gentlemen (most were Unitarians) and executed by many of the same sculptors mentioned here, appears throughout the pastoral setting of Mount Auburn Cemetery. See Blanche Linden-Ward, *Silent City on a Hill: Landscapes of Memory and Boston's Mount Auburn Cemetery* (Columbus: Ohio State University Press, 1989), esp. 225.

47. Miller, *Patrons and Patriotism*, 111–120. On page 118, Miller claims, "Even when it was a question of Old Masters, Bostonians usually favored the paintings of the well-known, traditionally reputable Dutch and Italian artists of the sixteenth and seventeenth centuries."

48. Report on the Pictures Exhibition, 31 October 1831; and Report of the Committee of Fine Arts, 10 December 1833, both in BA Letters Collection.

49. *Bowen's Picture of Boston; or, the Citizen's and Stranger's Guide to the Metropolis of Massachusetts and Its Environs*, 3rd ed. (Boston: Otis Broaders, 1838), 37.

50. John Lowell to Colonel Henry Dearborn, 22 June 1823, BA Letters Collection.

51. In a thorough and thoughtful survey of the Athenaeum's archive of architectural drawings, Catharina Slautterback (*Designing the Boston Athenaeum*, 34–40) investigates what appears to be nepotism in the choice of Cabot. Slautterback hints at, but does not insist on, a rigged selection process. Dexter (1802–1872) clearly helped the youthful Cabot (1818–1901) immensely. My quick summary of the Beacon Street plan owes much to Slautterback's meticulous research.

52. Quincy, *History*, 240–241; Slautterback, *Designing the Boston Athenaeum*, 49; Erik Forssman, *The Palazzo da Porto Festa in Vicenza* (University Park: Pennsylvania University Press, 1973), 62. See also *The AIA Guide to Boston*, 148–149.

53. The facade of the Liverpool Athenaeum, which was founded in 1798, is of a simpler design; it features a first story of rusticated arches and a streamlined second story.

54. See Anthony Lejeune, *The Gentlemen's Clubs of London* (New York: Mayflower Books, 1979). For more on Barry (1795–1860), see *The Life and Works of Sir Charles Barry, R.A., F.R.S., &c. &c.* (New York: Benjamin Blom, 1972), by his son, the Reverend Alfred Barry, D.D. For more on Notman's buildings, see Constance M. Greiff, *John Notman, Architect, 1810–1865* (Philadelphia: Athenaeum of Philadelphia, 1979); G. L. Meason, *On the Landscape Architecture of the Great Painters of Italy* (London: C. Hullmandel, 1828), 91. Notman (quoted in Greiff, 23) was undoubtedly familiar with Meason.

55. James S. Ackerman, *Palladio: The Architect and Society* (New York: Penguin Books, 1966), 79, calls Andrea Palladio (1508–1580) "the most imitated architect in history."

56. Thomas C. Clarke, "Architects and Architecture," *Christian Examiner* 49 (July, September, November 1850): 283; *Philadelphia Public Ledger*, 26 August 1847, 2, quoted in Greiff, *John Notman*, 23; Slautterback, *Designing the Boston Athenaeum*, 50–51.

57. Neil Harris, *Building Lives: Constructing Rites and Passages* (New Haven, Conn.: Yale University Press, 1999), 3–4, 26–27; *Boston Daily Advertiser*, 28 April 1847, quoted in Quincy, *History*, 173–182; the excerpt appears in *The History of the Boston Athenaeum* compiled by the same Mr. Quincy a few years later.

58. [Charles Fairbanks], *Aguecheek* (Boston: Shepard, Clark, and Brown, 1859), 116–117, quoted in Wentworth, *Look Again*, 54. There were of course other objections to the Beacon Street building; for example, an abutting neighbor named Mrs. Robbins was apparently inconvenienced by the added traffic of visitors (27 June 1849, BA Letters Collection).

59. See *Mapping Boston*, eds. Alex Krieger and David Cobb with Amy Turner (Cambridge, Mass.: MIT Press, 1999), 230; *Ballou's Pictorial Drawing-Room Companion* 8 (March 31, 1855): 200–201. The fact that these images idealize the Athenaeum experience does not negate their significance; indeed, their obvious appeal as advertisements for the institution reinforces my observations about popularization. These images have been reproduced as note cards for distribution to twenty-first-century visitors to the Athenaeum, proof of members' enduring fascination with the institution's biography.

60. See Oliver Wendell Holmes, "The Stereoscope and the Stereograph," *Atlantic Monthly*, June 1859.

61. For more on Sumner, see Anne-Marie Taylor, *Young Charles Sumner and the Legacy of the American Enlightenment, 1811–1851* (Amherst: University of Massachusetts Press, 2001); see also chapter 5 of this book.

62. Lauretta Dimmick, "Thomas Crawford's *Orpheus*: The American *Apollo Belvedere*," *American Art Journal* 19, no. 4 (1987): 90. Thomas Crawford (1813–1857) had a studio in Rome and impressed both tourists and the expatriate community. He created the *Orpheus* from 1839 to 1843.

63. Charles Sumner, Boston, to George Sumner, 1 June 1845, in Sumner, *Memoir and Letters of Charles Sumner*, ed. Edward L. Pierce (Boston: Roberts Brothers, 1877), 2:334.

64. Reynolds, *Discourses*, 201; Sumner quoted in Taylor, *Young Charles Sumner*, 119.

65. Gianlorenzo Bernini (1598–1680) was the greatest sculptor and one of the greatest architects of the seventeenth century. For an image of the *Scala Regia* (1663–1666), see Howard Hibbard, *Bernini* (New York: Penguin/Pelican Original, 1976), 164. The official designer of the Athenaeum stairs was Hammatt Billings (1818–1874), whose gift for illustration made him popular among the architects who worked with him: Slautterback, *Designing the Boston Athenaeum*, 89–90.

66. See, e.g., *Boston Post*, 18 June 1888. One wonders whether the staircase acquired its name only after 1856, when, having delivered a passionate abolitionist speech on the Senate floor, Sumner received a brutal beating from a southern defender of slavery (see chapter 5).

67. Slautterback, *Designing the Boston Athenaeum*, 56. The copy of the statue of George Washington was a plaster cast commissioned in 1847 (Jean-Antoine Houdon [1741–1828] was a French neoclassical sculptor), and the statue of mathematician Nathaniel Bowditch (1778–1838) by Robert Ball Hughes (1806–1868) was also plaster.

68. Catalogue quoted in Slautterback, *Designing the Boston Athenaeum*, 57. BA Collections File, Art Department.

69. Again, for a transcontinental perspective on this trend, see McClellan, *Inventing the Louvre*, 2–8; and Carol Duncan and Alan Wallach, "The Universal Survey Museum," *Art History* 3 (December 1980): 448–469.

70. Exhibition Catalogues, vols. 5–6 (1854–1864), BA Art Department. In 1858, Alfred Ordway was designated as the Fine Arts Committee's superintendent; in 1859, Ordway was called "Director" (little is known about his role). As an agent of canon formation, the Athenaeum Gallery in the 1850s reproduced visions of the same works over time and thus contributed to a sense of cultural continuity. Yet as John Guillory might argue, the gallery's permanent collection only "lists" the art, as a syllabus lists books; true canonical works, only secondarily lists, are *primarily* texts and art to be read. See John Guillory, "Canon, Syllabus, List: A Note on the Pedagogic Imaginary," *Transition* 52 (1991): 36–54.

71. Even an 1858 exhibition of paintings from the Pre-Raphaelite school did not reignite the scene. The library needed space anyway, so by the mid-1870s most of the Athenaeum's permanent collection had been sent to the Museum of Fine Arts as rootstock for its exhibitions.

72. Exhibition Catalogues, vol. 5; Exhibition Catalogue, 1859, 60–61, BA Art Department.

73. Robert A. Ferguson, *The American Enlightenment: 1750–1820* (Cambridge, Mass.: Harvard University Press, 1997), xi.

CHAPTER FIVE

1. Bernard F. Reilly Jr., "The Art of the Antislavery Movement," in *Courage and Conscience: Black and White Abolitionists in Boston*, ed. Donald M. Jacobs (Bloomington: Indiana University Press, 1993), 49; *The Liberator*, January 17, 1831, quoted in Reilly, 49; illustration of banner in Henry Mayer, *All on Fire: William Lloyd Garrison and the Abolition of Slavery* (New York: St. Martin's Press, 1998). Much of the material evidence is now lost. The Emancipation Act passed in 1833 (effective August 1, 1834) would later abolish slavery throughout the British Empire, including Canada. See David B. Davis, *The Problem of Slavery in the Age of Revolution: 1770–1823*, 2nd ed. (New York: Oxford University Press, 1998).

2. Prominent elite men, most notably Edmund Quincy (1808–1877) and Wendell Phillips (1811–1884), did join the antislavery movement but were considered exceptional among their social class.

3. It is unclear exactly how many Athenaeum proprietors had female relatives who were abolitionists. A representative list must suffice: Abigail May Alcott, daughter of philanthropist Samuel May and wife of social philosopher Bronson Alcott; Eliza Cabot Follen, daughter of merchant Samuel Cabot and sister to businessman Samuel Cabot Jr.; and Susan and Eliza Jackson, daughters of merchant Francis Jackson. See Debra Gold Hansen, *Strained Sisterhood: Gender and Class in the Boston Female Anti-Slavery Society* (Amherst: University of Massachusetts Press, 1993), 4–6, 69–71. Hansen corrects the misconception that the Boston Female Anti-Slavery Society enjoyed only harmony and accomplishment; after 1837, she argues, the society became splintered and paralyzed by disagreements about race relations and women's rights. In fact, according to Hansen, the divisions developed along class and religious lines: middle-class members favored evangelical sponsors; upper-class members clung to secularized religious leaders. The society's internal disputes eventually resulted in an end to the fairs in 1860.

4. Mayer, *All on Fire*, 252, 347; Boston Female Anti-Slavery Society, *Right and Wrong in Boston: Report of the Boston Female Anti-Slavery Society, with a Concise Statement of Events Previous and Subsequent to the Annual Meeting of 1835*, 2nd ed. (Boston: Boston Female Anti-Slavery Society, 1836), 77. The proceeds went to a variety of institutions: schools and asylums for blacks, as well as William Lloyd Garrison's Massachusetts Anti-Slavery Society.

5. Maria Chapman was able to check out books on the share of Samuel May Jr. I thank Barbara Adams Hebard for clarifying the source of sponsorship. Two curiosities under Mrs.

Chapman's name are worth noting. Like the cotton manufacturers Nathan Appleton and Abbott Lawrence (see below), she borrowed books on aristocratic mores: *Lodge's Peerage, Introduction to Heraldry*, and *The Book of Family Crests*. Her interests evidently wide-ranging, she also took out a volume with the frank title *Evans on Genital Organs*. BA Charging Records, vols. 4–5.

6. Quotation about the merchandise from *Report of the Twenty-First National Anti-Slavery Bazaar* (Boston: J. B. Yerrinton, 1855), 32; Hansen *Strained Sisterhood*, 129. See also Jane H. Pease and William H. Pease, *Bound with Them in Chains: A Biographical History of the Antislavery Movement* (Westport, Conn.: Greenwood Press, 1972), 42–45. For more on the Weston sisters, see Clare Taylor, *Women of the Antislavery Movement: The Weston Sisters* (New York: St. Martin's Press, 1995).

7. See Hansen, *Strained Sisterhood*, 124–139; Elisa Tamarkin, "Black Anglophilia; or, The Sociability of Antislavery," *American Literary History* 14 (Fall 2002): 444–478.

8. James Brewer Stewart, "Boston, Abolition, and the Atlantic World, 1820–1861," in Jacobs, *Courage and Conscience*, 106. Betty G. Farrell, *Elite Families: Class and Power in Nineteenth-Century Boston* (Albany: State University of New York Press, 1993), 41–45. See also Thomas H. O'Connor, *Lords of the Loom: The Cotton Whigs and the Coming of the Civil War* (New York: Scribner, 1968); and Russell B. Adams, *The Boston Money Tree* (New York: Crowell, 1977).

9. The challenge of finding exact data on the Athenaeum proprietors' political alliances—what percentage were Cotton Whigs, or supporters of the Compromise of 1850—proved onerous; it became clear, however, that representatives of both sides were outspoken in private documents.

10. Boston Female Anti-Slavery Society, *Right and Wrong in Boston*, 28–35, 56.

11. *Boston Courier*, September 1835, quoted in Stewart, "Boston, Abolition, and the Atlantic World," 116. Harrison Gray Otis (1765–1848) served as mayor of Boston from 1829 to 1832; architect Charles Bulfinch designed three houses for him in and around the Beacon Hill area.

12. Mrs. [Eliza] Harrison Gray Otis, *The Barclays of Boston* (Boston: Ticknor, Reed, and Fields, 1854), 26. Called "the notorious Mrs. Otis" by her contemporaries, the novelist rebelled against her father-in-law and established a regular Thursday salon at her home. See Cleveland Amory, *The Proper Bostonians* (Orleans, Mass.: Parnassus, 1947), 122–123.

13. *The Liberator*, May 16, 1851, quoted in Stewart, "Boston, Abolition, and the Atlantic World," 122.

14. Carolyn L. Karcher, *The First Woman of the Republic: A Cultural Biography of Lydia Maria Child* (Durham, N.C.: Duke University Press, 1994), 1–15, 40. For more biographical material on Lydia Maria Child, see Deborah Pickman Clifford, *Crusader for Freedom: A Life of Lydia Maria Child* (Boston: Beacon Press, 1992). Child's letters and other papers are scattered at various institutions, including the Boston Public Library, the American Antiquarian Society, and the Massachusetts Historical Society.

15. Karcher, *First Woman*, 237–238.

16. Lydia Maria Child to Samuel J. May, 29 September 1867, in *Lydia Maria Child: Selected Letters, 1817–1880*, ed. Milton Meltzer and Patricia G. Holland (Amherst: University of Massachusetts Press, 1982), 473–474.

17. Lydia Maria Child to Anne Whitney, 25 May 1879, in Child, *Selected Letters*, 558. William Lloyd Garrison (1805–1879) worked relentlessly for the abolitionist cause until the passage of the Thirteenth Amendment, at which point he took on the issues of temperance and woman suffrage.

18. Lydia Maria Child, *An Appeal in Favor of That Class of Americans Called Africans*, ed. Carolyn L. Karcher (Amherst: University of Massachusetts Press, 1996). See also Sean Wilentz, ed., *David Walker's Appeal to the Colored Citizens of the World, but in Particular, and Very Expressly, to Those of the United States of America*, ed. (New York: Hill and Wang, 1995; Walker's tract was privately published in Boston in 1829).

19. Deborah Weston to Anne B. Weston, 8 May 1835, in Child, *Selected Letters*, 28–29; Charles Knowles Bolton, *The Athenaeum Centenary* (Boston: Boston Athenaeum, 1907), 41; see

BA Charging Records, vol. 1 (1827–1834; the stated dates on the volumes are sometimes misleading—this volume includes some records of 1835).

20. "The Distaff Side," *Athenaeum Items* 15 (February 1939): 1.

21. Child edited the *Juvenile Miscellany* from 1826 until 1830; it folded a few years later. See Karcher, *First Woman*, 192. Even an old friend, Emily Marshall, distanced herself from Child; Marshall had married into the Harrison Gray Otis family and could not risk embarrassing her in-laws: Karcher, *First Woman*, 191–192; Clifford, *Crusader*, 106. See also David B. Tyack, *George Ticknor and the Boston Brahmins* (Cambridge: Harvard University Press, 1967), 185–186.

22. James N. Wood, "The Authorities of the American Art Museum," in *Whose Muse? Art Museums and the Public Trust*, ed. James Cuno (Princeton, N.J.: Princeton University Press, 2004), 107.

23. The French example of sanctioned culture is even more pronounced. More fully under the patronage of government than any American arts institution, the Louvre received its authority principally from the "liberation from the king and the church." See Andrew McClellan, *Inventing the Louvre: Art, Politics, and the Origins of the Modern Museum in Eighteenth-Century Paris* (Cambridge: Cambridge University Press, 1994), 91–123.

24. See Charles E. Clark and Michael A. Baenen, "The Portsmouth Athenaeum," Portsmouth (N.H.) Athenaeum publication; and Jane Lancaster, *Inquire Within: A Social History of the Providence Athenaeum since 1753* (Providence, R.I.: Providence Athenaeum, 2003).

25. William Smith Shaw to William Ellery Channing, December 1799, Shaw Papers, BA. Channing (1780–1842) would become a leading Unitarian minister in Boston; by the 1830s he was addressing American slavery publicly but still gingerly, advocating a gradual resolution to the problem. See Dorothy Broaddus, *Genteel Rhetoric: Writing High Culture in the Nineteenth-Century Boston* (Columbia: University of South Carolina Press, 1999), 80–82.

26. John Kirkland, "Memoir of the Boston Athenaeum," in Quincy, *History*, 30–31.

27. This dilemma certainly distressed elite Bostonians of the antebellum era. See George M. Frederickson, *The Inner Civil War: Northern Intellectuals and the Crisis of the Union* (Urbana: University of Illinois Press, 1993 [1965]). See also Broaddus, *Genteel Rhetoric*, 79.

28. The Federalists' views on the problem of slavery are especially complicated. For example, Josiah Quincy's hatred of slavery was always linked to his distaste for southern expansionism; other Federalists came to hate slavery on purely moral grounds. See Linda K. Kerber, *Federalists in Dissent: Imagery and Ideology in Jeffersonian America* (Ithaca, N.Y.: Cornell University Press, 1980), 23–66.

29. Robert A. Ferguson, *Reading the Early Republic* (Cambridge, Mass.: Harvard University Press, 2004), 289.

30. Ralph Waldo Emerson, "Self-Reliance," in *Selected Essays*, ed. Larzer Ziff (New York: Penguin Classics, 1982), 179. "Self-Reliance" includes materials from journal entries dating as far back as 1832 and from lectures delivered between 1836 and 1839. For more on books missing from the collection, see the report from the Examining Committee in a letter from librarian Seth Bass to the Trustees dated July 11, 1825.

31. Samuel J. May Jr. (1797–1871) was a dedicated abolitionist who, among many other deeds, helped runaway slaves reach destinations in Canada; see Mayer, *All on Fire*, 103–105, 109. William C. Nell, "Farewell to *The Liberator*: A Valedictory to the Liberator and Its Editor, William Lloyd Garrison," broadside dated 21 October 1865, Boston Athenaeum (Nell published *The Colored Patriots of the American Revolution* in 1855).

32. Harriet Knight Smith, *A History of the Lowell Institute* (Boston: Lamson, Wolffe, 1898). Athenaeum lectures were undertaken largely by the Lowell Institute; Smith's institutional history lists the titles of all lectures, and none had slavery as its theme.

33. Samuel May Jr., to Charles Folsom, 19 April 1854, BA Letters Collection. See also "The Athenaeum and the Abolition Movement," *Athenaeum Items* 117 (July 1998): 1.

34. See Albert J. Von Frank, *The Trials of Anthony Burns: Freedom and Slavery in Emerson's Boston* (Cambridge, Mass.: Harvard University Press, 1998).

35. See page 198 of BA Strangers' Book, 24 December 1857, vol. 3. This ledger was used by members to record all "strangers" (i.e., visitors) to the Athenaeum—as well as recipients of annual reading tickets. Guests and guest readers were allowed into the library only under the supervision of the current subscribers who first "introduced them" to the book. I am grateful to Barbara Adams Hebard, a conservator at the Athenaeum, who introduced *me* to the Strangers' Book.

36. Mabel Munson Swan, *The Athenaeum Gallery, 1827–1873: The Boston Athenaeum as an Early Patron of Art* (Boston: Boston Athenaeum, 1940), 157. See also Bolton, *Athenaeum Centenary*, 85.

37. Karcher, *First Woman*, 6. Clifford, *Crusader for Freedom*, 49, comments that Child eventually paid her respects to Adams: "Maria befriended the old woman [Hannah Adams] in her last years and was in the habit of carrying her bunches of fresh violets. As the two talked, the younger could not help observing the elder's diffidence and timidity."

38. See BA Charging Records, vol. 1.

39. Karcher, *First Woman*, 389. Karcher observes that Child was not entirely at ease with the aristocratic tone of the annual bazaars, even though she enjoyed the ambiance and sisterhood that the events created.

40. John Coburn's gaming house, located at 2 Phillips Street, was run by blacks for the elite; the barbershop operated by John J. Smith at 84 Pinckney Street was another Beacon Hill meeting place. It is likely that Sumner frequented both establishments, sites where residents of the North and South slopes intersected. Museum of African American History, Black Heritage Trail Pamphlet (Boston: National Park Service, 2002).

41. I am indebted to Anne-Marie Taylor for her fine biography, *Young Charles Sumner and the Legacy of the American Enlightenment, 1811–1851* (Amherst: University of Massachusetts Press, 2001), which covers Sumner's public life in and around Boston before his election to the U.S. Senate. Taylor disagrees, pointedly, with the previous major biographer of Sumner, David Donald, who, she claims, "was not able . . . to escape the traditional anti-abolitionist and anti-New England bias" (3). See Donald's *Charles Sumner and the Coming of the Civil War* (New York: Knopf, 1960). To correct this error, Taylor explores Sumner's relationships with the New England thinkers of his day. Although I depended on Taylor's biography for much of the material on Sumner's youth and early adulthood, his manuscripts and collected works abound: Harvard University houses his papers, and his speeches, letters, and other works are available in published editions.

42. "The aspiration and the ambivalence" that characterize such travels are taken up in Bruce Redford's *Venice and the Grand Tour* (New Haven, Conn.: Yale University Press, 1996), which focuses on the experiences of young elite British men.

43. David Sears had commanded cadets in War of 1812. His granite house on Beacon Street, now the Somerset Club, was designed by Alexander Parris (1780–1852) in 1819. Cornelius Felton (1807–1862), dear friend of Sumner, was a professor of Greek at Harvard. See Charles Sumner to George Hillard, 13 January 1838, quoted in Taylor, *Young Charles Sumner*, 94, 116–117.

44. Diary entry of 16 January 1839; Joseph Story to Charles Sumner, 11 August 1838; Charles Sumner to George Hillard, 9 March 1839, all in Sumner, *Memoirs and Letters of Charles Sumner*, ed. Edward L. Pierce, 4 vols. (Boston: Roberts Brothers, 1893), 2:41, 2:10, and 2:78. Joseph Story (1779–1845) was appointed a Supreme Court Justice in 1811; his "Commentaries" are a standard work on the Constitution. In addition to being an attorney, George Hillard (1808–1879) was an editor, author, and legislator.

45. Sumner, diary entry, 16 January 1839, quoted in Elisa Tamarkin, "American Anglophilia: Deference, Devotion, and National Culture, 1820–1865" (Ph.D. diss., Stanford University, 2000), 111, 119.

46. Story and Pierce both quoted in *Memoirs and Letters*, Sumner, 2:147, 2:151. William Wetmore Story (1819–1895) was also a sometime poet and the ostensible subject of a book by Henry James (*William Wetmore Story and His Friends* [1903]).

47. Especially in 1843 and 1844, Sumner withdrew books frequently—including the works of Richard Sheridan and Tobias Smollett, Socrates' *Apology*, and Aristotle's *Ethics*. See BA Charging Records, vol. 2.

48. See David B. Dearinger, "American Neoclassical Sculptors and Their Private Patrons in Boston" (Ph.D. diss., City University of New York, 1993), 363–492; Taylor, *Young Charles Sumner*, 95, 120.

49. Donald, *Charles Sumner*, 78–79. According to Donald (54), Morpeth (1802–1864) was the oldest son of the Earl of Carlisle—and therefore a future Earl of Carlisle himself; Lord Morpeth was his courtesy title.

50. Charles Sumner, Boston, to Lord Morpeth, London, 15 April 1841, in Sumner, *Memoirs and Letters*, 2:177.

51. Charles Sumner to Lydia Maria Child, 14 January 1853, quoted in Karcher, *First Woman*, 385.

52. Taylor, *Young Charles Sumner*, 75–76, 83.

53. Charles Sumner, Boston, to Lord Morpeth, New York, 28 December 1841, in Sumner, *Memoirs and Letters*, 2:189.

54. Quoted in Taylor, *Young Charles Sumner*, 138.

55. These characterizations echo those in Tamarkin's study, page 102.

56. Charles Sumner to Francis Lieber, 29 January 1844, quoted in Taylor, *Young Charles Sumner*, 150.

57. Broaddus, *Genteel Rhetoric*, 101. Charles Sumner, "The True Grandeur of Nations: An Oration Delivered before the Authorities of the City of Boston, July 4, 1845," in Sumner, *Orations and Speeches*, 2 vols. (Boston: Ticknor, Reed, and Fields, 1850), 1:10. A note of clarification: the owner of the Old Corner Bookstore, William D. Ticknor, was a Boston publisher and a cousin of George Ticknor. Both Ticknors were suspicious of radical reformers. See W. S. Tryon, *Parnassas Corner: A Life of James T. Fields, Publisher to the Victorians* (Boston: Houghton Mifflin, 1963), 249–250.

58. Lydia Maria Child to Charles Sumner, 3 March 1846, in Sumner, *Memoirs and Letters*, 2:366.

59. Ronald Story, "Class and Culture in Boston: The Athenaeum, 1807–1860," *American Quarterly* 27 (May 1975): 182. Chapter 2 noted the highly idiosyncratic borrowing habits of Athenaeum member William Appleton, a cousin of Nathan and Samuel. Samuel Appleton's donation was the equivalent of half a million dollars in today's currency, based on Consumer Price Index statistics.

60. See BA Charging Records, vol. 3. For perspectives on readership during this era, see James L. Machor, ed. *Readers in History: Nineteenth-Century American Literature and the Contexts of Response* (Baltimore: Johns Hopkins University Press, 1993).

61. Charles Sumner, "Speech for Union among Men of All Parties against the Slave Power, and the Extension of Slavery, in a Massachusetts Convention at Worcester, June 28, 1848," in Sumner, *Orations and Speeches*, 2:257. See also Taylor, *Young Charles Sumner*, 265–270.

62. In 1837, Samuel Lawrence, brother to Abbott Lawrence, had contributed money to make Sumner's European trip possible. Also, after losing his first wife to tuberculosis, Nathan Appleton married Sumner's cousin, Harriet Coffin Sumner. Nevertheless, Charles Sumner risked these personal associations for the sake of antislavery policy.

63. Charles Sumner to Nathan Appleton, 31 August 1848, in Sumner, *The Selected Letters of Charles Sumner*, ed. Beverly Wilson Palmer, 2 vols. (Boston: Northeastern University Press, 1990), 1:248–249.

64. Stewart, "Boston, Abolition, and the Atlantic World," 107. For more on the merchant class, see O'Connor, *Lords of the Loom*, especially 42–76.

65. See BA Charging Records, vols. 4–5. Abbott Lawrence, apparently a fan of James Fenimore Cooper, borrowed many of the Leatherstocking Tales.

66. Founded in 1820, the Boston Mercantile Library never had the wide selection of books or the membership that its counterpart in New York did; however, it was in these institutions

that young men seeking their fortunes in the city found sites for free intellectual and ethical inquiry. See Thomas Augst, *The Clerk's Tale: Young Men and Moral Life in Nineteenth-Century America* (University of Chicago Press, 2003).

67. Charles Sumner, *The Position and Duties of the Merchant: An Address before the Mercantile Library Association of Boston, on the Evening of 13th of November, 1854* (Boston: Ticknor and Fields, 1855), 3, 12.

68. See David Tatham, "Pictorial Responses to the Caning of Senator Sumner," in *American Printmaking before 1876: Fact, Fiction, and Fantasy* (Washington, D.C.: Library of Congress, 1975). See also Catharina Slautterback, "Charles Sumner and the Political Issues of His Time," *Athenaeum Items* 132 (April 2004): 10–18. In the South, the attack was perceived as a brave defense of honor; Brooks became a hero there.

69. Bolton, *Athenaeum Centenary*, 10. There is an exception to the Boston Athenaeum's inhospitable attitude toward Sumner: in a rare instance of genteel protest, Josiah Quincy became active in the antislavery movement as a retiree (see chapter 6 of this book).

Chapter Six

1. The introductory section of this chapter draws from these sources: Josiah Quincy, *An Appeal in Behalf of the Boston Athenaeum Addressed to the Proprietors* (Boston: John Wilson, 1853); Walter Muir Whitehill, *Boston Public Library: A Centennial History* (Cambridge, Mass.: Harvard University Press, 1956); George Ticknor, *Union of the Boston Athenaeum and the Public Library* (Boston: Dutton and Wentworth, 1853); and Charles Knowles Bolton, *The Athenaeum Centenary* (Boston: Boston Athenaeum, 1907). I thank Richard Wendorf and Kathleen O'Neill Sims for their helpful comments; I am also grateful to the reference department of the Boston Athenaeum. A version of this chapter appears in Richard Wendorf, ed., *The Boston Athenaeum: Bicentennial Essays* (Boston: Boston Athenaeum, 2009).

2. See these sources: Michael Harris and Gerard Spiegler, "Everett, Ticknor, and the Common Man: The Fear of Societal Instability as the Motivation for the Founding of the Boston Public Library," *Libri* 24 (1974): 249–275; Lawrence Levine, *Highbrow/Lowbrow: The Emergence of Cultural Hierarchy in America* (Cambridge, Mass.: Harvard University Press, 1988); and, for an understanding of Levine's sociological framework, Paul DiMaggio, "Cultural Entrepreneurship in Nineteenth-Century Boston, Parts I and II," in *Media, Culture and Society: A Critical Reader*, ed. Richard Collins et al. (London: Sage, 1986), 194–211, 303–322. DiMaggio examines the deliberate separation of high and low cultures, arguing that Boston Brahmin "cultural capitalists" embarked on a campaign of entrepreneurship, classification, and "framing" in order to "sacralize" art and control its audiences.

3. Ralph Waldo Emerson, "Self-Reliance," in *Selected Essays*, ed. Larzer Ziff (New York: Penguin Classics, 1982), 185.

4. Ticknor, *Union*, 7.

5. Some forty years earlier, Quincy had even endorsed a proposal for uniting many local institutions into one large library to be called the Massachusetts Institution; the entity would have combined the American Academy of Arts and Sciences, the Massachusetts Historical Society, the Agricultural Society, the Massachusetts Medical Society, the Linnaean Society, and the Boston Athenaeum. "Massachusetts Institution," *North American Review* 2 (1816): 313–314 and n. 55.

6. There is no direct evidence clarifying this particular disagreement between father and son; however, it was not unusual for Quincy Sr. to engage in healthy debate both with his namesake (who became a staunch "Cotton Whig" before abandoning public life altogether) and with his son Edmund, a Garrisonian. Beyond any father-son conflicts, the brothers themselves simply despised each other's politics.

7. The phrase appears in a poem by Holmes read at the laying of the cornerstone for the new Boston Public Library building in 1888: "Behind the ever-open gate / No pikes shall

fence a crumbling throne, / No lackeys cringe, no courtiers wait,— / This palace is the people's own!" Quoted in Whitehill, *Boston Public Library*, 147.

8. One cannot help noticing that the statement is soon followed by the clarification "who are qualified to judge upon the subject." John Kirkland, *Memoir of the Boston Athenaeum*, 1807, in Quincy, *History*, 30.

9. Bolton, *Athenaeum Centenary*, 46–47. The number was the result of happenstance; new shares taken by subscribers from 1854 to 1858 brought the figure to 1,049.

10. Ibid., 43–47.

11. For biographical background on Ticknor, see *Life, Letters, and Journals of George Ticknor*, ed. George S. Hillard, 2 vols. (Boston: Houghton Mifflin, 1909 [1875]); and David B. Tyack, *George Ticknor and the Boston Brahmins* (Cambridge, Mass.: Harvard University Press, 1967). For biographical background on Quincy, see Edmund Quincy, *Life of Josiah Quincy*, 6th ed. (Boston: Little, Brown, 1874); and Robert A. McCaughey, *Josiah Quincy, 1772–1864: The Last Federalist* (Cambridge, Mass.: Harvard University Press, 1974).

12. Ticknor was the author of *The History of Spanish Literature* (1849): see Tyack, *George Ticknor*, 131. For a poetic interpretation of Ticknor's inner turmoil (and insight into his attitude toward the historian William Prescott), see Sheila Heti's slim but atmospheric meditation, *Ticknor* (New York: Farrar Straus Giroux, 2005).

13. BA Charging Records, vol. 5.

14. Josiah Quincy, quoted in McCaughey, *Josiah Quincy*, 212.

15. Tyack, *George Ticknor*, 229–230.

16. Ticknor, *Union*, 8.

17. Ibid., 9–12.

18. Quincy, *Appeal* 1, 4–5, 15. The Somerset Street lot would later be rejected as a site for the new public library, and the city sold the land at no loss. The Boston Public Library went on to be housed first in temporary quarters in an old schoolhouse on Mason Street (1854–1857), then in a purpose-built building on Boylston Street (1858–1894; sold and demolished in 1899), and, finally, in the so-called palace for the people, the stately building modeled after Henri Labrouste's Bibliothèque Sainte-Geneviève (among other sources) and designed by McKim Mead & White for the site on Copley Square (dedicated in 1895). See Whitehill, *Boston Public Library*, 38–41.

19. Quincy, *Appeal*, 4; Ticknor, *Union* 10.

20. "Growth of Libraries," *North American Review* 45 (1837): 140. See Marshall Foletta, *Coming to Terms with Democracy: Federalist Intellectuals and the Shaping of American Culture* (Charlottesville: University Press of Virginia, 2001). Foletta portrays the work of the *North American Review* as transitional. The journal's efforts, he argues persuasively, helped professionalize American institutions in medicine, education, and the law—making these paths accessible to all citizens (and thus, ironically, diluting the power of these self-appointed public intellectuals).

21. Whitehill, *Boston Public Library*, 5; Nathaniel Dearborn, *Boston Notions: Being an Authentic and Concise Account of "That Village," from 1630 to 1847* (Boston, 1848), 199.

22. "Growth of Libraries," 138–139; "Public Libraries," *North American Review* 148 (1850): 191.

23. Vattemare, who went by the stage name "Monsieur Alexandre," exhibited unprecedented energy for free libraries. He traveled as far as San Francisco to speak on the subject, offering city representatives dry Parisian documents for their holdings in exchange for natural phenomena, such as American rattlesnake skins, for European archives. Though a source of great amusement (Ticknor never took the man seriously), Vattemare's vision helped inspire Bostonians to define their own public library plan. See Whitehill, *Boston Public Library*, 3–5, 9–10; "Public Libraries," 200–202.

24. Whitehill, *Boston Public Library*, 13 (Whitehill remains the definitive summary of the library's origins).

25. George Ticknor to Edward Everett, 14 July 1851, in Ticknor, *Life* 2:301–302. Edward Everett (1794–1865) filled many roles—from pastor to professor of Greek literature to U.S. secretary of state.

26. Foletta, *Coming to Terms*, 46.

27. Buckminster to Shaw, 3 April 1807, quoted in Lewis P. Simpson, ed., *The Federalist Literary Mind: Selections from "The Monthly Anthology and Boston Review," 1803–1811, including Documents Relating to the Boston Athenaeum* (Baton Rouge: Louisiana State University Press, 1962), 30. Apparently, Shaw had wanted Buckminster to purchase the dry papers of various English learned societies.

28. An early indication of the swerve away from current literary trends is evident in this comment: "The Boston Athenaeum has made already a large collection of valuable works, and follows, we believe, though perhaps at somewhat too respectful a distance, the progress of the literature of the day": "Public Libraries," *North American Review* 45 (1837): 139.

29. George Ticknor to Edward Everett, 14 July 1851, and Edward Everett to George Ticknor, 26 July 1851, Ticknor, *Life,* 2:302, 303; Edward Everett to John Prescott Bigelow, 7 August 1850, quoted in Whitehill, *Boston Public Library,* 21.

30. *Report of the Trustees of the Public Library of the City of Boston,* July 1852, City Document No. 37 (Boston, 1852), reprinted in facsimile (from a copy with annotations held by the Boston Public Library) in Jesse H. Shera, *Foundations of the Public Library Movement in New England: 1629–1855* (Chicago: University of Chicago Press, 1949), 267–290. It is from this facsimile (282) that I quote.

31. George Ticknor to Edward Everett, 14 July 1851 in Ticknor, *Life,* 2:301; *Report of the Trustees,* 281, 279–280.

32. Ibid., 281; Joshua Bates to Thomas Wren Ward, November 1852, quoted in Whitehill, *Boston Public Library,* 38. According to the Consumer Price Index, Bates's bequest would be equivalent to more than one million dollars in today's currency.

33. See, for example, Whitehill, *Boston Public Library;* Phyllis Dain, *The New York Public Library: A History of Its Founding and Early Years* (New York: New York Public Library, 1972); David Kaser, *A Book for a Sixpence: The Circulating Library in America* (Pittsburgh: Beta Phi Mu, 1980); Abigail A. Van Slyck, *Free to All: Carnegie Libraries and American Culture, 1890–1920* (Chicago: University of Chicago Press, 1995); Kenneth A. Breisch, *Henry Hobson Richardson and the Small Public Library in America: A Study in Typology* (Cambridge, Mass.: MIT Press, 1997); Dee Garrison, *Apostles of Culture: The Public Librarian and American Society, 1876–1920* (New York: Free Press, 1979); Thomas Augst and Wayne Wiegand, eds., *Libraries as Agencies of Culture* (Madison: University of Wisconsin Press, 2001); Thomas Augst, *The Clerk's Tale: Young Men and Moral Life in Nineteenth-Century America* (Chicago: University of Chicago Press, 2003); and Matthew Battles, *Library: An Unquiet History* (New York: Norton, 2003).

34. See Harris and Spiegler, "Everett, Ticknor, and the Common Man," in which the authors attempt to correct what they describe as two polarized schools of thought about the development of American public libraries. On the one hand, "progressive" historians have written about a movement led by enlightened humanitarians who wanted the library to be a vehicle for popular democracy; on the other hand, "revisionists" questioned this "myth" and have described public library organizers as driven by fear and distrust of the lower classes. Harris and Spiegler try to understand the perspectives of Ticknor and Everett as a case study, testing notions of the elite's ulterior motives. Their conclusions most definitely put them in the revisionist camp, as they give evidence of Ticknor's increasingly anxious attitude toward the changing Boston community. (The article's pessimistic coda implies that even today's public libraries are meant to control, not to liberate.)

35. George Ticknor, "Memoir of the Buckminsters" (1849), quoted in Michael Harris, "The Purpose of the American Public Library," *Library Journal* 98 (1973): 258.

36. Ticknor's views on immigration, however, moved him to write of bringing "[the refugees] in willing subjection to our institutions." See Tyack, *George Ticknor,* 222.

37. *Boston Evening Transcript,* 7 September 1847, BA Collections File, Beacon Street Folder, Print Department.

38. Printed circular, 11 October 1848, and notation, BA Proprietors' Records. The proposal was only a formality to appease the mayor. See note of clarification from the Athenaeum president, Thomas G. Cary, 9 February 1849 in Proprietors' Records.

39. 1 January 1849, BA Letters Collection.

40. Ronald Story, "Class and Culture in Boston: The Athenaeum, 1807–1860," *American Quarterly* 27 (May 1975): 192.

41. See essays by Kenneth Carpenter and Barbara Adams Hebard, in Wendorf, *Boston Athenaeum*. Fine distinctions between the privileges of a proprietor and those of a life subscriber were not consistently made.

42. John Everett to William Smith Shaw, Boston, 28 December 1817, Shaw Papers, BA.

43. *Boston Newsletter and City Record*, 25 February 1826, 116, BA Collections File, Exhibition Reviews, Art Department.

44. In my effort to understand the shifting rules of access, I have benefited from the researches of Mary Warnement, reference librarian at the Boston Athenaeum. The rules regarding membership were always somewhat fluid; indeed, there is evidence that the institution felt ambivalence about denying people access to the bookshelves. For example, the poster of Rules and Regulations published January 20, 1815, clearly stated that annual subscribers would *not* be admitted to the library (they were permitted use of the Reading Room *only*). Yet someone later amended that published rule—in spidery penmanship—by crossing out the restriction and replacing it with this more generous guideline: "The Library Room is now open to all who have a right to visit the Reading Room." Perhaps John Everett's complaints (see end of Chapter 2) inspired such a shift, or perhaps the amendment came many years later. By 1822, the first year of the Pearl Street location, it is clear that "subscribers" (again, to gain status as a "subscriber" required money and/or connections) were allowed access to the shelves. Institutional worry about book theft and injury persisted, however, as expressed in numerous official records: see BA Trustees' Records, 14 October 1822.

45. "As this institution has, in appearance, the aspect of a private concern, your committee feel it incumbent upon them to state that it is, both in its origin and on the principles on which it is conducted, almost exclusively publick. The object of its establishment was to lay the foundation of a great publick library for the use and resort of all our citizens. . . . Being merchants . . . , their subscriptions can be viewed in no other light than that of benefactions": Josiah Quincy, "Massachusetts Institution," *North American Review* 2 (1816): 313–314;

46. Charles C. Jewett, "Notices of Public Libraries in the United States," *Appendix to the Fourth Annual Report of the Smithsonian Institution* (Washington, D.C., 1851):

47. In contrast, soon after the Boston Public Library was founded, according to Whitehill (*Boston Public Library*, 43), "All inhabitants of Boston over sixteen had access to it, where not only periodicals but all books in the library might be consulted."

48. A library historian dedicated to interpreting statistical data, McMullen observes that so-called social libraries (a category that contains the multipurpose athenaeum) continued to flourish even through the time of the Civil War—despite the growing popularity of tax-supported public libraries: Haynes McMullen, *American Libraries before 1876* (Westport, Conn.: Greenwood Press, 2000), 65–66. The trend differs somewhat for athenaeums specifically. McMullen (73) identifies seventy-four American athenaeums before the year 1876; he notes that almost none were founded after the Civil War but that twenty-four still operated in 1875.

49. Michael Wentworth, with Elizabeth Lamb Clark, *The Boston Library Society, 1794–1994: An Exhibition of Portraits, Views, and Materials Related to the Foundation of the Society and Some of Its Early Members* (Boston: Boston Athenaeum, 1995), 9; Whitehill, *Boston Public Library*, 124–125.

50. Levine, *Highbrow / Lowbrow*, 234, n. 2. Reading Levine with the Boston Athenaeum in mind, one can appreciate anew the singularity of the book as a medium. One's experience in a library differs vastly from one's experience in a theater or a music hall: a library has more potential for a private, immediate communion of subject with object. The "sacralization" of a library can be only partial. Any given library may appear glorified in scope, even architecturally daunting, but the reader-book intimacy always prevails.

51. The Athenaeum–Public Library debate cannot be seen as the *reverse* of Levine's argument, either. That is, it does not demonstrate that the elite antebellum institution (Boston

Athenaeum) gave way to the more democratic late-nineteenth-century institution (Boston Public Library). Both sites were deemed necessary, thus illustrating no definitive cultural shift—only the special situation of a somewhat redundant elite home for books and art.

52. Charles Jewett codified the distinction between mere reading and true study in "Report of the Assistant Secretary, Relating to the Library," *Third Annual Report of the Smithsonian Institution* (Washington, D.C., 1849), 39. See also Thomas Augst, "The Business of Reading in Nineteenth-Century America: The New York Mercantile Library," in *American Quarterly* 50 (June 1998): 267–305.

53. *Report of the Trustees*, 287; Ticknor, *Union*, 9; Quincy, *Appeal*, 15.

54. This means that at the Athenaeum some women were allowed to own shares decades before Massachusetts gave women property rights, in 1855. See Barbara Adams Hebard's essay in Wendorf, *Boston Athenaeum*. Hebard states that at the close of the institution's first century "hundreds of women had been part of the Library's history." It was not until 1967 that the Athenaeum elected its first female trustee: Susan Morse Hilles. At other New England athenaeums the trustees were both more and less enlightened. Five women owned shares in the Providence Athenaeum as of 1840, whereas at the Boston Athenaeum only one woman is listed as owning a share that year, and it was not until 1860 that a woman owned a share in the Portsmouth Athenaeum. See "The Portsmouth Athenaeum," Charles E. Clark and Michael A. Baenen, Portsmouth (N.H.) Athenaeum publication, 6–7; and Jane Lancaster, *Inquire Within: A Social History of the Providence Athenaeum since 1753* (Providence: Providence Athenaeum, 2003), 72–73.

55. George Ticknor to Edward Everett, 14 July 1851, in Ticknor, *Life*, 2:301–302. For more on the flexibility of a private-public model for cultural organizations, see Peter Dobkin Hall, " 'To make us bold and learn to read—to be friends to each other and friends to the world': Libraries and the Origins of Civil Society in the United States," *Libraries & Culture* 31 (Winter 1996): 14–35.

56. Jean L. Preer, "Exploring the American Idea at the New York Public Library," in Augst and Wiegand, *Libraries*, 151; John Kirkland, *Memoir of the Boston Athenaeum*, 1807, in Quincy, *History*, 30.

57. Committee of the Library Report, 1 January 1855, BA Proprietors' Records.

58. For the flavor of the original prospectus, see Kirkland, *Memoir of the Boston Athenaeum*, 31–34. (The stated mission of the contemporary Boston Athenaeum is "to serve its members, the broader community, and scholars throughout the world by preserving and augmenting its collections of books and art, by providing library services and cultural programs, and by preserving and enhancing the unique atmosphere of its landmark building.") For additional perspectives on the two libraries, I benefited from a public conversation between Richard Wendorf and Bernard Margolis ("Ownership of Cultural Property: Should the Boston Athenaeum Have Become the Boston Public Library?") hosted by the Boston Public Library, January 18, 2007.

Conclusion

1. Henry James, *The American Scene* (New York: Penguin Classics, 1994 [1907]), 172–173.

2. See Terry Eagleton, *The Idea of Culture* (Oxford: Blackwell, 2000), 128–131. I was inspired by Eagleton's wise overview. Building on the work of playwright David Edgar, he teases out four aspects of contemporary "culture wars"—civility, identity, commercialism, protest— and concludes with a reminder that the world's most pressing problems are material, bound up in cultural patterns, to be sure, but never solvable by books alone.

3. Brian J. Wolf, "How the West Was Hung; Or, *When I Hear the Word 'Culture' I Take Out My Checkbook*," *American Quarterly* 44 (September 1992): 418–438, discusses the trend of contemporary museum curators to stage exhibitions that interpret the powerful rhetoric of history. Using brazen labels that tease the viewer, such exhibitions expose the myths of manifest

destiny and other well-worn American tropes that, for example, deny the importance of indigenous peoples. The subtitle of Wolf's article comes from a 1985 untitled piece by multimedia artist Barbara Kruger. Yet—perhaps illustrating the strange circulation of motifs in the cultural realm—the phrase originated as "When I hear the word 'culture' I reach for my gun." This was a rough translation of a line from a little-known German play performed for Adolf Hitler's birthday in 1933; it has also been falsely attributed to Hermann Göring. In his 1963 film *Le mépris (Contempt)*, Jean-Luc Godard inaugurated the "checkbook" adaptation, obviously a comment on art and commerce. Some peace activists have reverted to the original phrase but turned it around to suit their message: "When I hear the word 'gun,' I reach for my culture."

INDEX

Page numbers in italics refer to figures.